DAYBREAK

DAYBREAK

BELVA PLAIN

Delacorte ▦ Press

To Matthew, David, Sarah,
Michael, Katherine, and Amy
with love

Published by
Delacorte Press
Bantam Doubleday Dell Publishing Group, Inc.
1540 Broadway
New York, New York 10036

Library of Congress Cataloging in Publication Data

Plain, Belva.
Daybreak / by Belva Plain.
p.   cm.
ISBN 0-385-31104-4
ISBN 0-385-31232-6 (large-print ed.)
I. Title.
PS3566.L254D38   1994
813'.54—dc20   93-43915
                                              CIP

Manufactured in the United States of America
Published simultaneously in Canada

May 1994

10 9 8 7 6 5 4 3 2 1

BVG

PROLOGUE

A man and a woman, facing a doctor at his desk, sat staring at the wall behind the doctor's youthful head—it was often surprising how young such distinguished research scientists turned out to be—where stood a case of medical textbooks in dreary brown and melancholy gray.

The doctor had turned his gaze away from them toward the window that framed the dogwood grove in the park beyond the hospital; through this newborn blooming whiteness ran the wind of the southern springtime; then, shifting his gaze but a trifle, he could see the brick edge of the wing in which this couple's son lay dying.

To die at eighteen, he thought, in such a spring, with the dogwood, the redbud, and the fragrant grass!

The woman was first to break an unbearable silence. "He has suffered so much, ever since he was born. The lung infections, the pancreas, the malnutrition, everything exactly according to the books. And now cirrhosis of the liver. It's too much."

And the husband added softly, "We didn't know this was part of the disease. We never expected it."

"It's one of the rarer developments, that's true." The doctor nodded, parted his lips as though he were about to continue, but closed them together instead, so that the silence, thick as wool, wrapped itself around them all again.

Then the husband produced a timid question. "Is there — do you think there's any chance that, after all, he might possibly—"

The doctor reflected that he had seldom felt so much pity. He had to riffle through papers on his desk before he could find an answer.

"Well, 'possible' is one thing. He has come through a good many battles. Babies, three-year-olds—I've seen many die. On the other hand, I had a patient once who held on till forty. It can happen."

"But not often," said the wife.

"No, not often. And in this case, where the liver is affected, you see—" The doctor paused. "But by this time you people must have learned all there is to know about cystic fibrosis."

"Oh, yes. A generalized disfunction of the exocrine glands. Fairly common among Caucasians. Its molecular basis unknown. My husband and I have all the words, Doctor. They're embossed on our brains."

Knowing better, especially because he could see that the doctor, out of compassion, was withholding the final hopelessness, the husband still coaxed and hoped.

"We thought maybe coming here with these genetic studies among so many different families, and with all the blood work on my wife and me, that maybe you had come up with something new."

"We're surely trying." The young man in the white coat was restless, shuffling little objects on the desktop, a paperweight, a pile of paper clips. Perhaps his patience was ebbing away. It must be hard to talk to the parents of a hopeless case, thought the older man.

"Oh!" cried the mother in her bitterness, "I'll never understand! A hereditary disease, and never before in either of our families. And our other child with no sign of it. Thank God," she added quickly.

The doctor got up from his chair, rising so abruptly that the chair made a little shriek as it scraped the floor. He walked to the window and stood there a moment with his hands locked behind his back, looking out upon the white sea of dogwood. When he turned again toward the room, it was with so strange an expression on his face that the parents were shocked.

"You found something," the mother said quickly. "Something in our blood?"

"Yes." The single syllable was very quiet.

"What? What?"

"We found, without the shadow of a doubt, that your son, that the boy upstairs cannot be, is not, your son."

PART
I

Peter

CHAPTER

1

This must be what they mean, thought Margaret Crawfield, when they say "It hasn't registered yet." Now, with the funeral over—black cars moving slowly from the house then back to it, hushed voices, handclasps—now at the end of the dreadful week, with the flowers faded, the funeral foods eaten and kindly crowds gone, the terrible fact reveals itself at last. Peter is dead.

She walked. Through the rooms, down the hall, in and out, she walked. The rap of her heels was loud. The hum of the refrigerator and the slam of a car door across the street made the silence quiver.

Suddenly she heard herself ask aloud, "What are we going to do?" The high, piercing voice, asking the passionate question, repeated, "What? What?"

She had no tears. There were, at this moment, none left, though there would be a lifetime of them for her and for them all, Arthur her husband, Holly her daughter, and the grandparents who had so dearly loved Peter.

On the dining room table, beside a bowl of brown daffodils drooping in stagnant water, lay a pile of condolence letters waiting to be acknowledged. She sat down, took the pen, began a sentence: *Dear Cousin Andy, thank you for your*—and put down the pen to stare out of the window.

Life was there, wind rippling through new leaves, crisp and

creamy-green; robins hopping stiff-legged on the lawn; a baby carriage parked on the neighbors' porch. Life.

She gave up. There would be no letters today. Not yet. Her hands, her arms, her shoulders were limp. Toy hammers beat lightly inside her head. So she sat, closing her eyes against the brightness.

"Mom?" said Holly. "Are you asleep sitting up? Are you all right?"

"No. Yes. I'm not asleep. I'm all right. I didn't hear you come in."

"I came in at the back door. I thought maybe you'd be taking a nap. Dad told you to lie down, didn't he?"

"I know, but I can't do it. I'm too restless."

Holly laid a hand on the nape of her mother's neck. "You're all tense, all knotted there. Let me rub it for you."

"Thank you."

The warmth was good. Her daughter's hand caring for her, loving her. It made the tears start up again, stinging and prickling the backs of her eyes.

"Thank you, darling. I should be doing something for you."

"I'm fine. I'm younger," said Holly, trying to tease, to lighten the heavy, heavy air.

Margaret swallowed hard and, making her own effort to lighten and brighten, remarked that it was Holly's afternoon for hockey practice, wasn't it?

"Yes, but I'm skipping it. Finals are coming up and I've missed so much that I can't take time out for hockey." Holly's eyebrows drew together, giving her pretty face a look of anxiety. "I hate to leave you alone, so deserted, but I really should run over to Allison's house. She has all the book assignments in Latin and chemistry that I missed."

Margaret stood up. "Of course you should. Go over. I'm all right. We all are, you and Dad and I. We have to be."

"I won't be long, Mom."

Margaret watched her go down the walk, with her books under her arm, her long hair flying in the wind and her long legs running. Not many months from now she'd be away in college. But not to think of that this minute.

"I'm all right, we all are," she had just said to Holly.

Oh, brave words!

Ordinarily, at three o'clock in the afternoon Margaret Crawfield was busy, either at her part-time work as a tutor to housebound children or as a volunteer at the hospital. But not yet, not today while those toy hammers were still tapping in her head. . . .

She went upstairs and wandered, emptied a waste basket, put away a pink jacket that Holly had thrown over a chair, and straightened Arthur's tie rack. She combed her hair; it wouldn't do to look depressed, depressing Arthur to see her so when he came home. He never complained, he was a rock. . . . Her eyes filled again.

Presently her wandering brought her to Peter's room, which she had been avoiding all week. Now she was drawn in. Facing her there was the closet door that, ajar, displayed shelves and empty hangers. She reached in and touched the hangers, remembering the shape and color of the clothes that had hung on them, the brown tweed jacket, the red windbreaker, and the good navy blue suit. All these had been given away on the day after the funeral, when thoughtful friends had come to clear out the closet and the drawers.

The rest of the room was untouched. Books, records, pictures, and posters remained, so that the room still looked as though Peter might walk in at any minute, sit down at the desk or lie down on the bed with his hands locked behind his head, while he listened to the New Orleans jazz he loved and could himself play so well. The piano downstairs was silent now; he had been the only one, in a family that cared very much about music, who had the skill to perform it.

She lay down on his bed. The room was filled with sunlight. On the opposite wall she stared at the outline of Mont-Saint-Michel on the poster between the windows. How happy he had been only two summers ago when they had all spent that month together exploring France! He had had such a great capacity for happiness! And that, in spite of everything he'd had to endure from the very moment, almost, of birth.

Her mind—my crazy, tormented mind, she thought—went back and back over the same worn path. Where the bed now stood, the crib had stood, across from the chest of drawers and the rocking chair, all of them adorned with painted ducklings in procession.

"For our first grandchild," said Grandmother Frieda, "nothing is too good."

And Grandpa Albert joked, "A beautiful boy, even though he has my son-in-law's sandy hair." He had put his hand on Arthur's shoulder in affection.

It had been raining when they brought him home, but in this room, safe from the torrent, the baby had been snug. Nothing could harm that baby. Nothing.

Yet something had. . . .

Night after night he cried. There are few sounds as bewildering, she remembered, as a baby's wail. Nothing had stopped Peter, not feeding, changing, or rocking.

"What can be wrong?" they asked the doctor and their friends and themselves.

"Oh, nothing but colic, it usually is just colic." So the formula was changed, and that did work for a time. But only for a time. It had to be changed again and yet again. Then the doctor himself began to seem uncertain. . . .

One night Peter began to cough. Like any mother of a newborn, Margaret slept so lightly that the least murmur from the room across the hall sent her bounding across that hall in seconds.

The night light, a white kitten with illuminated eyes, shone on a tiny, purple-faced creature in torment. The cough was terrifying; he was struggling for air; the gasp, the snore, were like a death rattle—she had never heard a death rattle, yet that was the expression that leapt to mind.

"Oh, my God," she said, and picked him up. But no, that was stupid. This was not a baby who was asking for comfort. This was—a dying baby? And she laid him back in the crib.

Arthur, whose deep, healthy sleep was what you might expect in a man so rational, so unflustered as he, had as yet heard nothing. She ran back and shook him awake.

"The baby! The baby," she stammered. "I think he—I don't know—"

On either side of the crib they stood. They looked once at each other, and with that wordless look each knew that this was the ultimate moment of decision, that they could not wait another minute.

"Wrap him up," Arthur said. "We'll throw on some clothes and take him. I'm afraid it's pneumonia."

She thought, as they rode through vacant streets, past darkened houses, "He will die before we get there." And with her fingers groping under the wrapping of blankets she felt for the little heart.

Rain was flooding the city with an iridescent eerie gleam. It beat upon the windshield, and the wipers, madly sweeping, could barely keep up with it. In just such a storm they had brought Peter home when he was three days old. So happy, so proud they had been with their firstborn son!

The lights of the emergency entrance shone like a beacon to a ship at sea. Distraught, with their shoes untied, they rushed in. Competent hands took their baby from their arms; strangers took charge; the parents were helpless. . . .

"Yes," the doctor said, "it is pneumonia. We have to keep him here, of course." He looked over a chart, frowned a little, paused and remarked, though kindly, "He's quite a little fellow for his age. But—well, I can't tell you it's not serious—but with antibiotics, you know . . ."

He was fumbling for something tactful to say, a way of giving these parents some encouragement for the night and the bleak ride home, but not too much encouragement. They knew all that.

"We can't stay here?" asked Margaret, hopefully.

The doctor shook his head. "No point in it, anyway. He'll be in an ICU. Better for you to go back and get some rest."

So they went back, to lie awake together and wonder how

the baby could have contracted pneumonia. He was never taken among crowds, and no one in the house had even had a cold. Nevertheless, such things did happen. . . .

When Peter recovered, he was only a handful, so thin that Margaret's mother cried when she saw him.

"My pretty boy," she kept saying, and held his head against her cheek. "Grandma will fatten you up, she'll make you big and strong."

He took a long time to become "big and strong." His appetite was poor, he grew slowly, but eventually he did do all the right things, sat up, walked and spoke his first words as babies are supposed to do, and was, in short, normal.

"Are we just a pair of fatuous parents?" asked Margaret, "or does he really have an exceptional disposition? It seems to me, when we're at gatherings with lots of children his age, that Peter's the smartest and the best behaved. Really and truly."

"Foolish parent," Arthur said, laughing at her.

But Margaret's own mother said, "He's going to be a rare man. Can't you see he's Arthur all over? Looks like him and acts like him, even at this age."

"If he's going to be like his father I'm twice blessed," Margaret answered, and that night, in bed, was overcome with the love that had struck her when first she had seen Arthur across a crowded room.

She liked to think that was the night Holly had been conceived; the date seemed right, anyway.

They were so happy. Two babies in two years! They had everything, the whole world in their hands.

But one night in the seventh month of Margaret's pregnancy something happened. They were awakened again, this time by dreadful cries. When they rushed to him Peter was lying with his legs drawn up to his stomach, turning and turning in obvious pain from one side of the crib to the other. So then they were back in the hospital, and there, on that anxious night—how many anxious days and nights they knew!—a clever young resident was the first to make them aware of some facts.

"The child is very, very seriously ill. I suggest you call in Dr. Lear," he said. "Lear's one of the best internists in the state."

Arthur begged him: "What do you think it is?"

"I have no right to say," the young man answered. "I've made no tests."

"But you have some idea. Please give us your idea. I understand your position, and I won't repeat what you say to anyone. Please."

There was something irresistible about Arthur's quiet appeal and so, after several minutes had passed, the doctor relented.

"It may be cystic fibrosis," he told them. "But remember, that is only a hunch, a guess, and I should not be saying it."

Nevertheless, that clever young man was right. After him, they embarked on a long journey of discovery.

First there was Dr. Lear, "one of the best internists in the state." In his white office, under bright lights, the little body of Peter Crawfield was X-rayed, tested, prodded and probed by gentle, expert fingers.

"I'm afraid it is what we feared," the doctor told them finally. His glance went from Arthur's face to Margaret's, passing quickly over Margaret's by-now-enormous abdomen; his expression seemed to say that this was a sad place for a woman in her condition to be. "As I told you, before I become certain, this will be a hard road to travel. I always believe in being frank."

"He may be expert, and he certainly was nice, but I don't believe him," said Margaret, going down the steps from the office.

Arthur said only, "Shall we try elsewhere?"

"Of course we shall. Anyone with a brain in his head looks for a second opinion."

So they looked and so they received it: the same. The baby might live for a year or two or maybe into young manhood, or die anytime in between. He could be subject to pneumonia, diabetes, heat prostration, intestinal distress, or heart failure; he will need extensive, prudent, careful rearing and watching . . . After the fourth or fifth try they knew it all by heart.

Patiently, Arthur, knowing better, acceded to Margaret's pleas; by car, plane, and local train they went with their bundled baby from doctor to doctor, and came at last full circle to where they had begun.

"Enough," Arthur said. "We've come to the end. Now accept."

It was, in a way, a relief.

The family, parents and grandparents, gathered on that final evening in Arthur's den. The grandparents were shell-shocked.

"I looked it up the minute you got off the phone," said Albert, the grandfather. "Cystic fibrosis runs in families! No one, as far back as I can go, not any of us on Margaret's side, ever had it. What about you, Arthur?"

"Nobody," Arthur said miserably. "Of course there can be some ancestor so far back that no one even knows his name. Anyway, it doesn't always have to be inherited. It can just happen."

"Supposedly everything we are is in the genes," responded Albert, in equal misery.

"What's the difference?" cried Margaret. "What is, is, and there's no changing it. I'm worried now . . ." Her voice trailed off. Her hands rested on the rounded heap where the next baby lay waiting soon to be born. . . .

But Holly was strong and well from the moment she made her appearance. With her there were no crises, no worries or daily cares about pneumonia or diet or diabetes — or anything, certainly none of the symptoms or effects of anything as dire as cystic fibrosis. She was a joy, although not an easy joy like Peter! Headstrong, affectionate, argumentative, warmhearted and stubborn, she was certainly not like him.

"Holly is you, as Peter is Arthur." That was the informed opinion of relatives and friends.

"Informed opinion," said Margaret, lying now on Peter's bed in the waning afternoon. Like Arthur. Arthur's boy.

And it was not true! He was . . . whose boy? Her hands, lying at her sides, made fists. Her wedding ring cut her flesh. Not true! So there was another grief! How many kinds of grief was a person supposed to bear? How to resolve the conflict?

"My heart breaks over Peter," she whispered. "Breaks, do you hear? But that other, that other who is also mine, was mine . . . oh God, how much, how many sorrows?"

She was still lying there when Arthur came home. She heard his keys jingle as he laid them on the hall table and heard his call.

"Margy? I'm home. Where are you?"

"Upstairs. I'll be right down," she said, not wanting him, on his first day back at work, to come up and see her weeping in that room; she must be strong for him, must help him.

But he was already at the top of the stairs. When he saw where she was, he came in and put his arms about her, holding her without speaking.

"All those years," she murmured. "Our Peter. Nineteen, this summer."

"Yes, yes. A short life. My God! And all the time he knew, I'm sure he knew, it would be short."

"Can you absorb in your head or your heart that he was not born to us? He was so much ours! How can it have happened, Arthur?"

"Who can say? A careless nurse breaks the ID bracelets, that's all. It's happened, and it's happened to us."

"I feel," she said, "I feel this is a double death, as if—" And she put her hand on the place where her womb lay, where she had nurtured a child. "Isn't there—can't we find out what happened to the—the other one?"

"You know the Barnes Clinic closed down years ago," he reminded her gently.

She persisted. "The records had to be transferred somewhere."

He was silent.

"Don't you *want* to know, Arthur?"

He replied, so low that she hardly heard him, "I guess maybe I don't."

"But why? I don't understand!"

"Because—because what good will it do?"

"I need," she whispered, and gulped to control the lump of tears that was determined to rise in her throat, "I need to know whether he—the other one—has a good home. Suppose they are terrible people, alcoholic or cruel, or he's sick or hungry somewhere—"

Arthur had released her and stood now, with his back to her, at the wall. Peter's high school diploma hung there, but he was not looking at it. After a minute or two he turned about and answered her plea.

"Let's assume we can be successful in our search, and that's quite an assumption in the circumstances, rather like the needle in the haystack; what good will it do? If the home isn't a good one, there's nothing we can do about it. The boy's an adult. It's too late."

"Still, I want to know."

Arthur continued, reasoning deliberately, "And if the home is a good one, we will be disrupting it. Think of the lives we will overturn! The boy's life most of all, but his family's too, and probably Holly's as well. Here she is now. Let's leave this room."

They were in their own bedroom when Holly came up the stairs. Her cheeks were pink from running. Her legs, below the red miniskirt, were slim and strong. Clear sky and fresh air, thought her father, looking at her.

"Hi, Dad." She kissed his cheek. "I've got a load of work to catch up on. How was your day?" Embarrassed, she corrected herself. "I mean, how could it be? I mean, I hope it wasn't too awful, your first day back at the office. Oh Lord, I guess I don't know what I mean."

"It's all right," Arthur said tenderly. "We all know what we mean. Can I help you with anything? Latin? I used to be pretty good at it."

"No thanks, Dad. I'll let you know, though, if I need you."

"She's all we have now," he said, after she left the room.

The tiny hammers had started up again in Margaret's head.

"All?" she repeated. "Can you really forget about the other?"

"Forget? Of course I can't. Do you think I haven't thought about him, even before Peter died? From the day we were told about it, I've thought. And I believe, I do believe, better let it lie, Margaret. Let's accept the accomplished fact, as we must accept the fact of Peter's death, and go on living as well as we can. Take care of Holly. Pick up the broken pieces and try to put them together."

"I don't know whether I can," she murmured. And suddenly she cried out, "How I wish Peter would come back and tell us this is all a nightmare!"

"I know, Margy, but he can't." Arthur's voice cracked; he felt all her pain, the mirror image of his own.

Yes, thought Margaret, a double death, that's what it is. We brought you home, Peter, we loved you so, we cared for you and we followed you to your grave.

"And they tell us," she said aloud, "that he was never meant to be ours! That somewhere—where?—the other one—will you really not want to find out, Arthur? Never?"

"Margy, Margy, 'never' is a long time. Let me think, I'm so tired and confused. I'll have to think. I *should* think, and I can't."

PART
II

Laura

longed to her and to their son Tom, there being no other readers in the family. The photographs that were on the shelves and tables belonged to them all.

Here was her father, a young major in his cap with a sweep of hair just barely visible. "The hair of the black Irish," Aunt Lillian said. Her mother's thin face, tense and witty, regarded him from the other half of the double leather frame. There were the formal photographs of Laura and Bud together, taken last Christmas as a present for the family. Still fair-haired, she was not one pound heavier than she had been as a twenty-year-old bride. But Bud's thick fair hair, receding, had heightened a high forehead, and he had gained through the years a portly stomach. Yet he could still compete with Tom at tennis.

Something compelled her now to carry Tom's picture to the light. It was as if by examining the face beneath the dark silky hair that fell across one eyebrow, the strong face with the high cheekbones, the wide-open gold-brown eyes and the obstinate mouth, she might find some answers to the questions that so troubled her, although they did not trouble Bud.

Tom was so—so *determined*! He was so bright, so keen, and could be so dear, but was yet so stubborn. With bulldog's teeth he held to his convictions, and she despised his convictions. They were the ugly inventions of political fanatics, of men like Jim Johnson, who was now running for election to the state senate; a man old in spirit, he must be filled with God only knew what secret angers. That such a man should be able to corrupt the young, to corrupt my nineteen-year-old son! she cried in silent outrage.

Far to the rear of the house in the great kitchen, Betty Lee was polishing silver and humming gospel songs. Three times a week she graced the house with her healthy cheer, with her very presence. And Laura wondered how much she might know about Tom, whom she had fed and diapered. He had been ordered to keep Jim Johnson talk to himself, but there were all those books in his room. . . . Yet he was affectionate to Betty Lee. His heart was warm. She knew it was. Surely he did not belong with those people . . .

How different he was from his brother! His tall stance contrasted to Timmy's, who stood half a head shorter than his eleven-year-old peers. His confident gaze beside the half smile on the small freckled face, that smile which with a touching pride concealed Tim's fears.

And should Tim not be fearful? He knew too much about human suffering already, and knew what still awaited him when cystic fibrosis had run its course.

These thoughts, as always, made her pulses race. What if by some unlikely chance he should outlive Bud and me? she thought again. And she reminded herself: *But Tom would take care of him.* Tom loved him, Tom got up at night when Timmy coughed; Tom knew all the medications and cautions; he never let Tim get too tired or too hot. You could depend on Tom. He meant what he said and did what he promised to do.

Good sons, both. And each of them a gift of joy, each in his way a painful sorrow.

A sudden weariness born of these thoughts and of the dark day overcame her, and she lay down on the sofa, something she never did in the daytime, to wait for the four o'clock lesson. A plaster frieze of fruit and flowers ran where the ceiling met the wall. Idly her eyes followed it from grapevines to acorns, pine cones, wheat sheaves, and back to grapevines. The hard, monotonous rain beat on the roof of the porch. Powerful outside forces beat on the family . . . I hate these moods, she thought, closing her eyes. I shall will this one to pass.

Nevertheless, there were times when the will was never enough, when the questions persisted as if they were written in tall red letters and even closed eyelids could not shut them out.

Who is this woman, this Laura Paige Rice, and how did she get from there to here?

❖ ❖ ❖

Adults think that a child building a castle of blocks on the floor in the next room is too absorbed in play to hear their talk or even if she should hear it, to understand it.

"Poor little soul," said a visitor, commiserating. And then briskly, brightly added, "But how lucky to have you girls to take over."

The Paige sisters, Cecile and Lillian, would always in their circle, and should they live to be ninety, be "the girls." But they were far from the stereotype that that term brings to mind: "ladies who lunch." They were just as thin and fashionable in their expensive suits, but more significantly, they were out in the world; they were keeping their inherited place at Paige and Company.

"What did we know about wholesale building supplies? Lumber and wire and cement?" Lillian would say to anybody who would listen, and many did. "First our father, then our brother, and finally no one but us two girls to run that huge spread out on the highway. Well, if you've got a brain, it's a challenge to use it. Besides, we had Laura to think of."

They liked, these two aunts, to talk about Laura with their friends while the teacups clinked on the saucers on Sunday afternoons. Unmarried and already in their forties, they had been given a present of a pretty child, a responsibility, a beloved toy.

"She must have an inheritance. That's the main reason we worked so hard to expand. It will mean security. A woman needs security." People still talked that way about women in the 1950s. They took Laura's picture under the enormous sign that read "Paige and Company," and while she was still in nursery school, taught her to spell out the words.

"Yes, if it hadn't been for Laura, who knows? We might even have sold out and retired."

"But she is an enchanting child, isn't she?" Cecile's lovely voice rang with pleasure. "I do hope her hair stays blond. Blond hair," she mused, "fastened back with a black velvet band, or navy blue."

They had their own anxious, fussy way of loving Laura, not

sparing a moment's energy on her behalf. From the pediatrician to the dentist to the French lesson they drove, and as soon as her talent for music was discovered, to the music lesson, too.

"They gave me everything. They gave me their whole lives," she said to Bud years later. "I was completely spoiled."

And he refuted her. "If they tried to spoil you, they didn't succeed. You're the least spoiled person I ever knew."

"We must be careful not to let her get too bookish," Cecile reflected when Laura was ten. "I think I'll arrange for tennis lessons on Saturday mornings. What do you think?"

"Yes, it's a healthy sport, and very useful socially, too. You can play it all your life," agreed Lillian, whose only exercise was a walk from the house to the car, then from the car to the office desk.

And Cecile: "Perhaps we should put in a tennis court. There's a good level place back of the garage."

"Yes, and while we're at it, we might enclose the vegetable garden, the way they do in England. A trellis, perhaps?"

They were always doing things with the house. It was a house for the generations. They liked to dwell on some idyllic future for Laura in this dear place.

"Someday you will marry a man who will take over the business and will live here with you," they would often tell her.

Touched by their goodness, amused by their blindness, she gave them in reply her secret smile.

I am going to marry Francis Alcott. You don't know that yet, but you will.

Lying here now so long afterward, she felt the gathering of another smile, this in nostalgic recollection of that peace and innocence.

But are children, was I, ever innocent? No, Laura, you know better. . . .

A thick privet hedge grown taller than a man divides the properties. Toward one end some damage, either by disease or storm, has made a gap in it through which a child can peek, or, if permitted, slide. But Laura is not permitted.

"Dr. Alcott really should fix that," Aunt Lillian complains. "It's unsightly. They've not been keeping up the place as well since Francis went away."

"Poor folks," says Cecile. "It's a pity they haven't got a daughter. Francis is never home anymore."

"He's on his way home now, didn't you know? I heard this morning. He broke both legs skiing in Colorado during spring break. Or maybe it was both ankles. Anyway, we should go over there this evening."

Laura asks how a leg can be broken. In her mind there's a picture of a broken cup lying in small pieces on the floor.

"No, no, it's not like that," says Lillian.

"Well, I'd like to see one, anyway."

Cecile promises, "When Francis has had a chance to rest awhile, you may go over with us one afternoon. We'll bake some cookies for him. He's such a nice boy."

Laura is in the yard the morning after. She is sitting on the rim of her sandbox when a screen door slams and voices sound far off at the end of the Alcotts' lawn. It might be the boy with the broken legs, she thinks, so she goes to investigate. What she sees is a man with fat white legs stretched out on a long chair. There is a little table beside the chair on which she can see a pitcher and a glass. Lemonade? she wonders. And she watches closely, spying from the gap in the hedge as the man takes up his book, puts it down, drinks from the glass, runs his hand through his hair, which is dark and wavy, and picks up the book again. She would like to know whether those white things really are his broken legs; probably, though, they aren't because they don't look like legs, and anyway, the aunts said Francis was a nice boy, and this is not a boy. He's a man, so he can't be Francis. She's pondering all this when the man sees her and calls.

"Hello. How are you? Come on over."

"I'm not allowed to."

"Not allowed? Why not? We're neighbors."

"I'm not supposed to annoy Dr. Alcott. He's busy."

The man laughs. "You'd never annoy Dr. Alcott. Anyway, he's at the office now. And I'm his son. I'm Francis."

"Are those your broken legs?" asks Laura, already on the other side of the hedge and halfway toward the chair.

"Yes, and they're an awful nuisance. I'm missing half a term at college on account of them."

She draws nearer and suddenly solves the puzzle. "The broken part is under those white things, isn't it?"

"That's right. The white things are casts. Like bandages."

"Oh. Do they hurt?"

"Not anymore." He has put the book away and is smiling at her. "I'll guess your name, shall I?"

She nods. "But I'll bet you can't."

"Let's see. Is it Caroline?"

She shakes her head. "Nope."

"Susan?"

"Nope."

"Fuzzy Wuzzy?"

This seems very funny, and it delights her. "I said you couldn't guess!"

"Oh, but I can. You're Laura, and I knew it all the time. My father told me about you when you came to live next door, only I haven't seen you before this because I've been away at college in California."

"Where's that?"

"It's far away."

"Oh. Like Korea?"

"Not quite."

"My father went to Heaven from Korea."

Francis says gravely, "I know. He was nice, your father."

"Did you know him?"

"Very well. He lived here where you live now."

"Oh."

"You look like him except that your hair's blond."

She considers that for a moment. Then Francis touches her

hand, saying still gravely, "He bought me my first ball and bat when I was a little boy."

"I thought," she says, "you were still a boy."

"What makes you think that?"

"Aunt Cecile said, 'Francis is a nice boy.' "

"I see. Well, she's very nice herself."

Laura considers that, too. "But I miss my mommy."

"Of course you do," says Francis.

She likes the feel of his warm hand on hers. When she peers up into his face, his eyes look into hers with the same smile that Aunt Cecile has when she says "I love you."

"How old are you?" he asks now.

"I'm four. How old are you?"

"Nineteen."

"That's old, isn't it?"

"Kind of, but not awfully."

"Laura! Laura! Where are you?" It is Aunt Lillian standing at the hedge.

"Oh dear, you shouldn't— Francis, I'm sorry, is she bothering you?"

"Bothering, Miss Lillian? She's adorable."

"But you have to study, you said, and—"

"I've got another six weeks to be laid up with the books. Please, let her come over whenever she wants. I mean it."

So it begins.

It was Francis who taught her to read even before she entered kindergarten. All that spring while the casts were on his legs and even afterward when he began to walk again, he made a game of the alphabet and the words in his big books.

"Show me a word with three letters," he would command. " 'Sun,' that's right. Tell me, is the sun cold?"

"No, silly, it's hot."

"Okay, can you find 'hot' on this page?"

And Laura's plump finger would slide along the lines until, triumphantly, she would find it.

" 'Hot.' There it is!"

"What a fine young man," the aunt remarked. "So patient, so very gentle. He'll make a marvelous doctor, you can just see it in him."

For the Christmas when Laura was six, somebody gave her a copy of *Alice in Wonderland*.

"But I can't read it," she complained to Francis when he and his parents came to dinner during the vacation. "The words are too long."

"Come here, and I'll read it to you," he offered.

"That child takes such advantage of his good nature," said Aunt Lillian, who was serving after-dinner coffee on the other side of the room.

To this remark Dr. Alcott replied that Francis never offered anything unless he wanted to give it.

"He likes children, and besides, there is something especially appealing about Laura. You must know that."

Well, yes, she had to admit that she did. Her sigh was contented. "Cecile and I consider ourselves blessed. So many people seem to have such problems with their children through no fault of their own."

Always, Laura would remember *Alice in Wonderland*, its gray binding, the illustrations of Alice with her flowing hair, and Francis's long fingers resting on the page.

"You remind me of Alice," he said.

And she would remember, as the years passed, every detail of every book that was in some way connected to Francis. *The Secret Garden* because he gave it to her for her birthday when she was eight, and *Treasure Island* because he had visited the real island on a sailing trip.

When he returned, he showed photographs of the boat and his friends and the island that lay like a great green whale asleep on blue water.

"Someday you'll see these places," he told her. "You must see as much of the world as you can while you're young. The world is so beautiful, Laura. You can't believe how beautiful it is."

Whenever he was home, he gave her books and listened to

her opinions about them. They agreed and they argued. He taught her to play chess. He gave her a camera and taught her the art of using it so well that she won a contest for her still life of rain on magnolia leaves. Sometimes in the evening when he and his father came visiting, she played the piano and was pleased when everyone praised her.

Yet at the same time she knew that all of them except Francis were overpraising. "My aunts think I'm going to go around the world giving concerts," she complained to Francis. "It's embarrassing. If I were going to be famous like that, I would be now. I'm twelve, and that's already late."

"You have a talent, and that's more than enough to bring you happiness. There's no need to be famous," he said gently.

She loved his voice when he was serious like this. It had tones in it, deep, soft notes like the lowest piano key when the left hand barely touches them.

"You're wise, Laura. It's wise to see yourself so clearly."

Curiously, she asked, "What do you see when you look at yourself?"

"I? A pretty good student who always wanted to be a doctor like my father. That's all."

Laura shook her head. "No, you're not seeing everything. You're going to be great."

He laughed. "Good God, no. Never."

"Oh, yes. Everybody says so."

"Who's everybody?"

"My aunts say that everybody says so."

And Francis laughed again. "Well, tell them I'll try my best."

Sometimes while Laura did homework in her bedroom, the aunts would be talking in the upstairs sitting room. They knew everything that was happening in the neighborhood. "Internal medicine," one said. "Rare diseases, I think. Or tropical, maybe? I'm not sure."

"He's going on to a fellowship after a three-year residency, Mrs. Alcott told me."

"He won't be coming back here to settle, mark my words. It'll be New York or Boston, more likely."

"Well, probably. He won't be home at all this summer. No time off, Mrs. Alcott says."

"The Baker girl will be disappointed, that's for sure. He's been seeing her for the last three years whenever he's been home."

"They make a good-looking pair. She's a stunning girl, don't you think so?"

"But he's not ready to be serious, his father says. He won't even consider marriage until he's finished his training."

"She won't wait for him. She's twenty-six, and thirty is looming up."

"That remains to be seen. You never know."

She had better not wait for him, thought Laura, and scoffed: *a stunning girl.* The Baker girl with that foolish constant smile that made your cheeks ache to look at? Why ever would Francis want her?

From a group snapshot that had been taken one Fourth of July, she cut out his head and put it into her gold locket where before her aunts had been. Then she had to wear the locket day and night so that they wouldn't find it in her room. It was not that they would be angry or hurt; no, of course not; they would be merely amused, and she could not have borne that either.

They thought she had a crush on Francis. "And why not?" Aunt Lillian said to the cook. Her voice, unlike Cecile's, was loud enough to carry up the backstairs from the kitchen. "With his looks—those eyes of his—he can turn any woman's head if he wants to."

"And even if he doesn't want to." The cook laughed. "Any woman from eight to eighty."

They were cheapening her love. A crush, they called it, a feeling you might have for one boy in March, for another in April, and still another in May. And opening the locket in front of the mirror, Laura studied Francis's face, which seemed to be looking back at her with love. But then, I am only twelve, she thought. If only she were older . . .

Unexpectedly, one weekend he flew home from Boston. When she saw him coming across the lawn from his house, she dashed out, banging the screen door behind her, and threw her arms around his neck. She had always done so, and when she was still small enough, he had always lifted and hugged her. She was hardly small enough now; so taking her arms down from his neck, he held both of her hands and kissed her forehead.

"Oh, it's good to be back! How are you, Princess?"

"You're too big now to hug Francis like that," Aunt Lillian reproved her that night. "Laura darling, you're not a child anymore."

Hot with humiliation and knowing what was meant, she did not answer. What was meant was: *You have breasts.* He felt them when you pressed against him.

"She may be tall for her age, but she is still a child after all," Cecile said.

Would they never learn that she always overheard them when they were having their coffee in the sitting room?

"I sometimes think you read too much into things, Lillian."

"And I sometimes think you don't read at all."

That was Lillian. Cecile was the sweeter, the romantic one. But Lillian was the smarter of the two. And so Laura learned care and caution.

Then suddenly she was fifteen. Long ages seemed to have passed, not just three years, since she had been an impetuous girl of twelve. She had a quiet manner. The promise of height had been kept; she was slender, and her striking hair was still blond. Thanks to the aunts who, knowing how to dress, had taught her well, she had fine, subtle taste. Her clothes were simple. She wore a necklace of gold links, a small ruby ring that had belonged to her mother, and a man's wristwatch that the army had sent home from Korea. And hidden under her collar, she wore also Francis's picture in the locket, although it was two years since she had seen him last.

There were many parties that year, and she went to them all. People liked Laura, as people always had done. She was, in a sense, a leader, for which she was thankful, but also surprised because she could see nothing special about herself, nothing different from most other girls except that she was able to entertain people at the piano.

Dressed in red velvet for somebody's formal dance at the country club, she was waiting to be called for one evening when Francis rang the doorbell.

"You always come home unexpectedly," she said with her new calm smile.

"I covered for a fellow at the hospital last weekend, and this is my payback. I'm so darned glad to be here, Laura. But I'm holding you up. You're on your way out, I see."

Her heart was wild, and yet she was able to keep that practiced calm.

"Yes, to a dance, but not till half-past. Sit down and keep me company."

He drew up a chair near hers so that their knees almost touched. "Do you realize it's two years since I saw you last? You're so changed that I almost don't know you anymore."

"I'm fifteen now."

"If I were fifteen, I'd bar the door to the fellow who's taking you, and I'd take you to the dance myself."

"Your father says you're working too hard."

"Oh, I've had a few twenty-four-hour stretches between sleeps. But that goes with the job, and I love the job."

"Is that why you don't come home anymore?"

"Dad says he has more free time than I have, so he'd rather visit me. He's going to enjoy California again when I go back there for my fellowship." Francis smiled. "He loved the ocean."

"How long will you be there?"

"It's a two-year fellowship. Then maybe I'll go abroad for research. I want to specialize in rare diseases, then come back and teach."

"Elephantiasis and stuff like that?"

"Like that. How do you know about elephantiasis?"

"I pick things up when I read, and I read everything. Ever since you taught me."

"I'm proud of you, Laura. Glad and proud."

And with a touch of her own pride, she told him, "I skipped a year. I'll be sixteen and a half when I graduate."

The dialogue came to a stop, although there ought to have been so much to say after their long separation. Indeed, Laura's head was crammed with questions, but she could not ask them.

After a moment, Francis asked one. "What's been happening in the neighborhood? Anything interesting? All I've heard is that George Buckson's bank has sent him to Hong Kong, and that Carol Baker's engaged."

"But not to you?"

His eyebrows rose. "Me? Whoever gave you that idea?"

"My aunts."

"Of course, who else?" And they both laughed.

The laughter restored them to where they had been two years before. A light relief moved through Laura's body, an involuntary smile touched her lips, and wanting to display her lace cuff and the pink shells of her newly manicured nails, she rested her hand on the arm of the chair. If only the doorbell would not ring, if only they might stay alone like this.

He was looking at her, eyes meeting eyes, and she saw in his that he found her beautiful.

"You—" he began when the doorbell rang.

"Oh darn, here they are," she cried.

Francis went to open the door on the cold air and the noisy little troupe. Jeanie was with Rick, Cissy was with Fred, and Hank had a corsage—a white one, thank goodness—for Laura.

"We're late," Hank said in a rush. "I had to wait for the station wagon, so we all decided to meet here and save time."

Self-conscious in their clothes, they stood waiting while she made a quick introduction to Francis and hurried herself into her coat. Suddenly they looked like such kids, such awkward kids. They had never seemed like that before. And Laura's feeling of elegance evaporated; she partook of their awkwardness.

Francis loomed over them, although the boys were almost as tall as he.

"Have a great time, you kids," he said. "And Laura, tell your aunts I'm sorry I didn't get to see them, but this is a short visit. I'm going with my parents to visit relatives in the country tomorrow, and the next day I leave. So give them my best, will you?"

They piled into the car, and Laura watched him walk away across the lawn.

"That's a good-looking guy. Who is he?" Jeanie asked.

They were all so noisy that they didn't even give Laura a chance to answer.

"Good-looking! For Christ's sake, Jeanie, the guy's *old*. An *old* guy," mocked Fred, who had pudgy cheeks and a queer, flattened nose.

"Well, he doesn't look old," Jeanie said. "Who is he?" she repeated.

Laura was hot and cold. "A family friend. A neighbor," she said dully.

Have a good time, you kids. Kids. Yet the way he had looked at her . . . And he had been about to say something. Now she would never know what it was. Probably she would never know. He might not even be back here for another two years. And so much could happen while he was away.

She dreamed about him. At parties boys kissed her, but her dreams were of being kissed by Francis, and they were sorrowful dreams, filled with longing.

Time, time, thought Laura. Her eyes followed the plaster flowers on the wall. The grandmother had ordered the thistle and the rose, but the grandfather, being of Irish descent, had in rebellion squeezed a few shamrocks into the corners. "Old passions, old pains," she murmured, thinking: Francis is over fifty now. I wonder what he looks like.

People said he was a famous doctor in New York, a researcher, a teacher. The neighbors said, "We got a Christmas card from Francis Alcott. Of course, we were such friends of the old doctor's. Do you get a card, too?"

No, she never did. Not a card or anything else.

At the other end of the state was the university at which Laura was to major in music. The aunts were probably relieved that she was not a fitting candidate for a conservatory, for any one of these would have taken her too far away. They made mild lament over even this much distance from home.

"You promise, Laura, to call home twice a week? It's easier for you to reach us than for us to reach you in that enormous place. Call collect at dinnertime, hear?"

Their possessiveness could have been a burden, and to many girls away for the first time to savor independence, it would have been. But Laura had treasured love since the age of three, and she made allowances.

As always, the aunts were eager for news and eager to spread it.

"Carol Baker had a huge wedding. Ten bridesmaids, imagine! A good thing she didn't count on Francis Alcott, isn't it, or she'd still be waiting. It doesn't look as if he'll ever marry and stay in one place."

For a pair of single women past middle age, they were fascinated by marriage, Laura thought with affectionate amusement.

"The Alcotts just came back from California. They say Francis is doing well. But he was always outstanding, so it's only to be expected. He may be traveling to India with some medical group in a year or two, did we tell you? And he wants your address, Laura. I think he has a present for you. Books, Dr. Alcott said."

And books did arrive, the lives of Mozart and Beethoven, with a note enclosed.

Foraging in a bookstore as usual, I saw these and thought you might like them. So you see how you people at home are always in my mind. But I have to admit it's wonderful here. I've made great friends, the work's going well, and of course the climate is perfect. Dear Laura, I hope you're just as pleased with where you are.

His handwriting looked like him, the letters orderly and even until a capital appeared, tall and swooping like the punctuation of his sudden laughter. And as always, she remembered his hands, the narrow, pale tan hands with the Greek lettering on the seal ring. Now in the California sun, she supposed his hands must be brown.

"I'll be coming home in July for a couple of weeks," he wrote. "I'll want to hear all about your freshman year."

That was the summer the aunts arranged a trip to Alaska. Laura's protests were useless.

Aunt Lillian exclaimed, "Summer courses! What on earth for? With your grade average, you deserve a vacation, Laura. It's all planned anyway, from Anchorage to Nome. Bears, eagles, ice fields—we'll take our time and see it all."

So they went, and indeed it was as marvelous as promised. But when they got home, Francis had been there and gone.

And the same thing happened the next year, when they went to Montreal, down the St. Lawrence River and into Nova Scotia.

"It's too bad we missed Francis," said Aunt Cecile when they arrived home. "He went back just three days ago."

If she had not known Cecile so well, known that she was utterly incapable of dissembling, Laura might have thought that the dates had been planned to turn out that way.

Occasional letters came to her from Francis. Since she saved them all, she was able to compare and so to discover how often he wrote about "thinking of" or "missing all you people at home." Who were "all you people"? Did he possibly mean: "I miss *you*"? But if he did, he should have said so.

And one afternoon on a solitary walk, Laura had a sudden astonishing sense of herself as she might appear to an analytical observer: a foolish adolescent obsessed with an imagined romance. Seen so, she was a figure of embarrassment. This picture was so startling that it brought her to a halt in the middle of the sidewalk. My God, she must bring her mind under control! Must make a strict, enormous effort! She was letting Francis Alcott rule her life. . . .

At Christmastime, Dr. and Mrs. Alcott joined their son on a trip to the Yucatán. From there came a letter from Francis with a snapshot of the three standing before the pyramid at Chichén Itzá. The letter was cordial and as vivid as a travel brochure. No, there is nothing here for you, Laura said to herself; you are beginning to see that, aren't you? This will fade, you are an adult woman now, at eighteen. You are getting over this.

And still there was not a day, even if only for a moment, when she did not think of Francis.

In her junior year she met a man who stood apart from the crowd of her peers, the Freds and Joes who had gone through high school with her, the fraternity men, the jocks, the scholars, the whole assortment with whom she went to football games or chamber music concerts with equal enjoyment. She was adaptable, and she liked being adaptable. One had a wide choice that way, and it was challenging.

Homer Rice was in the graduate school working toward an MBA when they met. She had seen him a few times walking across the campus, and once, for no particular reason, someone had pointed him out in passing.

"There goes Bud Rice. He was a great quarterback a few years ago. He looks it, doesn't he?"

Powerful, was the word. He was large, tall and broad without a trace of fat. He might have been a symbol of good health in an advertisement for nutritious food; his skin was pink, and his strong teeth, well displayed by a short upper lip, were so flawless that one might believe they were false.

She knew that he had observed her. And one warm spring day when she was alone on a step reading an assignment, he came over to her and introduced himself.

"My name's Bud Rice. I've been noticing you for a long time. I'd have gone up to you if you hadn't always been in a crowd or if I'd had more nerve."

This shyness, especially on the part of a football star, surprised her. He was almost humble. And so she replied with
special gentleness. "My name's Laura Paige. I'd have been
glad to talk to you."

"Would you? A girl who looks like you sort of—well, sort
of makes a man hesitate. Mind if I sit down?"

"Of course not. Come on. I've no class until three."

By the end of an hour when they parted, Laura had learned
probably as much about Bud as, in those days, there was to
know. He came from the real backcountry, where his father
was the pastor of a small church. She had seen enough of
those to picture a board structure probably in need of paint,
on a two-lane blacktop highway at the edge of a crossroads
village. She had read enough to feel the shuddering poverty
and bleak isolation. And from that place he had managed to
win a scholarship, had then earned honors and also earned
money by doing odd jobs, enough to pay for the MBA. He
was ambitious and earnest; his respectfulness and his formal,
old-fashioned courtesy were "backcountry." He was certainly
different, and therefore interesting. Deciding that she liked
him, she agreed to see him again.

Her friends were impressed. It was "cool" to have a boy-
friend in graduate school, a person who already had his feet
poised to go out into the world of real jobs, of adult responsi-
bilities. Maybe it was the admiration that he inspired in her
friends that made Laura keep on seeing him; often, later, she
thought about that. Certainly there had never been any leap of
the heart. . . .

Then, too, she had been wooed by his own open admiration.
"You know so many things I never even heard about," he said
one night after she had taken him to a concert.

When she asked him whether he had enjoyed it, he gave a
candid answer. "I can't say I liked it, but I didn't mind it too
much, either. I guess that high-class music is something I
should learn about," he said with his appealing white smile.

"Why should you?" And wanting to be very kind in return

for his simple honesty, she added, "A person should like what he likes. There's no need to please other people."

"But I'd like to please you, Laura. I've had girls run after me, you know. Mostly because of the football business, which is absurd, isn't it? And yet, absurd as it is, I've enjoyed it. I've just enjoyed being wanted. I suppose it's natural, isn't it? Maybe it's because I can't be sure of what you think of me that I—" He floundered and stopped.

She was both flattered and touched by such confusion in someone who was otherwise so alert and competent, so sure of himself. He was a straight-A student, could do incredibly fast calculations right in his head, followed every trend in politics and finance—all areas where she felt stupidly blind—and yet there was such *esteem* in his long look at her.

"What I think of you? Why, if I didn't like you, Bud, I wouldn't be sitting here with you."

She was arch, she was flirting, but nevertheless, she was telling the truth.

"How about going out to the country for lunch on Saturday? I can borrow a car."

"I can't. My aunts are getting up at the crack of dawn to be here in time for lunch." When she saw his disappointment, she made a quick offer. "But I'd love to have you join us at the hotel."

"That's awfully nice. I think I'll be in the way, though."

Although she had instantly regretted the invitation, there was only one thing to say. "Of course you won't be. Do come. I only hope you won't be bored."

"Bored? No," he said in his proper way. "I'll be pleased to meet your aunts."

Bud and the aunts took to each other at once. To begin with, he looked as if he were going to church in his good dark blue suit and paisley tie. Cecile and Lillian, who had no doubt expected to meet a college boy in jeans, would approve of this businesslike appearance, Laura knew, for she had often enough heard their disgusted exclamations over what they called "radical youth" with their ponytails.

"Clean jeans are one thing," remarked Aunt Lillian. "That's just comfort and informality. But the scenes you see on television at some of those northern colleges make you wonder where we're all heading."

Bud agreed. "On this campus, it's law and order. That's why I like it. I guess I'll be sorry to leave it next year."

The talk was lively, and Laura settled back to listen. Bud presented himself well. He was interested in hearing how the two women had taken charge of the family business, and they were interested in his theories; concepts of taxation, the free market, and debt reduction passed across the table. At ease in his knowledge, Bud was impressive.

"The corporate recruiters will be coming, and you'll have your choice, I'm sure," Cecile said.

"Well, ma'am, I sure hope so."

They would like that "ma'am," thought Laura. It was falling out of use these days, but the son of a country preacher hadn't yet found that out.

When the lunch was over, the aunts agreed that he was a fine young man, so friendly, so polite, and so smart.

"Shrewd," said Lillian. "He'll do well, no question about that."

"Are you serious with him at all?" asked Cecile.

Laura frowned. "Good God, no. I'm not 'serious' with anybody. I have lots of dates. Lots."

Cecile was apologetic. "Naturally you do, dear. Why shouldn't you be popular? A girl like you with all your talents, piano, tennis, and so pretty and sweet besides." Wistfully, she sighed. "I never can stop thinking how happy you would have made your parents."

Lillian returned to the subject. "He surely is good-looking, Laura."

"In a way."

" 'In a way!' So tall and so manly, with that head of bright hair and everything about him so neat and clean? If I were your age—" And Lillian laughed at herself.

"I always think," Laura mused, "that he looks sort of military."

"Military? What does that mean?"

"Oh, spit and polish. Stand up straight."

"Your own father was a military man," Lillian said somewhat sharply. "I can't imagine what you're thinking of."

Actually, she was thinking of Francis. She had been trying so hard not to think of him and had been remarkably successful. But now, in this instant, for no particular reason, he returned to her with his flashing dark eyes, his fervor, and his delicacy that was at the same time so completely masculine. . . .

He had gone with a medical group to India, and evidently in a rare mood to write a long letter, had sent her six pages of exuberant description. In reply, she reminded him of a letter he had sent to her years before when he had visited a "treasure island" in the Caribbean Sea. *The world is so beautiful, you can't imagine, Laura,* he had written then. And he had written it now again.

Yes, even here among the violence and filth, the fearful diseases, some of these people are so beautiful in body and in spirit.

He wrote that he would be home in the summer. There was no vacation trip that year.

"I've been away since September, and now I want to be home," Laura told the aunts, and they agreed.

She acquired a few pupils and began to give piano lessons. She went swimming and saw friends. Bud Rice took a summer job about two hours' drive away, but several times on weekends he came for the day, always with chocolates for Laura and flowers for the aunts, huge heads of crimson peonies that Cecile would arrange in the center of the luncheon table.

There that first time in filtered green light from the half-drawn blinds, in the cool dining room, they spent a pleasant hour over Betty Lee's shrimp salad and lime pie. The aunts pressed several servings on Bud and fussed over him.

He thanked them. "You're awfully good to me. I'm not used to being fussed over. My mother died when I was seven."

Cecile said gently, "You and Laura. Except that she had us."

Bud smiled at Laura. "Lucky you."

The aunts asked questions.

"Do you have a family, or just your father?"

"Just my father. I had a sister, but she died when she was three years old."

The aunts made sympathetic faces and Cecile observed, "You haven't had an easy life, I see that."

"That's true, ma'am. But a lot of people have had it much worse. I'm healthy, I'm getting a good education, and I'm ready to meet the world." He laughed. "I'm out to make some money. But no tricks. I mean the good American way, fair and square." He looked around the table. "I hope I'm not shocking you with the admission."

Lillian almost snorted. "Quite the reverse. I have no respect for pious denials. You can't do anything without money in this world, and that's why everyone wants it."

And Laura read her mind: Now, there's a young man who could take over the business. Poor aunts! They were transparent.

They showed him through the house, related its history, to which he listened with great interest, and paused before the photographs.

"That's Laura's father. He was killed in Korea."

"Died for his country," Bud said. "You can be proud, Laura."

"I'd say that Bud Rice is a catch," Lillian remarked that night. "Some girl's going to get hold of him before long, you can count on it."

Such an old-fashioned concept, to think of "getting hold" of a man! And Laura said, "She's welcome to him."

"Don't tell me you don't like him!"

"I do like him well enough. I wouldn't have let him come here if I didn't, would I? Only—"

Not in the mood for explanations, she stopped.

"Only what?"

"There's more to people than what you can see, isn't there, Aunt Lillian?"

Immediately, Lillian pursued the subject. "What do you mean? He respects you, I hope."

"Respect" in the aunts' vocabulary meant "no sex."

"Yes, he respects me." And she recalled a crude attempt— she thought of such attempts as "wrestling matches"—that he had once made, and having been thwarted, had never made since.

"I am simply not going to let you," she had told him.

She had never "let" anyone yet. They might go so far and no farther. It had been quite a feat in 1971 for a nineteen-year-old woman to be still a virgin.

Bud had yielded. "All right. I'll wait. You're going to marry me, Laura. You don't know it now, but you are going to. So I'll wait."

In the middle of August, Francis Alcott came home.

"It'll be good to see him again. It's been almost four years," said Cecile. "Can you believe it, Laura?"

Yes, she believed it and remembered it well. Fifteen, and so childish that night! He must have seen that she was preening before him even while she was hoping to display her calm new maturity. But how absurdly she had posed in the big chair, thrusting under his very nose her manicured nails, her lace-flowered cuffs, and her "sophisticated" low neck, while all the time her heart was jumping so that it might just as well have been visible under the velvet dress.

"Dr. and Mrs. Alcott want us to come over this evening. They're having a little welcome home for Francis, just relatives and old friends," Cecile announced at lunchtime.

Laura looked down at her plate. "You go without me," she said.

Both aunts were astonished. "Without you? But why?"

"I won't know their relatives, and I hardly know Francis anymore, so what's the point?" This retort, given in a high-pitched voice so unlike her natural voice, contained a note of petulance that did not belong to her.

"Is it that you have a date, dear?" asked Cecile. "Something you'd rather do?"

"I'd just rather stay home."

"All wrong," objected Lillian, "when Dr. Alcott never even forgets flowers on your birthday. Really, Laura. Really."

Cecile rose from the table and drew back the curtains. "Look! They're hanging Japanese lanterns over there. What a lovely night for a party! Do get dressed up, Laura. You'll have a good time. You haven't worn that new white dress yet, and summer's almost over."

She was in great confusion, caught between a strange dread of seeing Francis and the challenge of letting him behold what she had become. For a moment or two, she was unable to answer them. And then, deciding that the dread was after all unreasonable, she told them that she would go.

Upstairs in her room she put on the white dress, red slippers, and the pearls that the aunts had given her for her last birthday. Her grandmother's pier glass told her that this was one of the "good" days that every woman has, in contrast to the days when nothing about herself is pleasing. Her eyes were large, her hair hung in long curves, and the white silk skirt swayed with grace when she moved.

Across the lawn and through the gap in the hedge that had never been filled in, the three women walked toward the lights and voices. There was laughter; it seemed to Laura that she recognized the gaiety of Francis's laugh among the rest. And the blood rushed up into her face.

He had been standing in the center of a circle. When he saw her, he broke the circle, came toward her with outstretched hands, and gave a little cry. "Laura! Laura!"

Everyone turned to look at her, and she was exposed. All her planned poise evaporated and, foolishly, she gave him her hand to shake.

"Oh no, a handshake? For me?" And he pulled her to him, pulled her into a warm, strong embrace. He whirled her about as if to display her with pride. "This girl, excuse me, this young woman, has been my friend since she was four years old. These are my cousins from Monmouth, you've never met, this is Mary, Don, my uncle Dave, Laura Paige, Miss Lillian and Miss Cecile, you people remember each other—"

Most within the circle were old, or, if younger, were married and had brought their children; the little ones ran around like rabbits, and the older ones were bored except at the buffet table, where they clustered.

"Come take your plate over here and talk to me," said Francis. "We need to get acquainted. The last Laura I knew was a young girl playing grown-up in a velvet dress."

"You remember that!"

"Of course I do. You were charming. You are charming. When I read your letters, I would think, 'Now she's seventeen, and she must be thinner; now that she's eighteen, she's stopped growing,' and I figured that you'd stop at five feet seven."

"Spoken like a doctor."

"Well, am I right?"

"You are."

"So then, tell me things. You'll graduate next year. And after that?"

"I'll be teaching piano, and I'd like to get a master's in music, too."

"Unless you get married first and start a family."

Laura's blood had sunk back into her heart, and her face had cooled, but now the flooding blood surged into it again.

"I have no plans for that," she said, and then because the sentence was so flat and final, questioned pleasantly, "And you? Are you finished with California, Boston, India, and wherever?"

"Yes, finally. I'm going to be in New York in private practice with a partner, and also I'll be teaching at a hospital."

"No more traveling," she said with a conventional smile.

She was waiting. Waiting for what? It was absurd.

"Yes, it's time that I stayed in one place with a permanent plan, don't you think so?"

"I guess it is."

A small night breeze struck the paper lantern so that it swayed, cutting a shadow across Francis's face, revealing now the gentle cleft of his chin and the corners of his lips, which having been shaped with a cheerful upturn, always contradicted his dark, heavy-lidded eyes with their thoughtful gaze. And the lantern tipped again, now lighting the upper half of his face and the thoughtful gaze directed upon Laura.

"You make me feel old," he said.

"Why? At thirty-five?"

He shook his head. "I suppose it's because I've watched you grow almost from your beginning. The years are not so many, it's true, but the changes are. I look at you and I don't seem able to grasp that you're the child whom I taught to read, the girl who learned tennis with me in her backyard, and now—"

"You're monopolizing Laura," said Dr. Alcott, "and I want to ask a favor of her. Will you go inside and play something for us? A party needs music to liven it up."

The interruption was provoking, but she responded with enthusiasm. "I'd love to. Just tell me what you want."

"Some show tunes. Or jazz?" the old man asked hopefully. "Can you play it?"

"Well, I did take a class this year, and I can manage. I'm not really good, though, I warn you. No one's invited me to New Orleans to play."

"Let me warn you that the piano's not all that good, either. It needs tuning."

The music floated out onto the lawn, so only a few people, chiefly teenagers, went into the house to hear it. After a while as they lost interest, they drifted outside again, leaving Francis standing alone in the curve of the piano.

He was watching her face, not her hands on the keys as one usually does; with his head held in the listening posture that she suddenly remembered, he studied her face. There was no way of telling what his thoughts might be.

"Are you tired?" he asked when she paused.

"Just tired of jazz. It's not what I like to play. And it doesn't fit this night, anyway."

Outdoors, voices had faded under an incessant wave of sound, the monotonous throb and chirp and tick of a thousand hidden insects, a wave as languorous as the lapping of low tide.

"Wasn't it Henry James who said that 'summer afternoon' are the two most beautiful words in the English language? But I think 'summer night' will do as well."

"Then shall I play 'Eine Kleine Nachtmusik'?"

"Yes, do."

And while her fingers moved across the keys, and while he stood there, still with the slight watchful frown that drew two vertical creases between his eyes, a question, in rhythm with the music, kept repeating itself in her head: Can this mean anything?

"That was perfect," Francis said when she came to the end.

"No, no, far from it. If I had a record here, I'd have you listen to a real pianist, and you'd hear the difference."

"Maybe so, but I'm not a musician. You touched my heart, and that's enough."

"You and Francis had a long talk this evening," Cecile remarked as they picked their way across the dark lawn going home.

"Yes, we stayed in the house. It was quiet, away from all the kids."

"His father's disappointed that he's not going to practice here in town."

Lillian said, "Well, he's aiming high, and he's got every right to, but still it's too bad. I hope you'll never get it into your head to fly off to New York or someplace, Laura."

"I'm not thinking about it."

This was the answer they wanted. But suppose—just suppose Francis were to ask her? The way he had looked at her tonight . . . And they had stayed indoors talking for two hours . . . Was it possible?

The little chime clock across the hall in the upstairs sitting room struck half-past one. When the clock chimed three, her thoughts were still running forward and backward: I want him to love me, I *know* he doesn't, I don't *know* it, his eyes, I want him to love me . . . And the clock chimed four.

"My, you slept late," Aunt Lillian remarked in the morning.

"I was awake half the night, that's why."

Cecile shook her head, reproving, "You had coffee at eleven o'clock, and it wasn't decaffeinated. I asked. You should always ask."

The sun poured over the grass, turning its tips brown. The morning was loud with the drone and drill of locusts, and although it was not yet noon, the heat was already enough to take one's breath away.

"So nice of the doctor's cousin Claire to invite us to their lake house," Lillian said. "After all, we don't know her that well."

Cecile said, "Don't forget a plastic bag for your wet suit, Laura."

She had been reading the newspaper, not paying attention. Now she looked up. "Oh, am I included?"

"Well, naturally you are," said Lillian. "Didn't you hear them last night? The cousins stayed over at the Alcotts' and they're going to drive Cecile and me and the Alcotts. That's already six, so it leaves you and Francis to go in a separate car."

"How far is it?"

"About an hour's drive, they said. Maybe a bit more."

A whole hour in a car with nobody to interrupt. A whole hour.

Laura yawned, took a long stretch like a cat, and spoke lightly. "I could use a cold dip in a lake on a day like this."

Often afterward, even now more than twenty years later, she wondered about the power of a minor, ordinary mishap to alter an entire life.

"You'll undoubtedly be there before we will," said Francis's cousin Claire. "I've driven with you, Francis, and you make my hair stand on end. So take the keys to the cottage and put the lunch in the refrigerator when you get there."

The car, a two-seater with the top down, climbed into the cooler hills and sped along a narrow road under dark shade. The radio played, and between the music and the rush of wind, you had to shout to be heard. After a while, they stopped talking. It seemed to Laura that a mood had settled upon Francis, a quietness, as if something had gone wrong. It troubled her, so she laid her head back on the seat, let her hair fly in the wind, and kept the silence as though she were simply listening to the music.

The cottage stood at the far end of a small oval lake. There was a dock and a stretch of sandy, man-made beach on which a canoe had been drawn up. A hammock and rocking chairs filled the front porch. When they had stowed the lunch away, they took some Cokes and sat down on the porch to wait for the others. Where the lake lay in this hollow of the hills the air was still. A single sailboat heading toward the shore barely moved.

"Can't make any headway," remarked Francis almost as if to himself.

"No," she said.

What could have changed him since last night? He had turned away from her to concentrate, or make believe to concentrate, on the boat. The one cheek that she could see was furrowed, and his lips seemed to be pursed, as if he were annoyed. He wasn't the same man that he had been. Maybe last night had been enough, and now he was angry at having been inveigled into this outing. A day with relatives, neighbors, and the neighbors' "nice young niece"! He must have had a dozen better things to do, and now he was bored. It's not my fault, she thought miserably, and he needn't be so sulky about it. . . . She sought for something to say that might break the mood, but her muddled head offered nothing, nor was there inspiration anywhere, not in the halfhearted garden, the neglected chrysanthemums and aster beds that dwindled down along the path to the dock, nor in the hot, vacant sky. The rocking chair creaked at her least move, offending the silence. Her hands lay heavily in her lap like useless things; not knowing what to do with them, she examined them, the bruise on one finger, the tiny ruby on another, and the whole hand splayed on the cotton skirt, the pretty skirt the color of ripe raspberries . . .

When the telephone jangled, Francis went in to answer it. "Oh, that's awful," she heard him say. And when he said next, "What hospital?" she followed him to the telephone.

"Not your aunts," he told her. "It's my cousin Claire. They stopped for gas, Claire got out of the car, took a fall down a step and gashed her leg open on a mess of gravel."

When he had hung up the telephone, he presented Laura with a choice. "The accident happened before they were ten minutes out of town, so they're taking Claire back to my house as soon as she's through at the hospital—Dad wanted a plastic surgeon to do the job. So we can either go back home or stay here for a swim. You decide."

"No, you do."

"No, it's up to you."

"Then I'll say let's start back."

"Why? Do you really want to?"

This posture of his was ridiculous. And a sudden reckless-ness, like that of a gambler risking his last, made her answer, "I don't, but you do and I don't want to stay here with some-body who doesn't like being here, so let's go."

He stared at her with a look of instant shock. "Who said I don't like being here?"

"You didn't *say* it. You didn't have to."

Shock turned to remorse. "Oh Laura, I didn't mean—" And he fumbled, he whose speech was so clear and fluent, saying, red-faced now, "I'm sorry, I didn't mean, didn't intend, you must know I couldn't have, I was only—things on my mind. Please understand." He seized her hand. "Please let's stay. There's a good lunch, and we'll have a swim. Okay?"

She nodded, and he repeated, "Forgiven?"

"Forgiven."

The accident gave them a way to begin a conversation. From tetanus shots and antibiotics the talked moved naturally to medicine or the lack of it in India and other places, exotic to Laura, where Francis had spent the last years. But she was hearing and responding only with the surface of her mind. Its sharp cutting edge was seeing *him*, the sudden lights in his dark hair, his eyelashes as thick and curved as if they had been curled, his cotton sport shirt open at the throat showing a tawny arc against white. A trail of disconnected pictures— Francis carrying a tennis racket, Francis reading with his cheek resting on his hand—unwound and took her to the day when, stopped in the middle of the sidewalk, she had resolved to think of him no more.

So they were to have this whole private afternoon, and she was perversely unsure how she felt; excitement and a certain queer anxiety tumbled together in her chest.

"You're far away," Francis said abruptly.

"No, I've heard every word."

"Let's get out of the sun. Your face is burning. Put our suits on and sit under a tree until you've digested this lunch."

When they had rested and had a swim in cold water, they went back to the warm little sliver of beach. In her yellow bikini she half expected him to speak some compliment—men always did—but he did not and now remarked only upon the pendant that lay glittering above her cleavage.

"Does it open?" he asked.

She felt an awkwardness in the question, as if, having for some reason become ill at ease as they lay there, he was merely making conversation. Surely he could not care whether a gold trifle opened or not.

"Yes, there's a picture inside. Do you want to see it?"

And she leaned forward so that the pendant dangled near enough for him to reach it. When he had seen the picture, he drew back and dropped his hand as if it had been stung.

"Me," he said.

Well, tell him. Why not? Maybe it's the sun that's made me a little drunk, but anyway . . .

"When I was just a child, oh ten or twelve, I was in love with you. Didn't you know?"

He sat up then with his arms around his knees and looked straight ahead across the lake. Then she sat up, too, for a sudden change in atmosphere had taken place, and she was afraid she had made a fool of herself.

"I hope you're not angry," she said, affecting a light tone as if really, this was all too amusing.

"No, of course not."

But he did look angry with his face so tight, just staring across the lake, while seconds passed in silence.

Now there was nothing to do but continue the joke and laugh her way out. "It was about then, yes, I must have been eleven, when you told me that you'd marry me if I were older."

At that Francis turned toward her with astonishing vehemence. His dilated pupils had turned his eyes black. "Did I? I don't remember. But I shouldn't have. It was wicked."

Really alarmed now, she cried, "Wicked! It was only a teasing little compliment. I knew you didn't mean a word of it and never would."

"You knew nothing, and neither did I."

She did not understand this, and said so; he did not answer but got up instead, walked to the rocky barrier at the end of the beach, and returned.

"We should start back," he said sternly. "Let's go up and dress."

Her heart was hurt. Something terribly ugly had happened, a senseless contrast to the previous night when at the piano he had stood watching her with that soft, thoughtful look. And now there was this queer, harsh voice, this determined stomping up the steps ahead of her, past the pungent odor of wilting hot chrysanthemums, past a tiny brown toad blinking in the dust, and up to the screen door.

It was when he stood aside to let her through that he noticed her tears.

"My God," he said, "my God, don't cry. Oh Laura, don't. The last thing I want to do is to hurt you."

At this her tears did flow. He put an arm around her shoulder and she hid her face on his shoulder, wetting his warm skin with those embarrassing tears. They stood quite still, his hands patting, comforting her back until her tears stopped.

And still they stood. Silence tingled in the room. Never in their lives except for the longing in her dreams had they been so close, their bodies fitting one to the other, then straining and swelling, she feeling the run and race of a heat she had scarcely been able to imagine.

Closer, tighter they pressed, until abruptly Francis broke away, putting from him the arms that wound around his neck.

"No, no," he cried.

Then, frustrated, she would have broken into a fury of humiliation if he had not cried also, "Darling Laura! Oh, darling Laura!"

Before his fearful face she drew back, whispering, "What is it?"

He shook his head. "No. Let's get dressed. Leave here."

"You're not telling me something." She sank down on the couch. "You have to tell me."

He shook his head again. "It's nothing. Things run away with themselves sometimes, that's all. A moment ago—"

"You called me 'darling.'"

"Yes. And so you are, so you always were. A wise, sweet child. I loved you then in the way one should love a very special child." He stopped, seemed to struggle against a wish to say no more, or perhaps to say much more, and sat down beside her. "All those dear letters while I was away. In my mind I saw you at fifteen wearing your grown-up dress and going to a dance. Little Laura. And yesterday when you came across the grass toward me, I could not believe what I saw." His voice ended in a murmur, and he looked away.

A great joy, streaked with a subtle sadness, filled Laura's body so that the blood ran faster and drummed in her ears, choking her words in her throat.

"You love me."

"I mustn't. Laura, let's leave."

"Why mustn't you? I don't understand."

And she grasped his hands in both of hers, bent over him and kissed his mouth. She felt him tremble. When he tried to move, she released his hands and held his head while she clung to his mouth. She felt his arms around her, felt him straining toward her and knew that he was overwhelmed.

He wore one piece of clothing, and she wore two thin wisps that fell to the floor when they lay back. Through the pounding in her ears, she heard his voice muffled in her neck: "I love you, I didn't know how much." She heard her own voice answering: "I've loved you so long. All my life."

And then the voices faded into wordless cries.

In the aftermath she lay resting, drowned in a thoughtless bliss. A long trail of sunlight dazzled, and she closed her eyes against it. When the glare passed, she saw that Francis had moved to a chair and was sitting with his head in his hands. Hearing her move, he raised a face filled with pain.

"What I have done," he said. "What I have done."

"Why? Because it was my first time?"

"Much more than that."

"I don't care what it is. I only care that you love me. It's what I've wanted."

He groaned. "Someone should take me out and beat me."

"What are you talking about?"

"You'll never forgive me."

Surely he was playing some game, some mockery of a nine-teenth-century lover who has deflowered a maiden, and she smiled.

"You're right. I will still be scolding you about this when I'm seventy years old."

"Laura, I don't know how the hell this happened just now. I didn't want it to happen, I've been partly crazy since I saw you yesterday. Everything flashed back and piled up, years and years of living. I didn't want to come today, but I wasn't able to get out of it. I didn't want to see you again because I—"

She saw him swallow what must have been a hard lump in

his throat, and she knew in that shivering instant that he was going away.

"You might as well tell me," she said evenly.

"Oh Christ, oh God, I'm going to be married on the four-teenth of next month."

I'm in shock, she thought. He's breaking me. And suddenly conscious of her nakedness, she seized the sofa pillow, the only covering in reach, held it over herself, and sat quite still.

"We didn't—my parents thought we shouldn't tell anyone here until it was over, because the relatives would want to be invited, and there's not going to be any wedding because she's British and her mother's too ill to travel, so we're going to have a simple ceremony in New York, so that's why— Laura darling, don't look like that, say something!"

This was not happening. There was no sense in it.

"I'll say I am not your darling and I don't give a damn about your ceremony."

"Oh God, do you know what I kept thinking all last night? It ought to be Laura. I kept asking myself how I could make that be. Yet I knew it was too late."

I kissed him first, said her inner voice. And she despised herself.

He talked as if he could not stop, as if he were purging himself. "She's a doctor. Isabel. We were in India together, before that for two years in the fellowship program. We have our office ready. Partners. And I care for her, I could never hurt her. And yet, you, you are—"

"I don't give a damn about your office or your Isabel."

"Hate me, Laura. You've every right to."

"Let me alone, I'm going to vomit," she said, and holding the absurd pillow in front of her, walked to the bathroom and was sick.

The tile, the porcelain, were cool on her cheeks. She put her head down on the windowsill. When she raised her eyes, she saw that the sky was still a pure, perfect blue. And that was queer; it seemed that the world ought to have changed. When she had gotten her breath and cleansed her mouth, she steadied herself and put on the white shirt and the raspberry skirt, the same clothes that had been put on that morning with such anticipation.

Francis was waiting on the porch, just sitting and staring out toward the lake, where now three sailboats went skipping in a fresh, joyous wind.

"Are you all right?" he asked.

"Just fine, thank you. Never been better."

His eyes pleaded. His words pleaded. "I'll never forgive myself for what happened here."

Quite probably she should be saying "It was my fault, mainly," but regardless of who had stuck it there, the knife was in her heart, and she could not say those words. So they rode back home all the way without speaking.

All night she lay awake. And now alone, she wept, stifling the wretched, racking sobs in the blanket. Through the trees, whenever she raised her head, far yellow lights shone like cats' eyes in the dark; they came from the Alcott house, from his room most likely, for there was probably not much sleep in him either on this night. She imagined him trying to read with his cheek resting on his hand as was his habit. She remembered going hot with the memory of his body lying on hers. From there her imagination painted a similar scene between him and his wife. She hated him.

And then she pitied herself for the cold, enduring loss of the love that had grown up with her.

In the morning her eyes were inflamed. She would have to hide in bed all day with the shades drawn so that no one would see this misery.

"It's my stomach. Something I ate, or else a virus," she told Cecile, who had come in because they had missed her at breakfast.

Cecile, a chronic worrier, wanted to call Dr. Alcott.

"I don't need a doctor. I've been up all night, and I only need sleep. Anyway, Dr. Alcott's already gone to the office by now."

"Then Francis can run over. I'm sure he wouldn't mind."

"Don't you dare! I'm not having him here in my bedroom."

Cecile laughed. "Heavens, don't tell me you're embarrassed in front of Francis! You sound like Queen Victoria. He is a doctor, after all."

"Francis has gone," said Lillian, overhearing. "He phoned early this morning to say good-bye. He went back to New York."

CHAPTER

3

One month after her twentieth
birthday, Laura graduated from college and in the following
week was married to Bud Rice. Why? She need not have
married anybody at all. But her best friends were engaged,
and Bud with his many graces, his kindness, intelligence, and
strength was more desirable than any of their men. Besides, he
had been asking her over and over all through that year. And
because he had wanted her so much, he had made her proud
again.

But how you drift into marriage! Not knowing what is
really *there,* inside the other, or what can develop as the years
pass. A man could be loyal, fatherly to the children, and sympathetic to his wife—if he was not all of these things, it would
be unbearably hard—and yet there could be no real communication between them. "Communication" sounds so electronic,
Laura thought, disliking a word that somehow failed to describe the way Bud listened willingly enough and still seemed
not to hear.

"Well, since there is nothing to be done about it, why talk
about it?" he would say.

He had been a passionate lover from the beginning. Even
though she had no basis for comparison aside from that one
encounter with Francis, which was too unhealthy to dwell on,
she knew he was. In fact, he was so vigorous that she used to

hope during the year when the aunts were still living in the house that they weren't able to hear him.

For them, Bud could do no wrong. His enthusiasm pleased them.

"It's not every young man who gets a thriving business handed to him," he told them. "Don't think I don't know it. I'll work my head off for it, you'll see."

He was excited about living in the city. "When I was a kid and we'd come in for something special, I used to wish I could live here in town. We hardly ever came, though. I think my folks used to see the doctor next door to you, Dr. Alcott, until a doctor opened up closer to home, and then they didn't even come in for that."

The aunts had seemed to find cause for pride in Bud's backwoods origins. It was, Laura thought, a kind of reverse snobbishness.

"There's nothing aristocratic about Bud Rice. No pretensions. Just good, conservative, decent stock. Old stock."

Bud loved living in a fine house so finely kept. He wanted to, and did, fit smoothly into its proper and rather formal ways. Chimes announced dinner, there were always flowers on the table, polished silver stood on the sideboard, potpourri cast fragrance into every room, and the tall clock on the staircase landing ran on time.

Before the first year was half over, Laura was pregnant. Bud was pleased with his own virility and absolutely certain that she would produce a boy who would shoot baskets with him, play touch football, go fishing, and be his buddy.

That was exactly what she had produced, and his name was Tom, Thomas, after her father. He was born on the day of Dr. Alcott's funeral.

"They all die young in that family. Bad hearts," said Cecile. "None of them sees sixty. It must be kind of a worry to Francis." She spoke to Laura on the telephone. "I know you don't want to be swamped with visitors while you're in the hospital, but I did tell Francis he could come this afternoon."

"You didn't! For heaven's sake, my baby's one day old. I refuse to see anybody but family."

"Francis is as good as family. I told him he has to see your boy," Cecile insisted. "He'll only stay a minute. He's got three days' work ahead of him going over his father's records, and then he has to rush back to New York. He'll be gone by the time you come home."

Laura was furious. No doubt Francis must be equally so, for Cecile had certainly made him feel an obligation. She was still wondering how she would act toward him, when Francis appeared carrying a box of candy, holding it awkwardly before him as one might hold an object that was about to break or spill. He laid it on the tray-table at the foot of the bed.

"I remembered that you're a chocoholic," he said, looking at the wall behind the bed.

Immediately she understood that he had not wanted to come, that he was afraid. He should have had sense enough to make an excuse, she thought angrily.

A terrible physical shame prickled all up and down her skin; she would have been glad to pull the covers over her head and hide; this was like one of those dreams in which you have forgotten your clothes and, out on the street in your underwear, you are looking in panic for cover. This man who stood uncertainly in the center of the room had brought with him so much more than a box of chocolates! He had brought recollections: There again was that idiotic sofa pillow with which she had run into the bathroom; there the shock, the disbelief and the sickness in the dingy bathroom with the summer afternoon outside.

"Your aunts tell me you have a beautiful boy."

She must retrieve her poise. . . . Let him know. Let him know that she was not destroyed. Torn apart, yes, but now recovered in full.

"Yes," she said, making her voice easy and light. "I can't argue with that. He is. He is like his father." And she raised her eyes for Francis to see that there was pride in them.

But he was still gazing at the wall behind her. She thought

he looked humble. And this humbleness, which was almost unmistakable, did restore her poise, so that she lifted herself against the pillows with her head high. He would see that she was established in the world, a cherished woman in a pink satin robe, in a room filled with flowers.

Good manners required now that she ask him to sit down. Yet why should she care? And he probably didn't want to stay.

"Do sit down," she heard herself say.

"Thank you."

His glance wandered around the room, settling nowhere. Still he could not fail to see how her hair shone, how lavishly it spread about her shoulders. Even against his will, he must be aware of it. Perhaps he was making a comparison. He had a wife, Isabel, a woman he had not wanted to hurt. How did she look, talk, act? How much did he love her? *It should have been you, Laura,* he had told her that day. And now he slept with Isabel.

Do they sleep entwined in one bed? Bud Rice, a man desired by women, lies close to me every night. His words are muffled into my neck: *your warm, sweet-smelling hair, you are the loveliest.* "Gentle Laura," he calls me. "You know so much, you do everything so well, where did I find you?" And he laughs. "I remember. On the library steps."

"Your aunts told me I must be sure to look at your boy," said Francis.

"You don't have to be so polite." She was gracious, magnanimous. "I know you have plenty to do right now at home, things more important than looking at a baby."

"I'm not being polite. I want to."

Then she remembered, and was embarrassed because it had taken her so long to remember, what had brought Francis home.

"We are all so sorry about your father. So many, many people loved him."

"Yes. He died too young." He paused. "Will you still give lessons now that you have a baby?"

As if he cared one way or the other! This stilted dialogue was absurd. They were not saying what they were thinking, that was sure. If Francis could have read her mind, he would have read defiance: *I suppose you thought I would never get over you.* The conceit of men! Every night I am loved, passionately loved, or when he is tired, loved with tenderness. And this baby, this marvel of a boy, is the result.

"I shall make time for both," she replied, and added then, "Your parents have told us how well you're doing."

Francis had written a textbook that had drawn praise. He was making a name for himself, and she was complimenting him as if he were a child who has brought home a nice report card. So, flushing with this realization, she added more. "But then, it was always expected of you."

"You try your best," he said simply, and stood up. "I mustn't tire you. New mothers need their rest."

Swift thoughts flashed. Was Isabel also a new mother? Probably not. It would be natural for him to say, if he had one, that he, too, had a child. And still, perhaps it would not be natural. This whole visit was unnatural, ridiculous, a passage of trivial words without substance. He should never have come here.

He went on making conversation. "My mother plans to sell the house and move west. She has a lot of relatives there."

"So much upheaval for her and for you! Really, it's so good of you to visit me at a hard time like this."

"I wanted to. I was thinking how my father would have enjoyed the sight of your boy. And he missed it by a couple of hours."

His departing footsteps made a lonely, hollow sound in the corridor. And suddenly Laura was aware of a tightening in her throat, a lump of pity or pain or loss, or maybe some of all. Yes, Francis, my baby could have been your father's grandchild. And isn't it curious, Francis, that I should be here in this bed while Bud Rice's baby is in his crib down the hall because of you?

Curious, too, all the little things, the trivial things, you remember, like the fried chicken and shortcake that Betty Lee made for dinner on the day they brought Tom home, or the giant stuffed panda that Bud had waiting for the baby in his room.

"Good Lord," Lillian said, "he'll be five years old before he grows up to the thing."

The aunts were moving out, leaving the house to the new family. Bud was doing so well at the business that they were able to foresee retirement before too long.

"You're on your own now," Lillian told them. "It's time for us to slacken off. I've been wanting to see some more of the world, anyway, and Cecile—I kind of think she may have some plans of her own."

Cecile had met a man, retired from the navy in Pensacola, an interesting man who was interested in her.

So there came another phase, the beginning of real adulthood for Laura Rice, responsible for a husband, a child, a house, and a burgeoning career. In the afternoons when piano pupils came, Betty Lee took care of Tom as she did on evenings when Laura and Bud went out.

He loved going out with his wife beside him, shining in her best clothes. A convivial man, he liked to dine and dance; a competitive man, he wanted the world to admire the woman he had won. And his pleasure warmed the atmosphere in which she moved.

It was a good life then in those first years, so busy that there was no time, let alone inclination, for introspection concerning the nature of true "happiness," or true marital compatibility.

In the bedroom, a lovely space enclosed like a garden by millefleur wallpaper, there in the grand bed with its airy white embroidered tester, they were together.

Always and exactly, Bud knew what to do. He knew how to hold a kiss, a soft, moist pleasure, never detaching no matter how their bodies twisted together. Never over too soon was this union, nor was it prolonged so far that the height of pleasure could be bypassed. His hands knew where and how to touch. Eagerly, she wound about him, all vigor, all desire flowing, giving and receiving.

It really was queer when you considered it. For those few minutes of total union, your mind literally left you. You were one force and one urge, so that whatever had pained your thoughts beforehand was obliterated in a total mindless bliss.

The business throve, for Bud worked hard; the roster of piano pupils grew so that the house seemed to ring all day with music. And most of all there was Tom, darling Tom.

"He's the image of your father," the aunts used to tell Laura when Bud was out of hearing. "So much emotion, with the temper and the kisses five minutes later. And the silky black hair—he's the black Irish all over."

The child was Bud's treasure. "A man's boy," he used to say as Tom grew and followed him around at his chores, watching while Bud hammered a loose board or mended a hose.

He was a mother's boy, too, as he leaned on her lap, listening with all ears and great, wide-open eyes to the tales of Winnie-the-Pooh. There was a sweetness in him; predictions of jealousy when a new baby arrived just did not come true.

"It's a question of intelligence," Laura told Bud. "I don't think most, or many, little boys would understand so much."

"Why does Timmy have to go back to the hospital?" asked Tom, for fair-haired, pretty Timmy had been sick from the moment they had brought him home. All night he cried; Bud and Laura took turns with him through exhausting hours. He did not gain. He caught one cold after the other, turning blue in the face as he struggled to breathe through his tiny stuffed nose.

"I told you I had no confidence in a woman pediatrician," Bud grumbled and snorted. "Women! Women doctors don't know which side is up. But you insisted."

Laura let this idiocy go unchallenged. The poor frightened man had to let off steam somewhere, had to blame somebody.

When they changed doctors, they fared no better. Some said it was colic, some said allergies. Before Timmy was eighteen months old, he had been twice in the local hospital with pneumonia. And meanwhile, Tom went off to school in his jeans and cowboy shirt, the tallest and strongest in the class. The contrast was poignant.

"There has to be a doctor on this planet who can tell us what's wrong with Timmy," Laura insisted.

And so, one bright winter day they got in the car with their baby, drove across the state to a teaching hospital, and there found someone who did finally tell them what was wrong.

The doctor was kind but blunt, for Laura had asked him not to spare them.

"Cystic fibrosis," he said, "is a fatal disease. With care and love, a patient can live into his twenties. But more usually—" He stopped because Bud's eyes had filled with tears, and Laura, too shocked to cry, was trembling.

When she was able to speak, she said softly, "Maybe we shouldn't have asked you for the truth."

With equal softness, the doctor replied, "I would have had to tell you most of it, and in time you would have found out the rest for yourselves."

Stunned in their grief, they had sat there trying to absorb instructions numerous enough to fill a thick booklet—which was handed to them anyway along with their delicate baby, wrapped for the journey home in his blue blanket that Aunt Cecile, with loving care, had embroidered with white rabbits.

So there began another phase, and here she was, eleven years later, lying on the sofa with her memory racing and the monotonous downpouring rain drumming on the window-pane.

In the kitchen Betty Lee was talking to Earl, Timmy's beloved mongrel, with a cocker spaniel's truthful gaze and the feisty spunk of a terrier. Timmy had chosen him at the pound to celebrate recovery from one of his worst sieges, that time his lungs had filled up and he had come so close to death.

"I don't want to call him 'Prince' or 'King,'" Timmy had said. "I want something different, but something noble." He had been nine years old, and very serious, his small face wrinkled in thought.

"How about 'Earl'?" Tom had suggested.

A less aristocratic dog would be hard to find, Laura thought now, a little rueful smile on her lips.

"Oh," said Betty Lee, coming in from the hall, "I didn't know you were asleep. I'm sorry."

"That's all right. I wasn't."

"I forgot to tell you that your lesson's been canceled. There's no one to drive, and the child can't walk over in all this rain."

Right now a cancellation was welcome. These foggy moods came rarely, but when they did, they sapped not only the spirit but the physical body, too. It would take real effort to get up now and go to the piano.

Still standing in the doorway, Betty Lee hesitated. "Is something wrong? You never lie down in the afternoon."

Well, sometimes she did. Betty Lee, who came only three days a week now—after forty-two years with this family, she was not yet willing to sever the connection—did not know everything that happened anymore.

"You worry too much," she warned, although Laura had not replied.

An unexpected crash and crack of thunder rocked the house, and the two women looked at each other in alarm.

"Timmy's picnic," Laura said.

"I'm sure they'll find shelter someplace."

"But if they've had to run for it? You know he mustn't! Oh," Laura lamented, "it's so hard to draw the line between coddling him and letting him live like other boys! 'Let him have as normal a life as possible,' they tell us. But what's 'normal'? Watch out for pneumonia, and diabetes, too. He must not be too hot, mustn't sweat because he'll get dehydrated and vomit. Be sure to keep salt tablets in his pocket. 'Let him have as much exercise as his condition allows, but don't let him over-exercise.' What on earth does that mean when a boy is crazy about baseball?"

"Don't you think he's improving, though? I know he's a little small for his age, but lately to me he looks healthier—"

"Oh Betty Lee, God bless you for trying, but you do know better."

"Well, well." The soft voice attempted to encourage. "Worry won't help, as your aunt Lillian used to say. And there's a car now, coming up the drive. See what I mean?"

A harried-looking woman came rushing to the door with Timmy. Both of them were soaked through, and Timmy was weary.

"He isn't feeling well. I'm sick over it, Mrs. Rice," she apologized. "But the storm came without warning, and we had to run for shelter. I know he isn't supposed to run. I don't know how to tell you—"

Laura had to interrupt. "Go upstairs, dry yourself thoroughly, put on pajamas, and get into bed. I'll be up in a minute," she commanded, and Timmy obeyed. These were the rules.

"I hope he won't be sick because of this. He's such a dear little boy."

At eleven, he could still be called a "dear little boy." Laura winced. Would she ever get used to it? People were always so kind to Timmy. They were so thoughtful and tactful because they knew he was going to die.

"Please. It's not your fault," she said. "You didn't know it was going to pour. And it was so good of you to invite him in the first place. Now, if you'll excuse me—"

Timmy was already in bed, leaning against pillows. Laura pushed the damp hair back from his perspiring forehead.

"It was so terribly hot, playing baseball," he murmured, "but nobody else minded it, so I had to play."

"I know. You didn't want to complain." There was no use remonstrating with him. He knew only too well the penalty he must pay for breaking the rules.

"My stomach's a little queasy, Mom."

"You're dehydrated, that's why. I'll run downstairs and get some water."

But Betty Lee was already halfway up with a pitcher of cool water, cool but not cold, and never with ice.

"Is he all right, Miss Laura? If you need me, I'll stay."

"No, no, you've done enough today. Go on home. Bud'll be here soon, anyway."

"You call me if you need me, hear? Don't forget, he's my boy, too."

There was that in Timmy that inspired love. Heaven knew he had cause for complaint over what life had dealt him, yet he never did complain.

"Drink half a glass at least. You need it. And I'll get—"

"—sodium chloride, taken orally," Timmy said, making a joke of the technical term. He knew all the technical terms, knew he must have high proteins and moderate fats because his pancreas wasn't functioning as it should. Naturally he had been told what he needed to know, but he had also gone to the library by himself and read there in a medical text that his life would be a short one. They had learned this from the librarian; Timmy had never mentioned it.

She sat down and watched him drink. Earl came in and bounded onto the bed, scattering raindrops from his rough gray coat. When Timmy put his free arm around the dog, drawing him close, the familiar gesture touched her today with a pain so acute that she had to look away. Yet her eyes, as they wandered from the oxygen tank, always at the ready in the corner, to the roller skates on the closet floor and finally to *Tom Sawyer* on the night table, found no comfort.

It was necessary to say something, to make some neutral, commonplace remark, and she said, "Oh my, you're sunburned, aren't you? People with such white skin have to be careful even on a cloudy day, you know. People like you and me."

"And Tom. Tom and I look alike, don't we? Except for our hair."

"That's true."

"Tom never had pimples, either."

"No, Tom didn't."

"That means I won't have."

"Probably not, but if you should, we can easily take care of it."

"But I'm like Tom, Mom, so I won't get pimples," Tim insisted. "I can't wait till he gets home. Is it Friday?"

"Yes. Dad's going to drive over to get him and all his stuff."

"So then he'll be home all summer."

"That's right. You and he will have good times together."

"I was thinking, you and Dad both went to the state U, and now Tom goes, so probably I'll go there, too."

"Of course, if you keep up your marks," she said cheerfully.

Timmy yawned. "When's Dad coming home?"

Laura looked at her watch. "In about an hour. You're awfully tired, aren't you?"

"I guess I am."

"Then have a little nap. You've had a long day. Shall I take Earl with me?"

"No, leave him here. He'll sleep, too."

At Timmy's age, a boy wanted a dog, a father, and a brother. Without the devastating illness, it would have been a simple time, its problems relatively straightforward compared with what could come later. . . .

Tom's room was near the top of the stairs, and the door was open. In a few days he would be back in it with his possessions stowed away again in their home: his clothes, books, guitar, and tennis racket, all the paraphernalia with which prosperous parents, especially where there is a generous, doting father, could possibly equip a son at college. And she was glad, for Tom brought health with him and energy and hope.

Hope. It rose whenever she thought of Tom's potential, and just as suddenly, like a stone, it sank. She walked inside and in the glare of the red sun that shone forth after the storm, stood feeling the stillness of the vacant room. The oak at the window dripped steadily, leaf upon leaf.

And she looked around the room, knowing what was there, wishing that through some magic these things would have vanished. The book entitled *My Hero Hitler*, in its bold, bright cover. And then, thumbtacked to the wall, the huge blowup of Jim Johnson's good-looking face.

Tom, Tom, what are you doing? she cried to herself.

She was still there when Bud came home and climbed the stairs, calling, "Hey, what's up? Where's Timmy?" For Timmy was almost always on the front porch waiting for his father every evening.

"In bed. He came back exhausted." And she explained what had happened.

Bud exploded. "Fool of a woman! She knows damn well that Timmy has to be watched. All he needs is another bout of pneumonia, the third since Thanksgiving, that's all. She ought to have her neck wrung."

"It wasn't her fault. That storm came like a gunshot. And they were way out near Hickory Branch. She felt awful about it."

"She had no business taking a kid like Timmy that far away. Damn foreigner didn't know any better, I suppose. Why a man like Rolandson had to go to Europe to find a wife I'll never know. Some Greek or Italian or whatnot."

"You're being ridiculous, Bud. She's a lovely woman, and for your information, she happens to be Portuguese."

"Well, at least she's not a Jew."

Laura sighed. "I wish you wouldn't say such things. I especially wish you wouldn't say them in front of Tom. How can you be so kind to people you know and at the same time sound so cruel?"

"Oh honey, come on. Let's not get into that business again. You're home, wrapped up in your family and your music, and that's how it should be. You're not out fighting your way in the world, you don't see the things I see. Anyway, is Timmy okay?"

"He fell asleep. He's not coughing, so I don't think his lungs are filling up."

"Good. What are you doing in Tom's room, getting ready for Friday?"

"I'm ready. No, I was just standing here for a minute worrying." She held up *My Hero Hitler.* "Look what he reads."

Bud shrugged. "You take it too seriously. He's a kid yet, away from home, exposed to all sorts of new ideas. At least he thinks, instead of being just a dumb jock."

"I'd rather he were a dumb jock who didn't have ideas like these." She pointed to Jim Johnson on the wall. "It's that man who's behind it, that awful man."

"Laura, I can't agree with you. Johnson's no Hitler. There's an awful lot of truth in what he says about conditions, the middle class being squeezed to pay for people who won't work, job quotas—"

"I don't like quotas, either. But he's full of hatred, he preys on ignorance and make a circus out of politics to attract the young. He makes drama for them, and frankly, he scares me."

"You'd better get used to him. He's around to stay. He'll be in the state senate next November. You watch."

"Not because of my vote."

"What? You're going to vote for Mackenzie?"

"I am. He's a moderate, intelligent man from Georgetown Law School, and he's a peacemaker, not a rabble-rouser. And even if he weren't any of those things," she said firmly, "he'd be better than Jim Johnson."

"So we'll cancel out each other's vote. So what? It's a free country. Anyway, I don't want to talk politics. Keep your opinions to yourself, I say, even with your wife. You never change anybody's mind, and nobody ever changes yours. Besides, in my position, it's bad for business. It makes enemies." Bud talked as he followed Laura downstairs. "Good thing is, recession or not, we've been busy. There's that mall going up, they've been buying stuff from us, and then there's a lot of home alteration, people fixing the place up instead of moving." He followed her into the kitchen. "And Laura, don't be upset about Tom. He's a good student, a serious kid. Never given a minute's trouble."

She whirled around with the salad bowl in her hands. "Have you read any of those books about blacks that he has in his room? I only hope Betty Lee hasn't. I won't have her hurt."

"Hey, he cares about Betty Lee. Has he ever been rude to her? No. So, okay, you don't agree with the books he reads, but as I say, there may be more truth in some of them than you know. And as long as he doesn't get into any trouble, I'll be proud of my son. I am proud of him."

No, you didn't change people's minds . . .

"Ah," said Bud, "I'm sorry we don't see eye to eye on all this." He put his arm around her. "But we do on most things, don't we? On the important things. On doing the best we can for each other and our boys. Right?"

That was quite true, and she said so.

"Then, come eat," he said, and they sat down at the table together.

The table stood in the path of a breeze sweet with the fragrance of wet grass. Outside, the evening was calm and bright, while inside the old house gave cheerful comfort. But a deep loneliness went sweeping through Laura so that she had to shiver, although she was not cold.

PART
III

Tom

CHAPTER

4

"And while I know you folks all are sorry Jim couldn't be here himself tonight—but he's trying to cover the state, every nook and corner that he can before November—I want you to know that I appreciate, and Jim appreciates, the attention that you've given me in his stead, and I want you to know that every word I've said here tonight is what he'd have wanted me to say and want you to hear because we're all in this together! All together, every last one of us!"

The voice boomed out of a throat gone raw; amplified, it ricocheted off the walls, exploded upward to the highest balcony and filled the darkened cavern below the glittering stage.

Two thousand voices roared reply: "All together! All together!" Then came antiphony: "What do we want? Power! Power!" And again the cry from voices now, so late in the evening, gone hoarse: "All together! All together!"

When they subsided, the speaker, a short man with thinning blond hair, resumed. His red forehead sweated and gleamed in the spotlight.

"We have a message for Washington. Yes, we'll get there, and don't think we won't. You put Jim in the state senate, then make him governor, then send him to Washington, to the top, and watch him turn this country around. That's our message to Washington, folks: Watch out. We're on our way!"

"On our way, on our way!"

"We're fed up with integration, busing, and reverse discrimination. Fed up with job quotas dictated from Washington by a government of foreigners. Let's get going! Less talk and more action. Stand with Jim Johnson and we'll show you action!"

"Action! Action!" bellowed the crowd, many of whom had now risen to their feet, roaring and clapping.

For a few minutes the speaker stood beaming his satisfaction. Suddenly he stretched up his arm in its short-sleeved shirt and gave a high, flat-palmed salute. The band struck a triumphant air, and the men who had been seated in the row on the stage behind the speaker marched out with jaunty steps.

"Military music stirs my blood," Tom said, looking down at Roberta, who reached to his shoulder.

"Fabulous," she murmured. "It was fabulous." Her black eyes sparkled with awe. "And that speaker! I was disappointed when we learned that Jim wouldn't be here, but I felt my blood stir, anyway. You've never heard Jim, though. Wait till you do."

They jostled their way through the crowd to the doors and out into the warm night. The long flight of steps to the street was lined with men dressed in a suggestion of a uniform, dark trousers, black leather belt, and a conspicuous red Jim Johnson button on the shirt.

"Most of them are armed, you know," Roberta whispered. "And see that girl in jeans? That's Flora Deane. She's the security chief. Been in politics for years. She must be about thirty. Now she works for Jim. You see how we have to guard ourselves? It's disgusting. You never know what these radicals will do. A bunch of wild blacks or God knows—hi, Lou, Jessie, Norma! Great, wasn't it?"

A little group made a circle around Roberta. Tom, half in and half out of the circle, watched; it pleased him that this tiny girl, this fiery, bright, black-eyed doll of a girl, was a leader of men and women; it delighted him that she, who could have had so many others, had chosen him to love. He was a year younger than she, who was a junior, and he had even taken her away from a senior who was mad about her. Last month at a dance he had simply walked over and taken her away from the guy. She was his first real girl; she knew the arts of love. She told him that he was the perfect lover, and she meant it.

When asked his age, he always answered, "I'm almost twenty." There was a much better ring to that than to "nineteen."

"But you look older," Robbie always told him. "You're a gorgeous man, you know that, don't you? And brilliant, besides. I'll tell you something, I can't stand being around stupid people, and half the people at this university don't belong here in the first place."

Robbie had a right to talk. Look what she had accomplished, scratching her way up from nothing! She was as well read as Tom's mother and practically all straight A's from the start. In tough courses, too. You couldn't bullshit your way through chemistry or physics; and she was a chemistry major, taking honors classes.

On top of all that, she ran *The Independent Voice*. A couple of fellows were hawking it right now on the sidewalk in front of the Civic Center.

Tom looked back up the slight rise on which the building stood. It had elegance. Low to the ground, it gave, nonetheless, a vertical effect with its tall, narrow windows, banked so closely that the structure, poised between sky-glow and its own artificial lights, seemed to be all glass.

It might be nice to be an architect, he thought, if I weren't already planning on astronomy. And if the country weren't possibly going to pieces. Who'd need architects? Who really could plan any future anyway?

But that's no way to talk, Robbie remonstrated when he said things like that. You have to get out and work for what you believe in. This rally here tonight proves what sprouts when you water the roots; that's what she would say later tonight when they talked about it.

"Let's get out of here," she said now. "Get the bikes and fly. It's not often that I have the room to myself for a weekend. Martha had to go home. Her mother's sick."

"I never have my room to myself in the dorm. Clem's a nice enough guy, but he's always there studying Latin and Greek. A classics major. We hardly ever talk." Tom laughed. "He has no time."

"But if he had time, could you talk?"

"You mean enlist him? No. He wears a Ralph Mackenzie button."

"That's the problem with the dorm, you can't choose your roommate. Did I ever tell you why I moved out and got a room in a boardinghouse? Well, on move-in day last September, I walk in, and who's there getting her stuff unpacked but this Jewish girl—can you imagine me? Me? 'Hello,' she says, friendly as can be. 'My name's Enid Somebody-or-other.' I can't even pronounce the name. 'My mother brought food, she thought the cafeteria might not be open yet. There's plenty for both of us. Try the chocolate chip cookies, they're great, and blah, blah, blah,' while she's unpacking enough for a trip around the world. Then in comes the mother with a diamond as big as a doorknob. And she starts, 'Blah, blah.' I was so mad, I was speechless. Then they drive away in a Lincoln. I looked out the window. Late model, top-of-the-line. Dad's a doctor, or maybe a lawyer. Some sort of crook, anyway. So I ran down to housing right then and there and got myself a room with a decent human being."

Tom winced. Dad was a car buff, and he bought the best. His latest was the Lincoln Mark VIII. Mom was still driving the small Mercedes that he'd given her when she'd turned thirty-five. Still, Dad was American. Been here for generations. Earned it honestly.

"Hey," he said, remembering something, "aren't you working tonight?"

"Oh yes, five nights a week. But I took off for the rally, called in sick."

"I don't know how you do it all." He had dropped in at the place where she worked, a real greasy spoon, noisy and jammed with jostlers at the bar. She'd been carrying trays of dirty dishes, squeezing her way among the tables, and he had felt guilty about the cash and the American Express card in his wallet. Once, very tactfully, he had offered to give her some money or even lend her some if she insisted, to help her out of a tough spot, but she had refused any help. She had a bold independence. And he repeated now, "I don't know how you do it all."

She gave a little shrug; he found the gesture charming.

"I have a lot of energy, don't need much sleep, and I learn fast. A matter of luck, that's all."

He asked curiously, "How did you happen to get into all this political stuff? Your family?"

"Nope. Just got hold of some books, mostly about race, that started me thinking. My family's too messed up to teach me anything. My dad came originally from New Zealand, why I don't know, nor why he married my mother, except that she must have been a beauty. Beautiful and stupid. You can't believe how stupid. He had the brains. I got her looks and his brains, thank God for that. Anyway, he used to teach school in New Zealand, and when he couldn't stand living with my mother—it was a battleground, I can tell you—he up and went back to New Zealand. Never sends me a dime except for a little something at Christmas and my birthday. What little I get comes from my granny and she's not far from being dirt poor herself."

"And your mother?"

"She met some man and went to Chicago. I hear from her now and then. Very now and then. I have an idea the man dropped her, because she's working now, in a cafeteria. At least she's working, which is more than my brother's doing. Twenty-four and never held a job for more than a month. Stupid. Takes dope. Takes after Mama. But I'm going to make something of myself. Teach chemistry or better yet, work in research."

Tom was silent. What a dirty deal the world had given to this bright, brave girl! And a sudden image of his home flashed before him, a picture of evening, with the books, the piano, and his mother's fair head gleaming in the lamplight. Dad was reading the paper, Mom had a book, and Timmy was doing his homework in the alcove.

Robbie sighed. "You're lucky you've got a good family."

"I know."

"Except, of course, for your brother. Poor kid. He won't live long, will he?"

Tom hadn't ever said that to Robbie, nor to anyone, for that matter. The words would have stuck in his throat. And he replied with another question. "Why do you say that?"

"You told me he had cystic fibrosis, and I looked it up. I like to understand things."

"So you know. It's a rotten deal." He burst out, "It's cruel. And he's the best little guy, good-natured, not like me—"

"Why, Tom Rice, you have a wonderful disposition. Don't say that."

"No, really. I've got a temper, and he's just so—so nice. And so smart. He knows what's going on in the world. You'd enjoy talking to him even though he's only eleven."

"Talking politics?"

"Well, not our kind. Not local politics. Not yet. I wanted to get a Jim Johnson photo for his room, but my mother got so upset that I dropped the subject."

"She's for Mackenzie?"

"Yes. Oh, my mother's wonderful, but I just can't talk to her about politics. My dad's different. He's a Johnson man, but quiet about it, not deeply involved."

"But he doesn't mind if you are."

"No, no, he's okay. He agrees with me about a lot of things. He's happy about anything I think or do as long as I behave. For himself, he's got too much on his mind, mostly my brother, naturally." Tom paused, remembering. "God, it's awful to see the kid looking at Dad's football pictures. And you know he's got to be thinking, I'll never do anything like that."

"You're a sweet man, Tom."

"Yeah, I'm sweet," and he grinned inwardly, wondering how long it would take to get her into bed this time. It wasn't that she was reluctant, she certainly loved it plenty once she got there! It was only that she could get talking with such enthusiasm about anything and everything that she forgot to stop.

They had pedaled away from the center of town and its traffic, out past the university's columns and red brick, past oaks in heavy leaf, into the meager suburban village and down the familiar street.

There were no lights in the enormous gabled Victorian except for the lamp that Robbie's roommate had considerately left lit in the bay window above the wooden gingerbread front porch.

Twin beds, two desks, and two easy chairs at the bay window filled the room. Stuffed animals lay on the pillows. An enormous blowup picture of Jim Johnson, twice as large as the one Tom had at home, hung on one wall. The room smelled clean, and it was clean; coming from the old Paige house as he did, Tom cared especially about that.

He grinned happily. "Two in a twin bed. I really like that."

"Oh God, so do I. I changed the linens as soon as I knew you were coming. Usual day is Wednesday. Bought lilac sachet, too."

She dimmed the light way down to a pale pink glow, although not far enough to hide the thrilling contrasts: the corona of black hair falling to pure white shoulders and the heavy breasts, ripe as fruit, above a waist so narrow that he was able to span it with his two hands.

Hungry and hurried, they rushed into the bed, collapsed into the fragrances of lilac and hot flesh, moved together in a perfect rhythm, rose and sank and quickened into a fine completion. And then they lay back, panting, to wait for the incredible arousal and repetition that would not be long in coming. . . .

Late at night the street had gone so quiet that they could hear the night wind rustle through the trees. When Robbie got up and blotted out the lamplight, moonlight swam in to replace it. Fulfilled at last and content, they lay close in the narrow bed and, although there surely was no one in hearing, spoke in the whispers that seemed to fit the mood of the gentle night.

"Nice here. I wish you had this place to yourself all the time."

"Greedy! But you can stay tomorrow."

"I've got two more exams next week. I've got to hit the books."

"Bring the books here. I've had my last exam, but I have to do an editorial for *The Independent Voice.* Last edition until September. That's another thing that's good about having this room besides its being cheaper. No snooping. My roommate's on our side, so I can feel really private. I don't have to hide what I write. I can even leave *Mein Kampf* right out on the table."

"Have you actually read it?"

"You won't believe it, but I've read it in German."

"German! That's pretty good after only two years. I'm impressed."

"It's easy for me to pick up a language. I have a good ear. I figured everybody's read books about Hitler, but I don't know one person who's actually read his own words, even in translation. So I decided to try. And it was fascinating, I can tell you. That was one brilliant man. Things would be a lot different if he had won, if the world hadn't ganged up on him. The lies they've told! The biggest propaganda fakery of all time, gas chambers. Six million dead." Robbie giggled. "That quote from *Mein Kempf* in *The Independent Voice*—I can't imagine who sneaked it in, can you?"

"I think maybe I can."

"Oh, they make me sick. That dressed-up thing I almost had to room with complained to the student council—in fact, I see she's gotten herself elected to the council for next year—all about unemployment among the blacks and the condition of the schools, and South Africa. A couple of us gave those big-mouths something to squawk about. Sent them a few sweet messages slipped under their doors on the Jewish holidays. Can you imagine the righteous indignation? Buzz, buzz, buzz. There's something about an anonymous letter or a message on an answering machine that can really get to people. They don't know who sent it and can't do anything about it. Really drives them crazy." Remembering, she began to choke with laughter. "We send dirty letters to the feminists. Half of them are lesbians, anyway. And we send condoms to the lesbians. Could you die?" The bed shook with Robbie's laughter.

Then abruptly she became serious. "You've got to fight these people before they turn the country inside out. I've known that for a long time, Tom. I've been political since I was fifteen. I've done a lot of thinking."

"I've just come to it. Didn't really firm up my thoughts till I got here. We never talked much about politics at home, anyway. My mother's wrapped up in music and Dad's wrapped up in his business, although it's clear to me that his basic sentiments are a lot like yours. You'd like my dad anyway, aside from that. He's big-hearted, smart, honest—the best father you could have."

Robbie squirmed and turned to kiss Tom's neck. He felt her eyelashes brush his skin, and he felt the soft movement of her lips murmuring, "You're so sweet, Tom. I'm crazy about you. I'm going to miss you all summer."

"Hey! I'll be seeing you! Working in the business, I can get time off pretty much when I want it. Dad's easy that way. And I always can get one of the vans. That's the reason I don't have a car of my own. No need to. How far is this bookstore where you'll be working?"

"Shouldn't take you more than an hour to get to. Straight out Highway Nine, then about three miles east, that's all. I'll give you directions. And I've got a room, not too bad, but the best thing is, no roommate. Got it all to myself."

"Summer's looking better and better." Tom chuckled. "How about some sleep? My eyes are closing."

"Sure." Robbie laughed. "We worked hard tonight."

His body lay easily, not the least bit cramped in this bed, just comfortably intertwined with Robbie, neatly fitted, like a pair of spoons. His thoughts floated peacefully. The day had been wonderful, from the morning's astronomy exam, in which he was confident he had done very well, to the blood-pounding rally at the Civic Center, to the last delicious hours in this room.

And he began to feel a sense of mounting power and joy. Home again! Working with Dad. His mother's good meals, a steak and a chocolate cake, for a change from college food. Sunday afternoons, he'd find a cool place and take Timmy swimming. Home. Five more days.

CHAPTER

5

Down the great central boulevard through the city's heart, they marched, they strutted, plodded, and swung. Some of them from time to time in response to cheers raised their straight arms in the fascist salute. But for the most part, they were stone faces, closed faces like those of men on their way to battle. Flanking them on either side came police on sputtering motorcycles, and behind these came more police in cars with top lights flashing. On the sidewalk their supporters, chiefly teenage boys, old men, and housewives in loose cotton dresses—for this being a weekday morning, ablebodied men were at work—kept up with them all the way to their destination at the monument in the center of the circle.

Unknowingly, Laura had come upon this parade. On her way back to the parking lot after shopping, she had been blocked here at the avenue. Now, fenced in by the crowd that had seemed to collect from nowhere—as crowds are always drawn to an ugly accident, she thought with scorn—she was unable to get away. She had, in fact, a ringside view of an event she had no wish to view.

The monument, a memorial to the dead young men of an old war, towered over the living men at its base. These, while waiting for the arrival of the parade, held American flags, hawked pamphlets, and shouted their slogans.

"Americans only! Whites only! Power! Power for Americans!"

As if someone had put some slimy insect or a wet garden slug down her back, Laura felt a shudder of disgust. Drab, angry, ignorant men! They were an insult to the flags they carried, an insult to the memorial before which now lay a wreath of dark green laurel leaves.

"My father wasn't fighting for the likes of you when he died," she muttered.

A woman standing next to her had overheard and, catching Laura's embarrassed glance, nodded in sympathy.

"Nothing but troublemaking scum, that's all they are."

"Who are they? I mean, what's the occasion today?"

"It's a national convention of right-wingers. Far, far right, like the Crusaders and the Guardsmen, that type. They're meeting this weekend at a motel out on the highway near where I live. My uncle's with the police. He says there are six or seven hundred of them. He says they're ready for trouble, too."

"Who are? They or the police?"

The woman smiled. "Both, I should say."

The vanguard of the procession now appeared. It began formation, lining the perimeter of the enormous circle. Slow feet trod with ceremonial solemnity, as if at some ancient religious rite. Only the words were incongruous to Laura's ears. "Power! Power!" they chanted.

And the many voices were indeed powerful, thought Laura. In unison, the straight arms shot up, Mussolini's arms and Hitler's arms; she had seen them often enough in old movies, and a chill went down her spine.

A bugle blared, commanding attention to a small gray man who was trying to begin a speech. At the same time there was a happening on the other side of the circle, a pushing and jostling altercation that drew attention away from the speaker.

"Boo! Boo!" From all sides more voices rumbled. "Boo! Boo!"

And now came ominous roars. "Quiet, down there. We can't hear. Shut up."

Whose side were they on? It was impossible to tell.

"Bastards!"

"Shut up!"

"Can you make me? You shut up, shut your dirty mouths or you'll find out what's good for you!"

Far up in front a group of men began to fight. One fell to the ground, and women screamed. Laura looked at the faces close around her; there were menacing scowls and curiosity and fright. She began to look for a way out of the crowd, but they were pressing and pushing in both directions. She felt the terror of being trapped. A police car broke into the circle with its siren wailing. She looked about in terror, looked into the face of a rather decent-looking man as if somehow he might help her.

"Ma'am, this isn't a good place to be," he said. "Follow me. I'm going to try to wiggle through to the back and get over to that side street if I can."

The pale sun strained through sultry clouds; in the humid air, fighting the pressure of stubborn, sweating bodies, all in uproar, all struggling, Laura struggled to follow the good citizen who had advised her. But the narrow passage he forged soon closed behind him and she lost him. The crowd surged and shoved, pushing her along, now here, now there.

The crowd was turning into a mob; people were trying to flee while others were forcing themselves closer to the center of the circle, where the action was. Anyone who stumbled in this melee would be trampled, and no one would care.

"Please may I squeeze through?" Laura cried, close to panic. "Please may I get through to the street, I need—"

And a terrible roar went up. "They've got the paddy wagon! They're bringing the paddy wagon!" People were panicking. At the same time there were those who were pushing toward the front to join the attack on the police. Out of the corner of her eye, as she clutched a stranger's jacket to keep from falling, Laura saw the man who had begun to speak, the gray little man—she was sure it was he—reach and snap the antenna from one of the police cars. A team of young fellows were rocking the cars; one, overturned, lay on its side with its wheels spinning. A club swung and a man toppled to the ground.

"They're arresting them!" someone cried near her ear as she ran. "It's the guy who laid the wreath. I've seen him before. There goes another into the paddy wagon."

In the swirl of escape, nothing mattered. Fear had become frenzy. Laura's breath was almost gone, and the heel of her right shoe had come off. But she fought her way through, losing her packages in her flight, and made her way to the side street. There for a few minutes she stood panting, leaning against a lamppost.

Then, recovering as her heartbeat came slowly back to normal, she made her way across the avenue, far beyond the turmoil, and headed for the parking lot.

A woman came panting up behind her. "Laura? I thought it was you over there. Wasn't this awful? My heart was in my mouth. It still is. I've never been so terrified in all my life." It was Lou Foster, the minister's wife.

"Of course I've read about what crowds can do, but being in the middle of one like this is something else again. I could never have imagined it."

"Johnson's people," Lou said contemptuously.

"I thought these were more Klan types."

"Same thing. Johnson's people talk more respectably, but as the Chinese say, they all eat from the same pot."

A child came pedaling his tricycle down the sidewalk. From an open window came the whine of a vacuum cleaner. It seemed that such a street, lined by quiet houses and shady oaks, could not possibly be so short a distance away from the hideous explosion of hatred that was occurring still on the boulevard. And Laura, reflecting on the other woman's words, said nothing for a moment.

"Yes, they're all the same," repeated Lou.

"My husband approves of Johnson. He says Johnson has

nothing at all to do with the Klan. He's a victim of malicious propaganda."

"My husband could tell him differently. Johnson was a fighting tough. Now he's remade himself into a middle-class gentleman. But you have only to look back ten years to when he worked for Fred Bartlett's printing press. You remember Bartlett? He went from the Klan to an organization of his own, the Sons of Zeus, some kind of crazy religion that he founded. He was on the Secret Service list of dangerous persons. They're all intertwined. No, I wouldn't trust Johnson any farther than I can throw your beautiful piano, Laura."

In the parking lot they paused before parting. Suddenly Lou said, "I'm worried, Laura. That black couple who bought the Blair house on Fairview Street are finally moving in and there's so much angry talk going on that I'm worried. No, not worried. Scared."

"What do you think is going to happen?"

"Heavens, people like you and me are the last to know. But there are plenty of agitators ready to make an issue out of something like this, you can be sure."

Laura sighed. "Well, it'll be a first for Fairview Street, that's certain." And recalling the fine classic facade of the old Blair place, she remarked that the new owners must be well off to think of maintaining it.

"I believe they are. She's a schoolteacher, but he's got a big executive job with Searle Computers. They're from Cincinnati, I heard."

"Well, let's just hope all goes well," said Laura.

Suddenly she remembered that she had no coffee ice cream, Tom's favorite. He could eat a pint in five minutes. "Lou, I've got to rush. Tom's coming home tonight. Bud went with a van to fetch him. And my aunts are driving up from Pensacola tomorrow to see him. They haven't seen him since Christmas vacation."

"Ah, a family dinner tomorrow."

"A big one, and I'd better hurry home and get busy. Maybe it'll take my mind off this horrendous morning."

❊   ❊   ❊

From the back veranda Laura and the aunts watched the touch football game on the lawn.

"Would you have believed that Clem at his age could keep up with Tom?" cried Cecile, proud of the husband she had, in late middle age or early old age, acquired.

Clem Hanson looked like the navy man he had been, tall, thin, silver-gray, and still crew-cut. A good-natured person, he accepted Lillian kindly when she moved to Pensacola to be near her sister. Indeed, Lillian often accompanied the couple at her own expense when they went traveling. Close knit, we surely are, thought Laura; to think they had all driven this distance to welcome Tom home from college!

Their coming made her aware of how much she missed the aunts, her twin mothers with their big hearts and their funny ways, the fussy domestic habits so out of keeping with their business persona, their determined, efficient hold on money, the getting and keeping of it.

"Tom gets handsomer every time I see him," observed Lillian. "And so like your father, Laura. More and more, the older he gets, with those eyes, those dark, haunting eyes," she said as if quoting poetry.

Laura smiled. It was true. Except when he was being stubborn, when his mouth got thin and hard, Tom was something to behold. And now, with his face laughing and gleaming as he swerved and darted, he gave delight.

Cecile clapped for Clem when he evaded Tom and clapped again when Tom caught up with Bud. Her pretty hair that had been pepper and salt was now mostly salt, yet she seemed to grow younger with each year of her marriage. Laura wondered if that was what happened when the marriage was wonderful. . . .

"It's good to be here in the old house," remarked Lillian, who had definitely grown older with each year. "Look at that magnolia! I remember the day I planted it. Nothing but a stick, it was, high as my waist."

"I wish you'd stay longer," Laura said.

"Can't. We have to start back early in the morning. There's a ton of packing to do. It's not every day we take a three months' cruise around the world."

"I'm dying to see India. Remember when Francis Alcott was there and sent us all those marvelous pictures? And he brought you a sari, Laura. So lovely. Pale pink and gold, wasn't it? Or was it blue and gold?" Cecile frowned slightly, concentrating on the memory. "Which was it Laura? I can't remember."

Wrapped in pink gauze, she had gone dancing around her room, had draped it to expose one naked shoulder, paused like an odalisque in front of the mirror, loving herself.

"I don't remember, either," she replied with a little shrug.

"Yes, I can't wait to see India most of all," Cecile repeated. She was dreaming of white marble and temple bells. Not beggars, not dirt, nor smells, thought Laura. Nor heartbreak. Dear Cecile!

"I'm getting tired," Bud said, tossing the ball toward the veranda steps.

He wasn't tired at all. He was thinking of Timmy, who, with Earl at his heels, had been racing to keep up, although the others had been careful to favor him. And Laura wondered painfully whether Timmy realized how much they favored him. Probably he did, although he would try not to admit it to himself; Timmy was proud. Proud, like his father.

The close tie between those two was sometimes frayed. Bud's kind of pride kept him exercising beyond the threshold of pleasure because he knew he tended toward fat, but he would never admit it. So it was that he never would admit his innermost feelings about Timmy, either, would never say that mixed with his fierce love there was also a bitter resentment. Why should this tragedy have come to him, Bud, who was capable of fathering a boy like Tom?

They should have had more children, another boy for Bud. Tom was grown and would go his way, as he should, she reflected now. But with Timmy in need of so much care, it hadn't seemed like a good idea to add another responsibility to the family. And besides, who could have known how another child might turn out? The chance of a sibling's being afflicted with Timmy's sickness was one out of four, a terrifying ratio.

"I'm starved," Tom said, clumping up the steps.

"Ten more minutes in the oven. Just time to shower. Then roast beef and a surprise dessert. One of your favorites, Tom."

"Can't be better than last night's lemon pie. You spoil me, Mom."

"As long as you know you're spoiled, it's okay."

Indoors again, the women could never refrain from making some remark about the photograph of Thomas Paige, which they had to pass on the way in. They paused before it.

"He looks so stern," said Cecile. "I don't remember him looking so stern."

"It's the military cap that changes the face. Put that cap on Tom and he'd look different, too," said Lillian.

"No, it's because he was on his way overseas. Anybody would look stern."

"Tom looks like that sometimes without going overseas."

"Tom's serious. Tom's good stock."

Thus refortified, content in the certainty of who and what the Paiges—and the Rices—were, the aunts proceeded toward the dining room and took their places, no longer at the head and the foot of the table because Bud and Laura sat there now.

Their complacency was contagious. Laura was feeling continuity. Her grandparents had bought this table in Ireland, a solid slab of West Indian mahogany, lustrous after thousands of patient rubbings and waxings. In one of these damask-covered chairs, her father must have sat through many a dinner's conversation, boring to a child who had to wait while adults lingered over their second cups of coffee. And here in celebration of their engagement he must have brought Laura's mother for a first dinner in this house; anxious to be approved, a young woman would have been careful to dress exactly right, neither too much up nor too much down. And here the young couple would have displayed their wedding silver . . .

Clem said, "I always tell Cecile that your boys have such fine manners. These days you seldom find a young man Tom's age who knows enough to pull a chair out for a lady. All that's gone by the board. I hate to see it."

Laura smiles. "If there's any credit due, it goes to Bud. He insists."

"Well, good for him, then."

Bud was pleased. "Tom's been worth every bit of effort. And one of these days very soon, I'm going to show him what I think of him. I'm going to print 'and Son' on our sign after 'Paige and Rice.' "

Laura amended, "And after that, someday you'll put the 's' after 'Son.' "

"Of course, of course, when Timmy's old enough," Bud said. He turned to the aunts. "Gosh, I remember the day you took down 'Paige and Company' and replaced it with 'Paige and Rice,' gold letters on black. I felt like bursting inside. It was like yesterday," he finished wistfully.

"There've been so many changes," said Cecile. "More now, I guess, than in any century before us. I see big changes in this town every time I come back."

Lillian remarked, "I heard on the car radio that you had quite a mess here yesterday."

Clem said, "We saw it on television. It's a disgrace. There's no law and order anymore."

"Laura was there," Bud told them. "She could have been killed. Scared the life out of me when she told me. Tell them about it, Laura."

She had been wanting to forget it, so she answered only, "It was awful. They were like savages." What decided her to say more, she could not have explained, but glancing at Bud, she added suddenly, "This will have been only the beginning, though, if Jim Johnson wins. Only the beginning."

"Nonsense!" Bud's exclamation rang down the table. "You call Johnson a savage? Listen, he may be a bit too emphatic at times, a bit extreme, but if you listen carefully and take apart what he says, you'll find he makes a lot of sense. That group yesterday could have had nothing to do with him."

Laura said stubbornly, "That's not what I was told. I was told it was Johnson, and that when you look behind him, you'll see the Klan."

"Oh, for God's sake, Laura, that's ridiculous. Johnson's got no more to do with the Klan than you have."

"Of course, we're in Florida," Clem said. "But we keep in touch with what's going on, and many of our friends from here have heard him, and they like him."

"What do you say?" Clem asked Tom. "You folks at college all vote now at eighteen, so tell me, what are people your age saying?"

Tom had been waiting his turn, and was ready for it. "Divided," he said promptly. "The people I go around with favor Johnson, naturally." He grinned, catching Bud's wink. "We wouldn't be going around together, otherwise. I know people close to him, and they have a lot of respect for him. Mackenzie's been slinging mud, that's all he's been doing. He won't deal with the issues, racial quotas and busing, high taxes on people who work, so—"

Laura had to interrupt. "I'm not in favor of quotas or busing, either, and I don't think Mackenzie is. He's a conservative person, and I am, too, and that's why I'm going to vote for him."

Now Tom interrupted. "Mackenzie won't talk about unpopular issues. He wants to please everybody. He won't come right out and say that our government has been supporting a bunch of lazy bums who don't want to work. That's what this is all about." And Tom ran his hand through his hair, which now fell slantwise like a black silk handkerchief over one-half of his forehead.

Bud clapped. "By God, he'll be governor someday. Hasn't my boy got what it takes? Right, Clem?"

Bud glowed and Clem approved. "Yes, Tom puts it very well," and then in the kindly tone that people use when speaking to a very small child, he asked, "What are your thoughts on the subject, Timmy?"

A delicate flush spread over Timmy's face. He glanced at his mother, then at Bud and Tom, finally back to his mother, and replied softly, "I think some of the things I've read, some of the things Johnson says, sound awfully mean. And Betty Lee told me he hates black people."

"With all respect to Betty Lee," Bud objected, "and we all love her, but I really don't think she has studied the issues enough to make a judgment. Naturally she listens to propaganda. It's not her fault, I understand that, but she's simply thinking what she's told to think."

"But people can always tell when other people hate them. And she's black, Dad, so she can feel it better than we can when somebody hates blacks. At least," Timmy said, suddenly reluctant, as if he had dared too much, as if he had felt some sharpness in Bud's objection, "at least that's what I think."

Deeply moved, Laura said, "Timmy's right. I see a terrible meanness here, too. This is an ugly election, and it frightens me."

"Well, I just don't know, Laura," said Cecile. "It seems to me you need a man like Johnson in this state. An educated man, we all agree, well-spoken—"

"That's just the danger, Aunt Cecile, he's so well-spoken and so well educated that he can talk convincingly before whatever audience he happens to be addressing at the moment. And when Johnson speaks against the Klan, it's only a mask for the kind of thing I witnessed yesterday, pain and hate and eventually, blood on the pavement. Nazi Germany. They started small, and look how they grew."

Tom objected. "You know something, Mom? You and millions more have been awfully hoodwinked. The whole story is a great put-up job." He spoke very patiently and very reasonably. "There never were any gas ovens, now that you mention Nazi Germany. There never were six million dead. Yes, there were camps and prisons where criminals, communist spies, and agitators were held, and they deserved to be. The rest is propaganda. Jewish propaganda."

"Right on!" Bud cried. "It's all a swindle, the whole blasted thing."

Laura felt the hot blood rising to her face, and she cried out.

"The Holocaust a 'swindle'! You dare to say that? When there are photographs in official German records, when there are eyewitness accounts by survivors and, yes, by American soldiers, too! When Eisenhower himself wept when he saw the human wreckage! As well say there never was a George Washington if you're going to deny history!"

"Ahh," Bud said, "you're always defending Jews. And why, I can't fathom. What do you know about them? How many do you even know?"

"What difference does it make whether I'm acquainted with them or not? But as it happens I have some darn good friends, girls I grew up with from kindergarten on. And I probably know more without being aware of it. I don't make a practice of asking people about their religion or their ancestry." Her own righteous indignation was making her vehement and proud. "I only want everybody to be treated decently and fairly. Isn't that what religion is all about? We go to church on Sunday, don't we? And it seems to me that what we hear there—"

No one responded. They were all looking at the empty air. In their code of behavior, the dinner table was no place for such vehement outbursts. It made the aunts uncomfortable. But she had not intended to be so emotional, so angry; her voice had simply risen, and without intending to, she had pushed her chair back from the table, clutching the edge with both hands. The events of yesterday must have affected her even more than she had realized. And she glanced at the faces, all of which, excepting Timmy's, seemed to have closed up.

A weariness drained through her body so that she relaxed her hands and dropped her eyes to her plate. No one understood; Bud and the aunts were one. "Fine women," he always said of them, and so they were. "A good man," they had said of him from the very beginning, and so he was. Yet when it came to something as deep as how a person felt about the world and what kind of world was building, a curtain fell that isolated her from the good man and the fine women. As for Tom, it seemed as if a curtain was about to fall before him, too . . . Or maybe not . . . She felt alone at the table.

Lillian spoke first. "I take it then that you'll be voting for Mackenzie, Laura."

She came to. "Yes, I think he's a decent, reasonable man."

"Silver spoon. Georgetown Law. Johnson's more of a self-made man."

And where's the sense in that? thought Laura. Who is Lillian to object to a silver spoon? It was absurd.

"We met Mackenzie," Clem said. "Did Cecile tell you? He was at a dinner party last winter when we went to Captiva. People found him very likable, very bright." He chuckled. "The women went for him in a big way. Thirty-seven, single, nice head of red hair—why not?"

Clem had neatly turned the conversation away from sober disagreement and Cecile would be grateful for that. They were well matched.

Laura jumped up. "The dessert's a chocolate soufflé, and it's ready just about now. Excuse me, I'm going to take it out of the oven, and then you'll have to eat it right away before it starts to collapse."

"Whipped cream with it, Mom?" asked Tom.

"Better than that. A great vanilla sauce. Help me clear the table, boys. No, Cecile and Lillian, you sit."

The atmosphere of celebration that had begun the day was now subtly diluted. It was like a time when you are absorbed in a pleasure, a mood of untroubled ease on a day when the world is vivid all around you, and then, abruptly, something startles, a reminder that you do, after all, have a nagging, lurking trouble. And now the topics at the table had changed the atmosphere, had tainted it.

"No more politics," Bud declared, when Laura came back bearing the soufflé in its bubble-glass bowl. And when she gave him a look of gratitude, he continued, "We aren't the only couple who cancel out each other's vote. Clem, shall I fill your glass again? This is a great dessert wine. Tom, too, now that you're nineteen?" He laughed, giving Tom his familiar wink. "It's nice to pretend you guys never drink at college, right? Oh, I remember."

Remarkable, thought Laura a few minutes later, how food can soothe. The soufflé, the wine, the coffee, the cheese and fruit, had spread contentment where only a short while before there had been polite hostility.

The evening ended early. Clem apologized, "We've had a long day, a long drive. I think we need to turn in."

"It always feels funny," said Lillian, "to come back and sleep in the house where you were born. It's as if you'd never been away. But I hate to walk out on your evening, Bud."

"Not mine. I have to go downtown, anyway. I've a meeting."

"What? On Saturday night?" asked Clem, who for all his punctilious manners tended to be curious.

"Always something, Clem. I've had emergencies on Sundays, too. When you're on a couple of executive committees, Rotary, Chamber of Commerce, Lions—you name it—you can be out every night of the week if you want to. Except, I don't want to. I keep it to a minimum. Tonight, though, I have to go. Really important business tonight. So I'll see you folks in the morning."

The boys, sitting with Laura on the back terrace, kept their voices low out of consideration for the guests in the bedrooms just above them.

And Laura's eyes went to Tom, watching and wondering— those ideas of his, those shocking remarks about the Nazis: who had implanted them? He had mentioned the crowd he "went around" with. And she reflected, knowing fully that every parent did the same, on the influences that might be shaping the son or daughter who has left home as a familiar person and has become, in a measure, a stranger.

But did Tom not really choose those influences? At every

university there is a variety of groups, a choice. So to a certain extent the foundation was laid before he left home. Yes. Face it, Laura, it was laid here by Bud. With a hundred little nods, winks, defenses, remarks and jokes—mean jokes—he has made himself quite clear. He has created an atmosphere, and Tom has breathed it in.

What a pity! The fine mind, the sensitivity, corrupted and led astray—

Tom broke into her thoughts. "Look. The polestar."

"Where?" asked Timmy.

"There, see?" Tom pointed. "Another name is the North Star. That's how sailors first learned to know what direction they were going in."

"Wagner's 'Pale Evening Star.' " Laura hummed a phrase. "So fair and mild."

"It's the only star that doesn't move. All the rest turn around it counterclockwise in twenty-four hours. Once you start learning even a little bit about the sky, you get hooked," said Tom. "You have to know more. I took astronomy last semester, did I tell you? It was only elementary, of course, so I want to go on with more. That means I'll have to take more math, too."

How can such an intellect fall for the garbage that was spoken tonight? she asked herself.

At the same time she spoke pleasantly, sociably. "I'm never any good at finding my way around the night sky."

"Look there!" Tom cried. "See that shape, Timmy? Follow my hand. Count seven stars—doesn't that look like a bear? It's Ursa Major, the Big Bear. And over there. Watch my finger pointing, see? Count seven stars again. That's Ursa Minor, the Little Bear. You know what boggles my mind about all this stuff? The precision. That's what I marvel at. It's all so precisely ordered. Regular and perfect. No confusion. Look at meteors, for instance. Isn't it amazing that you can predict their arrival? On August twelfth, maybe a few days before or after, but anyway, around then we're going to see a shower of meteors. You and I'll come out here, Timmy, and watch. Then on the fifteenth of November, there'll be another shower in the morning; can you believe it? They even know what time of day it'll be. Fantastic!"

Timmy stirred. "My stomach feels awful, Mom," he murmured.

She sat up instantly. "Is it pain or nausea?"

"Just sick. Maybe I'm going to throw up. I don't think so, though."

"He ate too much rich stuff tonight," Tom said. "The gravy, the chocolate and the cream sauce."

"Go on up and get into bed. Then I'll come and give you your medicine."

Tom intervened. "I'll go, Mom. You worked all day. Besides, Tim knows what medicine to take. Come on, kid, you and Earl. We've got a lot of talking to catch up on, anyhow."

Upstairs Tim began his familiar distressful, choking cough. From long experience Tom knew at once that there was a connection between the nausea and mucus-laden cough. And he knew what to do.

The shallow pan hung near the stove, milk was of course in the refrigerator and honey in the jar on the shelf. And as he stood watching the pan, he had a frightening vision of that intensive care unit on the seventh floor where the family had already had to watch and wait; you turned right at the elevator . . .

He shuddered and went upstairs with the milk.

"Drink it slowly, it'll soothe," he said, as if Tim didn't know all that.

And he sat down to watch his brother, to wait as the coughing gradually subsided. The two hands that grasped the tumbler were so delicate. Such a thin little guy, no doubt the smallest kid in his class. How that must hurt! And how, in a perverse way, it must hurt that nobody teased him, nobody ever called him "shorty" or "shrimp" because their parents had told them that he was very sick and they must treat him kindly.

"My coughing bothers Earl," Timmy said, for the dog, sitting upright at the foot of the bed, was turning a quizzical, bright look from Timmy to Tom in turn. "Do you know he's my best friend, not counting you, Tom?"

"I'm your brother. That's even more than a best friend."

"I know." Having finished the milk, Tim clasped his hands around his knees and regarded Tom intently, giving the latter to understand that he expected a cozy bedtime talk. "Have you got a girl, Tom?"

"Well, yes, in a way, and also no. I mean, in college you get to meet lots of girls. In classes and at dances and football games, I mean. So you have one for a month or a couple of weeks with another—you know." The kid would talk, and he didn't want to be questioned about Robbie, didn't, as a matter of fact, want to be questioned about anyone. "I guess I don't have any special one right now."

"You ought to have, Tom, it's nice."

"Yes? How do you know?"

Timmy, with a glance at the open door, leaned forward to whisper. "Because I have one. I'll tell you if you promise not to tell."

"I promise," Tom said solemnly.

"Her name's Mary Beth. I always have lunch at her table. Do you know why?"

"No. Why?"

"Because she asks me. Every day she asks me."

"She has good taste. I'll bet she's pretty."

"Yeah. She's the prettiest girl in the class. She's cool, Tom."

"What color hair has she got?"

"Sort of brown. Light brown with some yellow in it. She wears cool clothes, too."

"I'd sure like to meet her, Tim."

"Well, maybe you can if you'll drive me to a sixth-grade party some night. Dad or Mom always do it, but you can if you want to."

"I certainly want to."

That little face, that peaked, earnest little face with the wistful eyes! He has Mom's eyes, Tom saw. He hadn't ever noticed before. They were both so dreamy, Tim and Mom, as if they were thinking of something far off, even while they were talking to you. On the other hand, people always said he himself looked like Mom and like her father.

Tim yawned, yet still kept talking. He didn't want Tom to leave the room, that was why. "Dad got me a new Walkman. Want to see it?"

"Hey," Tom said, "look at the clock. I'd rather sleep now, and then tomorrow we can have the whole day. You'll show me the Walkman and we'll do stuff together. Okay?"

"Okay," Tim said.

"You're feeling all right now, aren't you?"

"Okay."

The smile, Tom thought, is like a 150-watt bulb coming on in a dark hall.

"See you tomorrow, kid."

Back in his own room he sat up in bed reading *The Protocols of the Elders of Zion*. It was a very old book, Robbie had told him, but it was constantly being reprinted and recirculated throughout the world because what it said was still true.

From every country, it said, the Jews sent representatives, old clever men, their most experienced, to a secret place, so secret that no one had yet been able to discover where it was, and there they hatched their plans to dominate the planet.

Tom hesitated. Well, maybe so . . . After all, you had to look at what these people owned in this city alone! The department store in the heart of town was Jewish. So were half the shops in the new mall, the stores where he bought his shoes and his suits, the sporting goods chain, the jewelry store where Mom bought the watch for his graduation. Yes, and at the cardiology department in the hospital where Aunt Lillian had her operation last year, the head was Jewish. Everywhere you looked, you came across these people living like princes.

This book was eloquent, powerful in driving home the facts.

People were too slow to recognize the facts, that their world was changing.

Dad knew it, though. But Dad had to be discreet. He had a living to make, this family to provide for, and the way they lived, it must cost plenty. They lived well, with the best of everything, and Dad couldn't afford to make enemies. Besides, he wanted to keep peace at home. Mom definitely was a bleeding heart, and there was no use arguing with her. And Dad loved her. He didn't want to upset her. She was an innocent, a gentle innocent, all wrapped up in her books, her piano pupils, and of course the family.

He looked around his room to savor the feel of it before turning out the light. Mom had put a single red rose in a vase on his desk. It touched him to look at that plump rose. She had been wanting him to come home, looking forward to him when she went into the garden to cut it.

"I shouldn't have said what I did at dinner today," he told himself, feeling regret. "It was mean to upset her."

His eyes roved farther. Maybe he ought to hide all the stuff that bothered her, the books on Hitler, even the photograph of Jim Johnson. What difference to his conviction did it make whether those things were out on display or not? He could keep them all in the room where he slept so often with Robbie. There with her was his other life, his adult, independent life.

He stretched, easing every muscle and bone into the comfort of the bed. Something in the motion sent a voluptuous throb through his loins, bringing the instantaneous thrill of Robbie's pneumatic body, hard in places, soft in places, resilient, as she clung.

Then, thinking, Timmy will almost certainly never know all that beauty, all that magic, the vivid throb subsided into sorrow, and he knew he must try to think of something else to lure himself into sleep and escape that sorrow.

Outside, the summer night was drowsy with the familiar sounds of insect life. Crickets were chirping as they had chirped for thousands of years. On some other planet, as it turned away from its own particular sun, some other kind of creature, according to the probabilities, must be awake in the darkness too. Scientists predict that, when catastrophe finally strikes down humankind on this planet of ours, only the insects will be left. Cockroaches? Ugh! Locusts, now, not too bad, although they do squawk and buzz. But crickets aren't bad at all, with their chirp and trill. Chirp and trill all night outside my window . . .

He slept.

Left alone in the vacant darkness, Laura was still sitting with her thoughts when Bud's car rolled up the driveway into the garage. The rear lights, two round red eyes, glared and closed as the garage door rumbled down. Bud's feet swished on the grass and he came up on the veranda.

"Hey, what's the trouble?"

"No trouble. Just sitting."

"Sitting here alone. What is it?"

"Nothing, really."

"I know your moods. You never fool me."

That was true, but she had no wish to start a discussion of any kind; her spirit was weary.

So she responded only with "How was your meeting?"

"Fine. Too much talk for a Sunday night. In love with the sound of their voices." He stooped to kiss her cheek. "You've got a new perfume."

"White Shoulders. Do you like it?"

"You bet. I love your white shoulders, your white breasts, the whole works. Hey, I'm hungry again. Got a sandwich someplace?"

The kitchen, like the whole house, had been planned to accommodate a big family. Its cupboards could hold three sets of china with two-dozen place settings each; across from the new electric stove stood the great old coal stove, still used, although seldom, but polished to a shine. Cedar logs lay neatly on the fireplace grate, ready for a winter evening. Copper pots hung from the ceiling, and a cascading spider plant hung at the window over the sink.

"I love this house. Our castle," Bud said. "A man's home is his castle. Yes sir, you bet. And he'll defend it with his life. I can understand that."

"It's good to know you'll never have to here in America."

"Don't be so sure of that. The old ways are under attack. There's a whole element in this country that doesn't know that. Blacks and Jews. Riffraff. And as for Catholics, I'm not too crazy about them, either, though some are all right. I've met a lot of pretty good ones. And yet even with them you have to remember that their first loyalty is to the Pope."

"Want a slice of pound cake?" she asked. "I made two. One's for the aunts to take home."

"Thanks, but I've got to watch myself. Already had a couple of beers tonight." He tipped back comfortably on two chair legs and chewed his sandwich. "I bumped into a couple of fellows who were telling about some blacks moving in on Fairview Street. Bought the Blairs' house. Can you imagine that?"

"Yes, Lou Foster told me."

"What a lousy trick to pull on good neighbors!"

"There are laws," Laura said.

"Sure, but you can get around them. Just raise the price so they can't pay."

Her fingers tightened around her coffee cup, but still she spoke mildly. "They may be, and they probably are, very nice people."

"So maybe they are, but for Pete's sake, Laura, be real."

"I think it's I who am being real."

"I'm damn glad it's not my problem. Well, the Ordways will just have to handle it some way, that's all."

"Handle it? And how will they do that, do you think?"

Bud shrugged. "Ignore them, probably. Give them the ice-cold shoulder. Look through them as if they weren't there."

Grace Ordway could certainly do that. She always looked as if she had just eaten a lemon. Yet they were a decent couple; they would never actually *do* anything. It was the spectacle of those marchers on the avenue, vicious and fanatical in their rage, that frightened Laura.

As if he could have read her fear, Bud continued, "I have an idea there may be a little trouble up on that street one of these days."

"What sort of trouble?"

"Who knows? All I know is, there's a pack of folks who don't take this kind of thing lying down."

A flicker of amusement passed across his face, and it was this that brought Laura close to fury.

"Yes," she said, snapping the words out, "yes, a pack of folks like you and—and to my sorrow, our Tom."

Bud's eyebrows rose in surprise. "Me? Tom? What have we ever done?"

"You haven't 'done' anything and I'm not saying you ever will, except to egg on with your words the people who do. That makes you almost, or just as, guilty as they are."

"I can't help it that you're a bleeding heart, Laura. Let any lazy black come to your door with his hand out, or any Jew with a piece of the Wailing Wall in his pocket—"

She put up her hand as if to control, to bring to a stop, the rush of his words. "I'd rather have a bleeding heart than a frozen one, or perhaps no heart at all."

"Of course, of course. I'm not against sympathy, for God's sake. Look at all the charity I give. Look at my checkbook if you want to know."

Bud's smile, showing his splendid teeth, was meant to be ingratiating, a peace-smile. He had a strong dislike of argumentation and would always try to end a discussion like this one as promptly as possible. But she was not about to let him end it.

"I can't do anything about you, I know that. Your mold was set long ago in the house where you grew up. But I'm damned if I'm going to sit by without a struggle, letting you teach evil —evil, Bud! to Tom. There's a terrible change in him, a hardness, a coldness, that doesn't fit him. And pretty soon it will be happening to Timmy also." An angry sob stopped her.

"You'd better lower your voice unless you want your aunts to hear."

"I can't talk to you. I'm only banging my head at a stone wall. Damn you, Bud!"

"Ah, come on, Laura, let's cut this out. You exaggerate everything. It's one of your few faults. Tom's a model son. He's got some ideas you don't approve of, and so have I, but we're pretty good people, both of us, and we'll all turn out right in the end. Come on up to bed. I'm tired."

"You go, I'm not."

"Not tired or not going to bed?"

"Both."

"I can promise you something nice if you'll come to bed."

" 'Nice,' " she said. "You disgust me."

He laughed and tousled her hair. "Okay, I'm going to sleep. Tomorrow you'll be over this nonsense and I won't disgust you."

She waited until she could be sure he was asleep; right now, she knew, he was naked and virile, waiting for her. If every room in the house had not been taken, she would have slept somewhere else.

As it was, she waited in the eerie quiet until the clock struck two and then, exhausted, crept onto the farthest edge of the wide bed, the "marriage bed." And she thought of how slippery the road was once you began to slide downhill. She could even have managed to bear with Bud's opinions, could have closed her ears for the sake of all that was good in him and in their marriage, if it had not been for Tom.

He was her last thought now, and was her first in the morning when, after a few hours of restless sleep, she awoke.

Tom.

CHAPTER

6

Two days later, Betty Lee had something to tell Laura. "Do you know that big brick house on Fairview Road, the one with the fancy iron fence around it?"

"Yes, it belonged to the Blairs. They were friends of my great-grandfather's, I'm told. Or their grandfather was, I mean."

"Well, they've sold it."

"Yes, I heard."

"You won't guess who bought it."

A glint of pleasure in the tone and the eyes brought painful recollections to Laura: her flight from the terrifying riot, Lou Foster's premonitions of trouble, and last Sunday's confrontation with Bud.

"I know that, too, a black family. That's nice, Betty Lee. Really nice."

"Isn't that something? They've got to have a big pile of money to buy a mansion like that. A sure-enough big pile."

The house was not, in Laura's view, a mansion, but with its pediments, its broken arch above the door and its balanced wings, it was a handsome specimen of Georgian architecture. And it was half as large again as this house. Betty Lee was rightly impressed.

"My brother-in-law drives a van for Gage Movers. He's

bringing their stuff from Cincinnati. They'll be moving in this week."

On Thursday morning Laura inquired of Betty Lee whether the people had moved into the Blair house.

"They got in yesterday. My brother-in-law said they had so much furniture, it took till past eleven last night to finish up. They had to hoist a big piano through the bay window at the back." Betty Lee was full of information. "He's in the computer business, a big executive with Searle, Wash told me. They've got a girl eight years old and two younger ones. Wash says you ought to see the house inside. It's got those stairs that go up in a circle. I always did admire stairs like those."

This move onto one of the finest streets in the city would be the subject of speculation for weeks to come among Betty Lee's people, Laura knew. And why not? It was a triumph, an example, a living proof that dreams can come true.

"What is the family's name?" she asked.

"Edgewood." Betty Lee laughed. "I've got cousins named Edgewood, but no relation to them. Don't I wish!"

Laura was thoughtful for a moment. Then she said, "Betty Lee, will you get out the picnic basket and dust it? I'm going to carry some dinner over to the Edgewoods. It must be a mess to move—I wouldn't know, would I?—and I think they'll be glad not to have to make dinner."

"If that isn't just like you! It's not as if you were next door to them, either. Those are the people who should do the welcoming." Betty Lee lowered her eyes, and her enthusiasm ebbed. "I wonder whether they will. I don't think so, do you?"

"No," said Laura. "I don't think so."

They'll get the message. Look right through them as if they weren't there.

She roused herself. "There's another cold chicken in the refrigerator. Will you dice it for me while I get some lettuce and tomatoes from the garden? I'll make some chicken salad, there's a corn pudding in the freezer, I bought fresh rolls yesterday, and it'll only take a few minutes to make some quick cupcakes. That should do it."

"You've always had a heart of gold."

It was early afternoon when she drove up before the Blair —no, the Edgewood—house and carried her basket to the door. A dark young woman, obviously in a hurry, with a broom in one hand answered her ring.

"I'm Laura Rice. I'm a neighbor, and I've brought a little supper so you won't have to cook tonight."

"Oh, how good of you! I don't know what to say. How good of you. And you're a neighbor? Which house is yours?"

"I'm not on this street. I'm on West Oak. It's not far, not more than half a mile."

"Half a mile? And you came all this way? Oh, here I am letting you stand there in the hot sun."

Laura moved inside where cartons and barrels, still un-packed, stood at random in the hall.

"I've been trying to sweep up after the movers first. They leave all these scraps, torn paper and rope. Then we'll tackle the rest. It's so good of you to do this. Mrs. Rice, you said? I'm Pauline. Pauline Edgewood." The woman was flustered, as if she had not expected any attention from the neighbors.

"Shall we put these things in the kitchen?" asked Laura. "There's chicken salad that needs the refrigerator. These are cocoa cupcakes in the foil. I'm told it was my grandmother's recipe."

"No mixes in those days. You took so much trouble—"

"Not at all. Baking relaxes me. This is a lovely house, with the marble fireplace and the high ceilings."

The rear windows looked out on a driveway and a lawn. A baby sat in a playpen on the lawn, a little boy pedaled a tricy-cle on the driveway, and the eldest child, a girl of eight, swung on a gym set.

Laura remarked, "The children are at home already, I see."

"Yes, we love the house because of the yard. They'll make good use of it."

"Somebody mentioned that you're a teacher."

"I was, and I want to get back to it when the baby's older.

It's hard to do everything at once, though, house and baby and job."

Across the hall, Laura, seeing a piano, asked who played it.

"Well, I suppose I do, very badly. We really bought it for Cynthia. She loves it, and we think, we hope, she has some talent."

"I teach piano."

"Really? One of the first things I planned to do here, I told my husband, is to find a teacher for Cynthia. May I ask—I mean—would you consider taking a child that young?"

"That depends. I'm at a stage," Laura explained with candor, "when I select. I really don't like to struggle with children whose parents are forcing them to play, who hate it and won't practice."

Mrs. Edgewood smiled. This time she spoke with fine assurance. "If you will hear Cynthia play, I think you'll know that won't happen to her."

"I'll be happy to hear her."

"I can bring her anytime unless you want to take a few minutes now."

This woman is charming, Laura thought. She has a quiet elegance.

"I'd like to hear her now," she said.

The child, a sprightly little girl with great black eyes and hair done in cornrows, was called in; when she was introduced, she gave her hand and sat down promptly at the piano when asked.

"I'll play a waltz, or shall I play a march?"

With equal seriousness, Laura considered. "A waltz. It fits a happy day like this one."

The child played neatly a tinkling version of "The Blue Danube."

"That's good," Laura told her when she was finished. "How long have you been taking lessons?"

"Not quite two years," said the mother.

"Then I'll change that to very, very good."

"Do you think you might consider Cynthia as a pupil?"

"If Cynthia wants to come to me, yes, I can."

The black eyes considered Laura. "I think you're very pretty," said Cynthia, "so I'd like to come."

The two women hid their amusement. Then Laura said, "You haven't asked me about my qualifications. I have a master's degree in music education."

"That's all right. I had a feeling about you regardless of that," said Pauline.

So the brief visit ended. Laura, on the short drive homeward, had a feeling too, a feeling of warmth for having given, and for having, in a larger way, received. But she did not plan to mention this afternoon to anyone. It was easier that way.

CHAPTER

7

Luxuriating in the tumbled bed that Robbie had just left, Tom watched her get dressed.

"It's more fun to watch you get undressed, but this is kind of interesting, too, in its way."

She flipped a towel at him. "Come on, what's making you so lazy today?"

"Not lazy, just relaxed. Sex in the morning does that to me. I wish you'd come back in here."

"You are just plain greedy, Tom Rice." She bent over him, he pulled her down, and they tussled, kissing and laughing until she pulled herself loose. "I promise you we'll be back here early this afternoon, but it's going to take twenty minutes to get there, and it's already half-past." She turned away to face the mirror, fluffing her hair. "Put on your good suit and your best tie. Jim Johnson's stylish." She stepped far enough away from the mirror to see herself at full length. "I wish I had a decent dress," she said, pouting.

"Why? What's wrong with that one? I like red, and it shows your shape."

"Ah, Tommy, you don't know anything about it. A girl needs *clothes*! If I had a father in some rich racket like that Jew Enid, I'd have a closetful, I can tell you. Well, I'll have to go on making the best of it as I always have."

The plaint continued. "I was thinking. If I can get my father to loosen up some more, I might be able to afford that room near the campus without having a roommate. Then you and I could have some real time together. I could fix it up with good curtains and a new bed. I hate cheapness. Look at this. Cheap. Dingy."

Tom looked where she was pointing. The dresser had lost two drawer pulls, and the bilious green paint that was supposed to cover the nicks and chips was peeling. He was reminded, looking first at this object and then at the sagging bottom of the easy chair and the ugly, faded purple bedspread, of his mother's household in which every object that could be laundered or waxed was cared for. Because he had always lived with such crisp cleanliness, he had never really thought about it until this minute in which the absence of it was suddenly depressing. And with equal suddenness, he felt the pity of Robbie's deprivation. She was herself so clean. It was one of the reasons—he realized that now for the first time—that she had so attracted him.

"Of course, this place is only for the summer, so I mustn't mind it too much. I was lucky to get anything at all so near to the bookstore. There's nothing else within five miles of it, you'll see."

And abruptly, in the quick change of mood so typical of her and so alluring to Tom, she became animated. Her face sparkled, and she spun around so fast that her full skirt rounded like an opening parasol.

"Isn't this the craziest, the most wonderful thing today? Me unpacking books in the back room when who walks in but Jim Johnson. And it was really nice of Mr. Dudley to call me out and introduce me as an editor on the *Independent Voice*. Really nice. Dudley looks grumpy, so don't mind him. He has to be on guard all the time against left-wing snoopers. They like to come in to look over our books. It's funny how you can always spot them. I suppose they think we keep bombs on the shelves. Actually"—Robbie lowered her voice—"he does have a thirty-eight in the desk drawer."

"You must have made some impression on Johnson for him to invite you to lunch."

"It wasn't really an invitation, nothing as formal as that. He just said something like, 'I have to be back here tomorrow, so if you're around, we can have a Coke and talk about your paper.' He's wonderful, Tom. Sexy. Wait till you meet him."

"I'm saving my wages to get a car by the end of the summer," Tom said as they climbed into the pickup. "In the meantime, this'll have to do."

"As long as it gets us there," Robbie said cheerfully.

Mom had offered him her car. "I know you're visiting a girl out of town, Tom, and since it's none of my business, I'm not asking any questions. I'll lend you my car overnight so you won't have to take her out in Dad's pickup."

That's how Mom was. Naturally he would have loved that car except for the fact that it was a Mercedes, and he knew in his bones that Robbie would have very mixed feelings about that.

The ride led down the highway, spotted on either side with clusters of new little houses; then, leaving the highway for an old blacktop road, it led through two or three shabby villages built a century or more ago, in which boxy large houses were interspersed with mobile homes scattered in dry brown fields. Tom began to wonder why anyone would want to open a bookstore here in this place.

In the third village at a two-story house where an American flag hung prominently, Robbie directed him to stop. The house had a deserted look; curtains were drawn shut at the windows, and in the meager plot of grass the weeds had grown knee-high.

"This is it," Robbie said. And no doubt because Tom looked puzzled, she explained, "We do mainly a mail-order business. We don't expect transient traffic way out here."

When she knocked at the door, it was opened by an elderly man who by reason of his surly, down-turned mouth Tom assumed was Mr. Dudley.

"This is Tom," Robbie said. "He's a good friend. Is anyone here yet?"

"He's on his way, though. You're early."

"Better early than late," Robbie said breezily. "Come, I'll show you upstairs."

The whole upper floor had been gutted to make one large room lined on all sides with bookshelves. The only pieces of furniture were a desk and a chair occupied by a woman who now stood graciously to greet them.

"Adeline, this is Tom. We're at college together. He's been a big help on the paper, and he's going to be a bigger help next year."

"I'm glad to know you, Tom."

She was a lady. That was the immediate word, almost outmoded now, that occurred to him as he took her narrow, light hand. Why, she looks like Mom, he thought. Her fine oval face, her fair hair, even the cream-colored linen dress and the delicate pearl earrings were like his mother's. There was a curious contrast between the woman and the place.

"Mrs. Irons is a volunteer," Robbie explained. "And she works harder than any of us."

"The name is Adeline, and I don't work harder than anybody else, Robbie. But I do work *hard* because what we're doing here is so important. What's at stake is the kind of country that young people like you are going to inherit. I don't mean to sound pompous, but it's the truth."

Tom glanced at a pile of books on the desk. There was one with "Hitler" in the title, another about World War II, another with the word "negro" —

Mrs. Irons interrupted his glance. "Feel free to browse. If you want to buy anything today, I'll be glad to recommend. Or maybe you'd like to show your friend our mail-order department in the basement. We generally keep fifteen hundred to two thousand books down there, ready to go."

"I'd like to see it," Tom said.

The three went downstairs. "Your friend knows, of course,

that we don't talk about this place," Mrs. Irons said, addressing Robbie, who replied that most certainly Tom knew.

"Not that we're doing anything illegal in this organization, but we do have enemies, and the less they know about our private business, the better."

A long row of cartons, partially filled with books, stood against the walls.

"We fill orders from every corner of the country. It's been quite amazing to see how the business in our own state has picked up since Jim Johnson started his campaign."

"Is he affiliated with you here?" asked Tom.

"Oh dear no, he's a completely independent man. Completely. Let me make that perfectly clear. Oh, there are plenty of points at which our philosophies do meet, but Jim has his own ideas. He only drops in here very quietly now and then when he happens to be in this part of the state. And when he does, it's only for old friendship's sake. He and I went to school together. I hear his car now. He always parks in back of the house and uses the basement door."

Jim Johnson was handsome. His pictures didn't begin to do him justice. From a clear, wide forehead, bright hair swept back in natural waves, as crisp as if they had been made with a curling iron. He was tall and fit. His light gray summer suit was obviously expensive, and Tom was glad he had worn his own best suit.

"Hi, Robbie!" Johnson said. "And you have to be Tom." He looked straight into Tom's eyes and pumped his hand. "Friend Roberta here tells me you're a first-rate man on that great *Independent Voice*."

"Well, sir, I don't know about being first-rate, but I try and intend to try harder."

"Good, good. Let me tell you, we need more right-thinking young people like yourselves in the universities. Need all we can get if I'm to reach the state senate this fall. I assume you want me to." And Johnson cocked his head in a gesture that was both humorously appealing and absolutely certain of receiving the right response. When they both nodded, he went on, "The important thing about your paper is that it has so much support from alumni who are scattered all over the country. Many of them won't be very aware of the election in this state, and your paper can make them aware. We have a program, we have things to say that make as much sense in the other forty-nine as they do here. Of course, the hope is that your readers will be induced to help along our campaign with their dollars. So that's where you young folks come into the picture, why I wanted to meet you together, answer your questions and say thanks."

"This is a great honor for us," Tom said respectfully.

Johnson smiled. "It's about time for lunch, and so why don't we go down the road a way for a hamburger. There's a fellow who knows me from when my wife and I lived in this part of the state. He keeps a couple of booths in a back room so people who don't want to attract a crowd—and I don't today, I want to have a little private time with you—can eat unseen. Come on, he's expecting us."

They squeezed into Johnson's car, which was piled high with papers and pamphlets, and stopped a couple of miles away at a barbecue shack set back among scrub trees. At the rear door they were admitted by a bulky man in a soiled apron who took their hamburger order; after it was brought, they were alone in the room. A large Coca-Cola poster hung on the wall opposite the booth, and from the ceiling there dangled a long strip of flypaper.

Johnson smiled. "Not exactly elegant, but I've been in worse." He put a notepad and pen in front of Robbie. "Make notes on what I'm going to tell you. These are the points you should include in your editorials." His eyes sharpened. "It probably is not necessary for me to repeat, but I will anyway, that on no account should my name appear on any personal piece of paper that you own. We don't want some snooper to find stuff like that and link me up with any organization, any at all, you understand? I am not affiliated with anything except the party that nominated me for the state senate."

Johnson paused. His eyes, between which a small frown

was gathering, looked off into space. He seemed suddenly to be trying to reach a decision. Then apparently he reached one.

"I'm going to talk straight from the shoulder. I trust you to understand this, Robbie. You've been very well recommended. And so, because of you, I am going to trust Tom. That's what politics is—a network of trust and obligation." He made a neat little steeple of his hands. "The reason I cannot have my name linked with any groups, even a—a bookstore like the one we were just in is that there already is a dirty smear campaign against me. The opposition has been trying from the beginning of my career to link me with the Ku Klux Klan. What am I saying? From the beginning of my career? I made enemies while I was still in college. The liberals didn't like me, the school-busing crowd didn't like me, the housing crowd didn't like me. I worked on a paper much as you do, and being of a talkative bent, I did a lot of talking. But I never belonged to the Klan, that I didn't."

Robbie said thoughtfully, "Certainly I understand what you're driving at, but just between ourselves, I often think there's a good deal of sense in the Klan's agenda. We have a heritage in this country that's being diluted by all sorts of foreign strains who haven't a grain of Americanism."

"Exactly," Johnson said. He smiled. "But it doesn't pay to say such things loudly if you want to get elected. You have to appeal broadly, and not offend. And the Klan *is* far too extreme. After all, I'm not an anti-Semite, and I don't want to lynch blacks, for God's sake. But you know," he said thoughtfully, "it does pay to read every point of view. I've been a reader since I was ten years old. I've read Hobbes, Nietzsche, Adam Smith, Taine, Schopenhauer—and what I found is that you can get a worthwhile idea from every single one of them, even though you may not completely agree. I daresay you can find worthwhile ideas even in communism—no, probably that's the one philosophy that's entirely wrong. But my advice to you is to read everything and then think hard. I already tell that to my children, young as they are. By the way, the bookstore back there has some fascinating material." He looked at his watch. "Uh-oh. I've got to get to a rally. Can I make one hundred fifty miles by four without getting a ticket? The last thing a candidate needs is a ticket for speeding. I'll drop you folks off so you can get your car at the store and get on my way."

"Now there's a real leader," Tom said as Johnson drove off. "A reasonable, articulate, educated man. I don't know how anyone can get the idea that he's a redneck populist."

"Yeah. Well, it was a nice day. And night, too."

"It always is. Will I see you Friday? I can drive out late Friday after I take Tim to a ballgame."

Robbie said sympathetically, "You really do care about the kid, don't you?"

"He's my brother," Tom answered simply.

"I heard," Robbie said over the telephone, "there's going to be a rally for Johnson next Wednesday in your city."

"There is? I haven't seen anything in the paper."

"It'll be there. A man came in the store this morning and told us. I want to be there and make a feature article out of it, something personal, something creative for our paper. I'll write it and save it for the first issue in the fall."

"Good idea. You do that, and I'll follow up on the next meeting."

"Yes, but you should be at this one, too. Dudley's going, so I'll ride over with him, and we'll pick you up at your house. West Oak Street, isn't it? What number?"

He didn't want Robbie to meet his parents, especially not Mom. When he asked himself why that was so, what difference it would make, he was unable to answer.

"No, I'll wait for you on the corner. The folks are having relatives here next week, and I'd rather slip out quietly. Make it the corner of West Oak and Tilden Street. Let me know what time, and I'll be there."

On Wednesday his parents sat reading in the living room. His father looked up from the newspaper. "Going somewhere, Tom?"

"No place special."

"Well, have a good time." As he went down the walk, he heard his father's laugh. "Going out to chase chippies. What else at nineteen?"

Under a lamppost where moths bumped and burned themselves on the weak yellow bulb, he waited. Before long, a broken-down sedan appeared with Dudley at the wheel and Robbie next to him. She opened the door.

"I'll shove over. There's room for three in the front."

"No need. I'll hop in back." There was something unappetizing, something greasy about Dudley, and he didn't want Robbie to be pressed up against the man.

The car began to move. "You'll have to direct me to Fairview. I don't know this town too well," Dudley said.

"Fairview!" Tom exclaimed. "I thought there was going to be a rally downtown in the Civic Auditorium."

"No," Dudley said. "Johnson had a conflicting date, so we're going to this instead."

"To what? What's happening on Fairview? You didn't tell me, Robbie."

"I didn't know until this morning when somebody came to the store and said we should go here. It seems some young guy is having a protest meeting at his house. It's not an official campaign rally, it has nothing to do with Johnson," she explained. "But he's a Johnson supporter. Young and rich. Name of Anderson. A very important supporter, it seems."

Greg Anderson. Tom had a general recollection of a flamboyant kid, said to be very smart, straight A's, who had left high school in his junior year and had been sent away to a prep school in the North. He had a sense of uneasiness. Whatever this was, it was too close to home.

"It sounds cockeyed to me," he said. "What's he protesting?"

"Maybe it is cockeyed, but we won't know until we see for ourselves, will we? Which way, left or right?"

In the few seconds while the car waited at the intersection, Tom's thoughts coalesced. A protest on Fairview; possibly, very possibly, it had something to do with those blacks who had moved in there. And if so—

He gulped. "Gee, this is tough on me. I live here, a couple of minutes away. My father's got friends on that street, his banker—gee, he'll kill me if I get mixed up in a protest meeting."

When Dudley turned around, Tom could see his eyes glitter. "Which way?" he demanded, cutting the two words apart as with a knife. "I'm not going to stand here all night while you shake like an old woman."

"Left. Then another four or five intersections and a tennis club on the corner. Turn left again there, and that's Fairview."

Alarm had definitely hastened Tom's heartbeat. At the same time, the very existence of this alarm infuriated him. He had allowed himself to be insulted. "Old woman," was he? He had shown weakness in front of Robbie, who was so vigorous and determined.

"I'm far from shaking," he said stiffly. "And I'm not thinking only of my father. I'm looking a whole lot further. It won't do our work any good at college, Robbie, or our work with the paper, if we get the wrong publicity, whatever this thing may be about."

"Tom's got a point, Mr. Dudley," Robbie said thoughtfully after a moment. "And Jim Johnson wants to use us in the campaign. If we get our names mixed up in any mess on that street, he's not going to like it at all."

"Okay, we'll drive along the street, see what's happening, park the car and walk, depending on what's going on. Should be interesting, anyway."

It was quite dark, a cloudy night made darker by the heavy leafage of the old oaks that, meeting one another, arched a ceiling over these fine streets. On either side of Fairview, two or three dozen cars and vans, mostly vans, were parked with nobody in them. Far down the street a crowd had gathered, vague shapes in the lighted circles thrown by the streetlamps.

Seventy-five to a hundred people were standing on a lawn that sloped up toward a great stone house. At the crest of the lawn on a podium improvised out of boxes, a young man wearing a red shirt was haranguing the audience. The scene was theatrical: the imposing house with its balustraded terrace and its flare lights on the corners that, illuminating the crowd, only deepened the blackness of shrubbery as dense, as secretive as a wilderness. The scene was eerie.

"That's Greg Anderson. I was in high school with him until he left," whispered Tom.

The speech must have been going on a long time, for the listeners were restless, milling about and whispering among themselves, while the speaker's voice as he tried to keep their attention and struggled to rise above the rustle of the wind in the trees, verged almost on the soprano.

"What do these people want? Preference in jobs, in the universities, in government—what else? Shoved ahead by the liberals, they'll end up owning us, body and soul. Look at that house across the street, turn your heads and take a good look at it. Then ask yourselves how many of you can afford to live in a house like that. How much farther do they want to go? To the White House, maybe? Well, and they will if we keep electing the dolts and fools who've been running this state and are running it right now. I hope you will all have brains enough to do something about the muddle we're in, to get out and put more men like Jim Johnson in office. Then maybe, just maybe, we will be able to turn this evil tide—"

As if the listeners had become one body, every head turned toward the street. For a second, Tom thought he was hearing the clatter of horses, but then came the hoot and cry of young male voices; a troop, no more than twenty strong, wearing heavy military boots and dark glasses, was racing down the middle of the street. In the next second, all twenty had vaulted over the low wrought-iron fence of the property that had once belonged to the Blairs.

The house had been dim, as if the occupants were readying for bed, but suddenly the entire front flared into light so that Tom could see the figures racing over the lawn with caps drawn down over their faces. They were screaming. The hideous, wordless cry raised gooseflesh on Tom's back. He saw their upraised throwing arms, he heard the crash of glass, and he heard the wail of a child. In seconds they had smashed every first-floor window of that elegant Georgian house.

"What the hell—" cried Greg Anderson. "Quiet, folks! Let's mind our own business, this has nothing to do with us, you hear?"

But his audience was already fleeing, melting away into the darkness. It was every man for himself.

"Who? What?" Tom panted as, with Robbie, he went stumbling back toward the car.

Dudley grumbled under his breath, "Damn idiots. Fools."

Cars parked on both sides of the street were trying to pull away, backing, filling and bumping, in a rush to vanish before the certain arrival of the police. A van tried to make a U-turn; drivers entering the street, who were naturally unaware that anything out of the ordinary was taking place, blew horns frantically and tried to back up, inching away from the chaos.

"We've got to get out of here," Robbie said anxiously, as they stood helplessly beside Dudley's car, which was blocked in.

Tom blinked into the headlights of a car that was slowly approaching. When it passed, he had a glimpse of the occupants and ducked.

"God Almighty, Robbie, that was the minister and his wife. She's a friend of my mother's."

"So what? You haven't done anything."

"My God, if she saw me!"

"Get in the car. Nobody saw you. It's black as hell unless somebody shines a light directly in your face."

"I'm sure she saw me, though."

"Get in the car, will you?" Dudley was in a rage. He got behind the wheel, started the engine, and began to rock the car back and forth until he had squeezed it out of the space.

"Listen," Robbie said, "you didn't break any windows. It's not the end of the world. If they did see you, well, they were here on this street, too."

"That's different. They live near here, just around the corner."

With furious defiance, Dudley had forced his way into a U-turn, and, grazing a fender, ignoring protests and curses, fled out of Fairview Street. Bent over the wheel as he sped, he said to himself, "Goddamn mess . . ."

The car screeched around a corner, raced and squealed around another corner. From a distance behind them, police sirens wailed.

Tom spoke. "You're going toward the highway. I live the other way."

"For Christ's sake, give me directions, then." Dudley was scared. You could smell his sweat.

"Next right and down the hill. You can stop at the bottom. I'll walk the rest of the way."

Dudley kept muttering. "Last thing we need is to be mixed up in an attack on blacks. Last thing."

The car went hurtling down the hill, and Tom gripped the seat. These last few minutes had the feel of unreality, the shattered summer night, shouts, cries, the running feet in unified attack upon that house, the broken glass . . . He saw his parents as he had just left them, reading in the silence and safety of their home, then stones slamming through the windows . . . His mother would scream . . .

"I wonder whether anybody in that house was hurt," he said.

"And if they were, what difference?" Robbie's tone was sharp.

"You can make your point without *hurting* people."

Dudley laughed. "Listen, those people knew they're not wanted there and yet they forced their way in. So you have to use force to get them out. Nobody *wants* to injure anyone, but that's the chance you have to take to get your message through. Those people don't belong in that neighborhood any more than you belong in Buckingham Palace."

Well, probably so. Those people really didn't belong there with the Ordways, the minister, and the Andersons, families like that. And as Dad always said, if this kept up, they'd be taking over the whole neighborhood. Everything would change, and Tom didn't want things to change. Things were fine as they were now.

That guy Greg has guts, he thought. My age, and he holds a meeting for Johnson on his lawn. His parents, naturally, are behind him. Not like my parents. Then he wondered aloud, "What do you suppose is happening back there now?"

"They'll arrest the guys if they catch them. And your friend Greg may be called as a witness. That's all," Robbie said. "But right across the street from a Johnson rally! Tough luck."

Dudley reprimanded her. "Don't worry about Jim. He can take care of himself. Here's your corner, Tom. You won't have to walk far."

The "Fairview incident," as it came to be called, was the talk of the city and beyond. Tom rose early the next morning to catch the newspaper as it thumped onto the front lawn. Stunned by the headline, he sat down on the veranda steps and read about the night's events.

By the time the police arrived, the stone-throwers had left. A photograph showed the shattered windows and the family gathered, huddled at the front door talking to the police. But that was not all. Much later, after the police had left, another attack had been made upon the house, this time with bullets that had gone through the broken windows and embedded themselves in a baby grand piano.

When Laura and Bud came out onto the veranda, Tom gave them the paper.

"We just heard it upstairs on the radio. Some excitement," Bud said.

Well, they have to be crazies to do that, Tom thought. Protests are one thing, but bullets are something else again.

"What do you think? The Klan?" he asked.

Bud shrugged. "Who knows? Maybe some neighbors — no." He laughed. "I can hardly imagine Ordway creeping out at night with a rifle slung over his hand-tailored shoulder."

"You're laughing?"

At his mother's tone, Tom, still seated on the steps, looked up. There were tears in her eyes.

"Those animals! No, that's wrong. Animals don't do such things." She wiped her eyes. "I will never understand. Not as long as I live."

"What won't you understand, Mom?" asked Timmy, coming onto the veranda.

"This. In the paper. It's unbelievable. If I could get my hands on those people, I would—I don't know what I'd do. Scum of the earth. They deserve to die."

"Death penalty? That's pretty strong. They didn't kill anybody," Bud said.

"I'm talking morals, not laws. I'm no lawyer," Laura said vehemently. "Oh," she cried, "don't you see, it's not only the cruelty to that one family? It's much more. It's a whole poisonous atmosphere, like a cloud." She made a wide gesture with her arms. "A cloud that spreads and spreads. Don't you see?"

"I see," Bud replied, "that if—listen, I'm not saying it's right to shoot up somebody's house—but if people upset the applecart, they shouldn't wonder why the apples are smashed all over the ground. Anyway, I'm sick of hearing about blacks. I'm sick of them, every damn one of them. Blow them all up into space or drown the lot in the Atlantic. I won't miss them."

Timmy had a puzzled, worried expression, looking from father to mother and then to Tom. The atmosphere was heavy; you felt, Tom thought, as if an actual storm were coming, when the wind stirs the quiet trees and the leaves turn inside out. With a glance at his mother he saw the storm rising. And then as quickly as it rose, it sank.

Her cheek muscles tightened; she spoke with measured calm.

"I've got the pancakes mixed. Blueberry this morning. So come on. The Rice family's front-porch arguments aren't going to solve the world's problems."

❀　❀　❀

"Your mother gets too upset. She takes everything too much to heart," Bud said as Tom and he rode to work. "I hate to see it."

"Betty Lee told me Mom brought cake and stuff over to those blacks on Fairview."

"She what? God Almighty. She never told me!"

"I guess she knew you'd make a fuss."

"Damn right I would! Suppose the Ordways had seen her! They're all wrought up over those people, and Mrs. Rice, my wife, brings a welcome basket. For all I know, they may have seen her. It's just when you don't want to be seen that you are seen."

This remark jolted Tom. Somehow he had managed to put out of his mind the image of Dr. Foster's wife. He had fallen asleep and awakened without thought of her; now, at his father's words, the woman's startled white face loomed in the air before him. Immediately, then, he squashed the image. With all the controversy over this neighborhood event, such trivia would be overlooked.

"So the visit was to be a secret."

"I don't know. Betty Lee didn't say so. She said Mom was an angel."

"She is an angel, I agree to that. She has the softest heart of anyone I know. The truth is, she's not very practical, though, not realistic. She'd better stay away from those blacks up there. If there's to be any more trouble, it'd be her luck to get hurt, God forbid."

They drew up at the plant, past the long sign over the entrance: PAIGE AND RICE.

"Yes, I remember the day that sign went up," Bud said.

He was proud of that sign. Tom thought, almost tenderly: I must have heard him say that a thousand times.

"There's a big load coming in from United Wire, Tom. Get the copper separated from the rest and set it in Number Two warehouse. There are two sizes, and the Austin Constructions man will be coming today or tomorrow to decide which size they want. Okay?"

"Got it," Tom said.

He liked working here. Certainly he was aware of many things that made it pleasant for him: the fact that he had the privilege, which he did not abuse, of taking time off whenever he wanted to, the fact that most of his time, when midday heat was at its worst, was spent in the air-conditioned retail shop, and the ultimate fact, from which these others derived, that he was the son of the owner.

Walking around the four-acre spread, he often felt the swell of pride. When his time came, he would be the fourth-generation owner. But this place was far different, Mom's aunts were the first to say, from the business that his great-grandfather had founded, and it was Bud Rice who had made it what it was today. Because of him, there was this bustle of arriving and departing trucks, these warehouses, these sheds crammed with tools, gravel, lumber, and cement, this parking lot filled up, this traffic of customers in and out all day. Bud had caused it, and his son was proud.

The workers were friendly to Tom. However uncomfortable they might feel about his presence, they naturally did not show it, so he hoped that they might sincerely like him. After all, he never shirked, he joined in their talk and jokes, he ate his sandwich lunch not in the office with his father but in a shed with them.

Today as they sat down in the shade, they talked about the incident on Fairview Street, and this time, remembering Bud's admonition about political discussions, Tom stayed out of it, which was just as well because the men were hotly divided.

Then one of them produced a transistor radio, and the twelve o'clock news came on.

"The police stopped a car at four o'clock this morning speeding eastward out of the northwestern section of the city. Ku Klux Klan regalia, hoods and gowns, were found in the trunk of the car, but no weapons or ammunition or any illegal objects. The occupants were given a ticket for speeding in a residential zone.

"Ralph Mackenzie, running for the state senate, deplored

the criminal attack upon the Edgewood family's home last night, condemning it as brutal, inhumane, and un-American. He expressed some wonder that it occurred simultaneously with a rally for his opponent that was taking place across the street.

"In an interview this morning, Jim Johnson expressed 'outrage' at Mr. Mackenzie's attempt by implication to link a legitimate political rally with what he himself called 'a criminal attack.' He said, 'Neither I nor any of my supporters condone any behavior that Mr. Mackenzie himself called "un-American." We are entirely and completely American.' "

"Good for Jim," someone said. "That's telling them."

Someone else said, "Telling them a lot of bull if you ask me."

"I didn't ask you."

"Well, I'm telling you all the same."

The first man laid his lunch down and made two fists.

"Hey," Tom said, "no sense fighting about it."

The words slipped out of his own accord, slipped out because violence repelled him, and violence was in both men's faces.

An older man spoke up. "Tom's right. We'll vote the way we want. A fistfight won't turn the vote one way or the other."

The second man got up and walked away, grumbling something under his breath that sounded like, "Yeah, get in solid with the boss's kid."

Obviously a Mackenzie man, Tom thought. His mother's words flashed: *This is going to be a nasty election.* Not necessarily nasty, he thought, but very, very emotional.

The owner of the radio switched it off, and the talk turned more happily to baseball. And a few minutes later, Bud unexpectedly appeared with an announcement.

"Knock off work for a second after lunch. We're having a little ceremony, kind of, that I want you all to see."

On the front of the main building the PAIGE AND RICE sign had been taken down. Two ladders were propped up on either side of the entrance, and a new sign lay on the grass ready to be hoisted. Tom craned to read it upside down: RICE AND SON, it said, causing a hot flood of embarrassment to creep up his back to the roots of his hair.

"What, so soon?" he blurted.

Bud slapped him on the back. "Why not? You are my son, aren't you?"

The men laughed, and Tom stood abashed before them as the sign was hoisted and fastened into place. It was so conspicuous, with its bold gilt letters glittering in the sun!

One of the men called out, "Hurray!" And there was brief clapping. The three women who worked in the office clapped, calling, "Speech, Tom, speech!" And when he shook his head, the old one, who had been there since his mother was a child, reproved him, smiling the reproof. "Come on, Tom, I knew you before you were born."

"I don't deserve this," he said. "Not yet, anyway. So I really don't know what to say."

Bud roared, "Of course you deserve it. You work here, don't you? You give us an honest day's work. Otherwise Bud Rice wouldn't put you up on that sign, you can damn well depend on that. Right, guys?"

The men laughed again, nodding, no, Bud Rice wouldn't. You sure could depend on that.

And Bud put his arm around Tom's shoulder. "This is my son, guys. He's good stuff. Otherwise, son or no son, I wouldn't reward him. I'd love him, yes, but a reward is something different. I just want to say this—hell, I'm being too sentimental, I know, but a lot of you have sons, so you know the feeling—I just want to say that if anything happens to me, Tom here will take over, and he'll be as fair and square, as decent as I hope I've been. I've tried to be, anyway."

A wave of love passed over Tom. Suppose it was sentimental! Suppose it was embarrassing! It was real. My father, he thought. If anything ever happened to him, I'd—I don't know what I'd do. And in that instant, he didn't care a damn what anybody else thought. He put his arms around Bud and hugged him.

"Okay," Bud said, "it's too blasted hot to keep you all here in the sun. There's beer inside to cool you off before we get to work. That's the celebration."

After Tom and Bud left, Laura was alone, for Timmy had been invited to a friend's house for the day. Or she had thought she was alone. For when she took the newspaper and went out to the veranda, she was followed by Betty Lee.

"I didn't hear you come in," Laura said.

"I know. You were all talking. And when you came to breakfast I hid upstairs."

The tone combined with the word "hid" was so strange that Laura put the paper aside and looked toward Betty Lee. The old woman's dark face was overcast with gray. She had been crying.

"What's wrong? What happened?" There must have been an accident or another death in her large family. "Tell me. Sit down and tell me."

"I almost can't, Miss Laura. It hurts my heart." And Betty Lee covered her face with her hands.

"Whatever hurts will hurt less if you let it out," Laura said gently.

The hands went down and the wet eyes turned piteously to Laura.

"I heard—heard what he—he said."

Not those words about blasting and drowning? Not those? "You mean—"

"When he said he was sick of every—every one of them, of *us*, he meant *me*. I never thought, I would never believe that anyone in this house— You're my family. You were. But now, not anymore." Betty Lee wrung her hands. "How can I stay here now, Miss Laura? I can't, I can't."

To be numb, to be stunned, is to lose the use of language. There were no words that could assuage this woman's grief and disillusionment; her world, the bright little world of her adopted family with its births and deaths, its celebrations, the flow of its days and years, had been wiped away. Bud, in a matter of seconds, had done it. And Laura was absolutely silent.

Then Betty Lee stood up and laid her hand on Laura's bowed head.

"You think I don't understand you have nothing to do with it? Oh, I've been sad for you! You were my baby girl. I took you in my arms when your mother died, I made finger curls in your yellow hair. I taught your Tom to walk, and I watched him grow, and yes, I opened a page or two in those books he has in his room. But I never told you. I thought, well he's young, they grow a bit crazy, with crazy ideas like our Black Power kids who hate all whites. Then they get out in the world and learn better, we hope. But when a grown man in a family like this one— Oh, if Miss Cecile or Miss Lillian ever heard that, they'd—I don't know what they'd do."

Over and over the warm hand stroked Laura's head, until at last she was able to look up and speak.

"If I could undo this, oh if I could undo what you heard today!"

"I know."

"Listen, listen, Betty Lee. He didn't mean you. What he said was awful, but often people say things they don't mean."

"He meant them."

"He didn't mean you! I promise! He knows how wonderful you are, he says so."

"What difference does it make after all whether he meant me or not?" Betty Lee's mouth was grim.

She is right, of course, Laura thought, and it was stupid of me to make the point.

"I don't know what to do," she said, with a question in her voice, as if to hope for an answer.

"I don't know what you can do. That's why I'm so sad for you. It's hard when a husband and wife—" Betty Lee did not finish.

"But he is really, really a good man in many ways. You've seen—" said Laura, and broke down.

Then Betty Lee put her arms around her, comforting with

the old, old refrain, "Don't cry, nothing's worth crying like that, it'll be all right, you'll see—"

"You didn't mean it when you said you can't stay, did you?"

It was a moment before the reply came. "Yes. I wouldn't be comfortable anymore. Would you if you were in my place?"

Another difficult moment passed. "No," Laura said. And another moment passed. "I can't imagine this house without you."

The other smiled sadly. "I was getting older anyway. Almost time to quit working."

"No, you're not that old. You weren't thinking of quitting. Let's admit the whole truth."

"All right, we have. You know I'll always be here for you just the same, don't you?"

Laura nodded and wiped her eyes. "And I for you . . ."

"Now maybe I'd better go." Betty Lee bent and kissed Laura's cheek. "You take care of yourself, hear? And call me if you ever need me. Will you?"

"I will," Laura whispered, and did not look as Betty Lee went out.

She heard her walk through the kitchen, call good-bye to Earl in his basket and close the back door.

Gone. The dignity of a dignified woman had been offended.

The world had so little mercy. Betty Lee, and that child with the cornrow hair, sitting at the piano . . . Why? Rocks and taunts and bullets. In God's name, why? And Laura sat there staring from the ghastly photograph on the front page to the receding shape of Betty Lee going homeward down the street.

After a while she got up and left the house. The morning was fresh and moist. When she reached Fairview, there was a brisk little wind beneath the arch of the trees. The street was quiet. A gardener trimmed a hedge. A lawn sprinkler sprayed diamond drops as it circled and spat, and it was hard to believe that anything ever could disturb the peace of a place like this.

A car slowed as it passed the old Blair house. Most probably it would be years before people stopped calling it the Blair house, for it had belonged to the Blairs so long. Another car passed slowly enough to get a good look, and then went on its way. Curiosity seekers. But I am more than that, Laura told herself. I know those people; at least, I mean, they are more than a name to me.

She came to the wrought-iron fence. A truck was parked in the driveway, and men were already working on the windows. Broken glass lay on the lawn, pointed shards as lethal as carving knives.

"Careful, lady," a workman warned as she went up the walk.

On the white front door there was a splash of black paint. Something had been written there, and someone had effaced enough of it so that it was illegible except for a letter that looked like an "n." Perhaps the father of the family had gotten up early to hide what had been written. She rang the bell.

She waited awhile and rang again. The door opened just enough for a child's head to appear. Startled eyes met Laura's.

"Cynthia," said Laura.

The door moved to close.

"Cynthia," Laura said again, "don't you remember me?"

"My mother said not to let anybody in except the men who are fixing the windows."

"Please tell her who it is. The lady who came the other day, the lady who's going to give you piano lessons. You do remember me, don't you?"

The child closed the door. She wants to make sure I don't force my way inside, Laura thought ruefully, waiting at the blemished door. A few moments later, the door opened again.

"My mother says she doesn't want any visitors. None at all," she says."

Well, that was understandable. Yes, yes it was. You had only to put yourself in that woman's shoes.

"I'm sorry," Laura said gently. "Perhaps another time."

"And no piano lessons, either," the child said.

The door closed with a muted thud as decisive as if it had

been slammed. And Laura went back down the walk feeling an unfamiliar shame. This was like watching an actor forget his lines. It was like being in a group where someone was making a terrible fool of himself; although it had nothing to do with you, you partook of the shame.

And she went on down the street past an ample lawn where little boys no older than seven or eight were playing baseball. So serious, so businesslike they were, with their mitts and caps, as if everything depended on their team's win. So innocent. At the intersection from behind the shrubbery that enclosed the tennis club, came the ring of voices, the whack and thwack of racket against ball. That, too, was an innocent, a happy occupation. An American afternoon.

Lou Foster came around the corner. "I walked up here to call on them," she said, "but no one answered my ring. I feel sick. Those people's terror last night—can you imagine it?"

"You and I seem to be meeting at bad times," Laura said bleakly.

"Jeff and I got a glimpse of something last evening. We were on our way home, and when we turned into Fairview, there was a commotion, people running, cars going every which way, honking and bumping. We had a hard time getting through the jam. Your son Tom was there in a car with some people. Did he tell you about it?"

A little shock went through Laura as when, while standing on a particular piece of carpet, you touch a light switch. It was a hot little shock . . .

"No, he and Bud were late this morning and we didn't have a chance to say three words."

"Well, he'll tell you what a mess it was. The way I see it is that the group who broke the windows must have scared the crowd across the street. They wanted to get away before the police came. But if you ask me, Laura, Greg Anderson's mixed up in it somehow. He's a follower of Johnson, and I don't put anything past Johnson."

"I don't know. I don't know anything anymore," said Laura bleakly.

"Greg Anderson's a bad egg. His parents had no control over him when he was five years old, and apparently, they still have none."

"You don't control people when they're nineteen," Laura said, wanting to get home, only to get home . . .

She went up the walk to her front door, her gracious, glossy green door with its polished brass knocker that no one used; knockers were of another century, before doorbells had been invented, but this one was pretty. There was no defacement on this door. The windows were not broken, either; in the sunlight, they gleamed, and you could clearly see a trailing pattern of vines and grapes on the lace curtains. Petunias, cream and crimson, cascaded out of wooden tubs beside the door. Earl had detected her approach, and she heard from way back in the kitchen his gravelly bark. He would be racing through the front hall to meet her.

She turned the key in the lock and went inside. There sat the dog, sweeping the floor with his joyous tail, as though she had just come back after a year away. He expected to be acknowledged, and she bent to stroke him.

"Yes, yes, I'm home."

The day was not oppressive, the walk had not been that long and besides, it had been mostly downhill; yet her blood was hot and craved water. From the kitchen where she poured a glassful, she could see into the dining room and beyond, where every familiar thing was in its proper place, the chairs aligned around the table, and the corner cupboards filled with the blue-and-white Wedgwood china that had been there for half a century. All was orderly, untouched, secure.

But was it? And a sudden sense of peril, of menace, passed through these dignified rooms, as though a cold wind had blown open all the doors. This house—no house—was safe. Terrible angers, fanned and fed, could blow it down, and everything would crumble into ruins, everything, whole streets and towns. Terrible hatred could do that. It was history.

She went upstairs to Tom's room. Jim Johnson's frank, attractive face hung between the two windows. Otherwise, it was an ordinary room, a college boy's room with the university pennant and a map of the United States thumbtacked to the wall. Above the desk there hung a diagram of the heavens. On the desk there were a heap of books and, in its cheap frame, the small photograph of the girl whose rather winsome face was almost eclipsed by a full mass of shoulder-length wavy hair. *For Tom with love* was scrawled across the corner.

Laura had a faint twinge of jealousy. But that was natural. All mothers, one read, feel that tiny hurt at the thought of taking second place in their sons' hearts. All mothers wonder whether the girl is a passing fancy or the "real" one, and if she is the "real" one, whether she is the right one. Who and what was this girl?

She picked up a newspaper from a pile. *The Independent Voice,* she read; then, always a rapid reader, she scanned the front page and saw at once that here was competent propaganda masquerading as journalism. Here were clever political satire, biting bigotry, and dangerous, scurrilous lies. She turned the pages and hurriedly read the names; coming to "Thomas Rice," she put the paper away and sat down.

It was one thing to have heard him speak his ideas out loud, and quite another to see his name attached to these ideas, and worse, in print. This must be the paper about which she had vaguely heard, a college paper financed by powerful alumni who had an agenda of their own. She looked over the masthead again. Masculine and feminine names were intermingled alphabetically, and because she had some totally unfounded idea that one of the feminine names might belong to the girl in the photograph, she studied them: Sue-Ellen, Jennifer, Roberta, Linda. But this was foolishness. What difference did it make?

"I am so sad," she said aloud. "I am so angry. I am so disappointed, and I don't know what to do. Oh, I could wring your neck, Tom. How can you do this? How can you, when all you ever saw, all I ever taught you, was decent and good?"

She was still sitting there when she heard the car come in and the garage door roll up. A minute later she saw Bud and

Tom take the hand mowers out of the toolshed. Bud was particular about keeping the edges of the beds mowed clean. It came to her as she watched them that there were two paths open to her; the easier was to ignore Lou Foster's words, as well as the paper, while the harder was to confront them both. Which of the two might accomplish more, or whether either would accomplish anything, it was impossible to know.

Having decided on the harder way, Laura was waiting when Bud and Tom came into the house.

"You're hot," she said. "I've made iced tea. Now sit down. I want to talk to you, Tom, but your father ought to hear it, too." And casting a furious glance in Bud's direction, she began, "Tom, where were you last night?"

Since he was fundamentally honest, he had never been a convincing liar, and now, as his eyes widened and his brows rose, making a crease across his forehead, she saw that he was alarmed.

"Walking around the neighborhood, catching up on people. Why?"

"I just want to set a few things straight in my mind. Tell me, did you catch up on anybody?"

"Not really. I passed a couple of guys, said hello, and never got any farther than East Oak. Then I got bored and came home."

"No farther than East Oak. Nowhere near Fairview?"

The beautiful eyes grew wider as he exclaimed reproachfully, "Mom! You aren't thinking I'm the one who broke those people's windows, are you?" And laughing at the ludicrous suggestion, he continued, "Or that I fired those shots?" He lowered his voice and looked about with a sly, suspicious expression as if conspiring. "I'll let you in on something. I'm really an international terrorist. I don't bother with trivial jobs like that."

"I'm not joking, Tom. Don't try to wriggle your way out with a joke."

Because alarm was obviously mounting within him, he pretended to be hurt. "I'm not trying to wriggle out of anything, Mom."

"Don't lie to me, Tom. You were on Fairview in the crowd. Lou Foster saw you. She and the minister were driving through."

Tom was silent. Bud poured another glass of tea from the pitcher and was silent.

"Well?" demanded Laura.

"Okay. I walked to Fairview, not East Oak. Is that okay?"

"No, because you lied about it."

"I'm not a child. Do I have to account for every step I take?"

"You know that's not the issue. Do I ever ask you to report to me? No one could have more freedom than you have. But those weren't ordinary steps that you took last night. Extraordinary things happened on that street. What were you doing there? I want to know."

"All right. I went to the Johnson rally. It's no secret that I'm for Johnson and that Dad is, too."

"Then why didn't you say you were going there in the first place?"

"Because you hate Johnson," said Tom, now with some slight defiance.

She flared up. "I don't 'hate' anybody. I strongly disapprove of him, but you have every right to vote as you please. No, Tom. You went because you didn't want me—us—to know whom you were with. You were in a car with a young woman and an older man. Who are they? What's the secret?"

Bud spoke up. "Let him be, Laura. This sounds like a third degree. And you're scaring the life out of Timmy."

For Timmy had come home and was standing there in bewilderment.

"Timmy is a member of this family, and he's old enough to know what's going on in it. And we have a right to know what company our son is keeping."

"No," Bud said, getting up from his chair, "no, Tom's right. He's not a child. He doesn't have to answer as if he were in kindergarten. If he wants to meet a girl, he doesn't have to explain to us what company he keeps." And he gave Tom a glance that she recognized; it was a glance of complicity.

"No? No? Well, look at this and tell me what you think." Reaching behind her, Laura took from a table a copy of *The Independent Voice.* "And you're an editor on this paper, Tom. This is the company you keep. Read it, Bud."

Bud read a column and handed the paper back. "Free speech, Laura. You can't quarrel with that."

"It's a revolting rag."

"In your opinion."

"And yours, too."

"Probably it is, but my opinion isn't the issue."

"How can this have happened to our Tom?" she lamented.

"Nothing's happened to him," Bud said impatiently. "He's got a head on his shoulders; he has his own thoughts. And it's a free country."

"Yes, I hope it stays that way. Don't you see that that's what this is all about? The Klan—"

"I'm not in the Klan, Mother." When he was angry or arrogant, Tom called her "Mother." "That paper doesn't support the Klan. Jim Johnson doesn't, either, as we have discussed two or three times before this."

"Indeed we have, and I'm still not convinced. A reporter at that rally last night says that Anderson reviled those black people across the street, said they had no right to move there. I heard this on the radio."

"Yes," Bud said, "and did you hear Johnson himself on the radio? He condemned the attack on that house in no uncertain language."

"Oh," Laura cried, "it was horrible! Those poor, terrified people! And this paper of yours is responsible for that kind of thing. You know it is, Tom. You know it."

"I don't know it at all, Mother. We never encourage anything like that. I personally don't, either, but I can understand how it happens."

"Some people say that about the Holocaust in Germany."

Tom gave an audible sigh. "You sound like a Jew. I'm sorry, but I have to tell you."

"Don't be sorry. If I sound like a Jew, I also sound like a lot of people at our church, including Dr. Foster."

He knows things, Laura thought. Maybe—even probably—he didn't know what was going to occur last night, but still he knows about undercurrents. Observe him, he is not comfortable. He fidgets with the empty glass and looks away. My voice has grown strident, an unfamiliar voice for him. He is aware that something serious now lies between us, too, and he is sad because he loves me. It is, in a way, like families split between North and South during my great-grandfather's time, or like collaborationists and the Resistance in France. Where will it end?

She got up and gently grasped his shoulders. "Is there anything you can tell me, Tom? What did you know? I want an answer. Please give me one."

"I went there, and I left. Believe me, that's all." Then he stood up, too. "I don't want to argue with you, Mom. We're not getting anywhere, so let me go."

"Good idea," said Bud, giving Laura a black look. "Come on, guys, let's get some exercise. Tennis? We'll play triples, Timmy and I against Tom."

Yes, Bud, you big, stupid, healthy lump of meat, she thought watching the two tall ones walk off, trailed by Timmy and the dog. She was hurt, baffled, and pained. He wouldn't understand. He wasn't capable of understanding. She would certainly have to tell him soon about Betty Lee, but not just now; it would only lead to another discussion that got nowhere.

They had dinner. The three talked about tennis, the stars and the tournaments, while Laura said nothing.

Later, she went to the piano for something to do; music was solace. Debussy was a spring wind moving through trees, the trickle of a brook. As she played, the strain began to lift from her shoulders.

Then Bud came in. "Will you leave that thing alone, Laura! It sounds like funeral music, and it's getting on my nerves."

"I didn't know you had any nerves," she said. "You never had any feel for music, did you? You're only pretending, when you ask me to play for guests. You're showing off. No other man around here has a wife who can play as I do. Isn't that right?"

He sat down beside her on the piano bench. "Come on, let's cut it out. Let's reach an understanding, as you always say."

His pleading tone softened her a little. Yes, she was soft, maybe too much so.

"I'm willing, but you don't help," she said quietly.

"Well, you don't either, Laura. You make too much fuss about things. That newspaper, for instance. You've got to compromise, see the other side of it. He's not married to those ideas—many of which I happen to agree with."

"That I know."

"Some of which I don't agree with. But I'm not going to hassle him over his politics. I stay neutral. Meanwhile, he's getting good experience. He's an excellent debater, you heard him in high school, and I'm sure he's improved at college. This experience in an organization is preparation for life. Meeting people, working with people. You can't tell what the future holds. He may turn this experience around one hundred eighty degrees and use it even in our business, who knows?"

"Meeting people?" she repeated. "The people who write the stuff that's in that paper? You disgust me, Bud, when you talk this way." With a weary shake of the head, she closed her eyes. "I'm tired. I'm going to bed."

"Do that. Let yourself unwind." He spoke kindly, cheerfully. "Poor little Laura! Worry, worry, worry. You can't take the world's troubles on your shoulders, you know. Those blacks will take care of themselves, and Tom will take care of himself, too."

Alone in the bed while Bud watched television downstairs, she lay awake. The boys were in their rooms, Timmy no doubt with Earl asleep on his feet, and Tom most likely trying to smother his anger. What future was there really for either of her sons? Our children hurt us so. . . . For Tim, the end was too clear. And Tom's future is up in the air. There is so much of Bud in him, she thought. The ambition and the stubbornness are both his. What if she had married some other man with different genes? He would still be her son, but he would not be Tom. What if, for instance, she had married Francis Alcott? Foolish, aberrant thought.

From the trees near the window a bird, awakened from sleep, gave a startled cry and subsided. This cry, followed by its silence, now suddenly brought to her awareness the insect chorus in the yard, a level sound as incessant and unremarkable as silence. Yet for an instant now she became aware of it as though she had never heard it before. And perhaps because Francis's name had slipped out of some locked box inside her head, something more slipped out: sounds of the summer night when she had played *Eine Kleine Nachtmusik* for him. The crickets had been loud that night. Another aberrant, foolish thought.

PART
———— IV ————

The Crawfields

CHAPTER

8

The mail always came in the late afternoon. Shoved through the slot in the door, it landed on the floor of the hall, a tumble of bills, postcards from the traveling aunts, appeals from charities, and slippery catalogs presenting kitchenware, hand-knitted sweaters, birdhouses, and everything that has ever been manufactured by man.

Among all these this day there lay a long white envelope. It looks stern, thought Laura, with its professional lettering: LONGFELLOW, BRYCE & MACKENZIE, COUNSELORS AT LAW. She didn't like the bold look of it, which was silly of her. And thrusting everything else aside, she sat down to read it.

Dear Mr. and Mrs. Rice:

A matter of urgent importance to you has recently come to my attention. My purpose in writing is to request that you respond by letter or telephone as soon as possible, so that we may set up an appointment at any time or place that is convenient for you.

Thanking you, I am very truly yours,

Ralph R. Mackenzie

A matter of great importance.

Really, really, it was ridiculous to be feeling this quiver of the nerves, this tiny lurch of the heart. People in business received letters like this one all the time. The man probably had something to sell. But—Mackenzie? Ralph Mackenzie, who was running against Jim Johnson, was not a salesman. What could he want?

There was no sense waiting to find out, so she went to the telephone and asked to speak to Mr. Mackenzie. "I just received your letter," she said, "and it seems so mysterious that I'm answering right away. What is this about?"

"It's a very personal matter, Mrs. Rice. It's not anything we should discuss over the telephone. I'm sorry."

Tom, she thought. The awful business that night. Oh God, could Tom have really had anything to do with it? Yes, maybe he could.

"I'd like to make an appointment with you and Mr. Rice. You tell me when."

The voice was a gentleman's, but that meant nothing; he could still be some sort of con man. "You are the Mackenzie who's a candidate for the senate, aren't you?" she asked anxiously.

"I am. I am the only Ralph Mackenzie in the book. If you want to make sure I am who I say I am, this office has several telephone numbers, all listed. You may try any one of them to check me out."

"Tell me, this worries me. Are we being sued for something? If this has anything to do with business, you should get in touch with my husband at his office."

"Don't be frightened. You're not being sued."

This gentle assurance made Laura feel foolish, and she said hastily, "I don't know why I said that. We don't owe anyone, we haven't done anything wrong."

"I'm so sorry to be worrying you, and I don't like being mysterious. Tell me what day will do. Tomorrow, perhaps?"

He was certainly in a hurry. And this sense of hurry conveyed itself to her, so she said promptly, "Tomorrow afternoon. It's Saturday, and my husband will be home." And remembering that it was this man and not she who had asked for the appointment, she said with dignity, "Three o'clock will be convenient for us."

"Thank you, Mrs. Rice."

"Oh, for God's sake," Bud protested. "The guy's a politician. He's collecting for his campaign. Going around begging. 'A personal matter.' Yeah. Personal for the bastard, and you fell for it." He laughed. "Well, I'll make short work of him. He's come to the wrong place. Any pennies I have go to Johnson."

"I don't know." And again there was that prickle of fear. "He said it was urgent. He was very nice."

"Aha! I've got it. Some third cousin, yours or mine, has died without wife or child and has left a fortune. And they've tracked us down as the nearest relatives. That's it, Laura. Wow! We'll go around the world. I'll buy you a diamond necklace that you can wear to the supermarket. How about that?"

"He's coming tomorrow," she said, not laughing.

Now Bud frowned. "You shouldn't have allowed it. Let him come to my office with whatever it is. I don't do business at home, and he ought to know better, a high-class attorney like him. Longfellow, Bryce and Mackenzie."

"I told you he said it was personal."

Ralph R. Mackenzie arrived on time at three o'clock. He was tall and thin and looked like a lawyer in his immaculate seersucker suit with his attaché case in hand.

"I'm sorry to intrude on your home," he said pleasantly. "But I think you will see it is the best way."

"Quite all right," replied Bud in the courteous manner that he could display so attractively. "We'll sit in the library. It's the coolest room in the house."

Mackenzie set the attaché case on the floor beside his chair, opened it, took two or three typewritten sheets out, and was about to speak when Bud spoke first.

"I might as well tell you, in case this has anything to do

with the campaign, that I'm a Johnson man. I always believe in speaking frankly from the start."

"I understand. But this has nothing to do with the campaign. I'm here as a lawyer, not a candidate."

Laura was frightened. The fright came over her like a cold draft. The events of the last few days had made her vulnerable to outside forces. There was menace in the world; she had never been so sharply aware of it. Her gaze was fixed on the man as she waited.

"This is, as I told you, Mrs. Rice, a personal matter, a very painful one. So I shall get directly to the point with no long preamble. I represent a family whose son was born in the Barnes Private Maternity Clinic, now no longer in existence. He was born on July 8, 1974. And you have a son, Thomas, I believe, born there on July 9. Am I correct?"

"Thomas Paine Rice," Bud said. His voice rose. "What is this about?"

Mackenzie, putting the papers back into the attaché case, had a moment's problem with the lock. This delay was maddening. Yet Laura saw at once that it was purposeful, because the man was tense. When he had adjusted the lock, he looked from Bud to Laura and back to Bud.

"Mr. and Mrs. Rice, this is the hardest thing I've ever had to do in the fourteen years since I passed the bar. There is reason to believe that a mistake was made at the hospital, and that the two families were given each other's babies."

Laura gasped, and Bud jumped up from the sofa where he had been sitting next to her.

"What? Are you crazy?" he cried. "Crazy, to come here with a cock-and-bull story like this?"

"I wish it were, Mr. Rice. But I can tell you—I represent a family—we've been exploring this situation for months now, and unfortunately—"

"I don't want to hear it!" Bud shouted.

Laura touched his arm. "Bud, please, please don't. We have to hear it." Thank God the boys were out of the house. Her heart hammered so—

"Look at my wife! She's going to faint."

Mackenzie shook his head. "I don't know what to do. I have to tell you this, but I don't want you to be ill, Mrs. Rice. What shall I do?" And he gave Laura a look of purest compassion.

"Of course you have to go on," she whispered.

"These other people, when they were told, came to me. They were as shocked and disbelieving as you are—"

"It's a trick," Bud interrupted. "These things don't happen. It's a fabrication, and I am damn well going to get at the bottom of it." His throat muscles bulged at the V of his open collar, and his cheeks were flushed. "Coming here like this to scare the life—" And then remembering himself, he said more quietly, "I don't say I blame you, Mr. Mackenzie. You're an attorney, and when people come as clients with some wild, tricky story, I understand you have to listen. But I don't have to."

"The story is wild enough," Mackenzie said quietly, "but it isn't tricky. That I can vouch for. I have known these people, they're my friends as well as my clients, and they are honorable people. Also, it goes without saying that I have made my own extensive private investigations. We searched the records that were transferred to Wilson General when Barnes was closed, we interviewed the only nurse from that section who is still employed there, and naturally she knows nothing. The sole fact we can establish clearly is that there was just one other male infant in the nursery at that time, and he belongs to Homer and Laura Rice. That's it."

Bud was breathing heavily, leaning forward with his tense hands on his knees. Still quietly, with a visible effort at control, he said, "No more, please. That's enough, Mr. Mackenzie."

Laura said, very low, "It's not enough, Bud. We have to listen. We have no choice." And she grasped the arm of the sofa as if to brace herself.

"About five months ago," Mackenzie began, "these people's son Peter, who had been a sick child from birth, had a crisis.

They had gone everywhere over the years from one great medical center to another—Baltimore, New York, Atlanta— all over. At the last place where he was hospitalized, it happened that some genetic study was being made, and for its purposes, extensive blood tests on the parents were made— DNA and so forth. It was then that they learned that Peter could not possibly belong to them."

"And laboratories don't make mistakes?" Now Bud's control vanished. "Some jerk in a laboratory decides that their child isn't theirs? Those people are big jerks themselves. And so they go creeping around to find out who *is* their son, and they decide that my boy is their son. Not on your life! What kind of a fool do you take me for?"

"I know this can sound something like a detective mystery, but—" Mackenzie started to say when Bud again interrupted.

"Half a mystery. My Tom is mine, and there's nothing mysterious about that. Period."

There were a few moments of silence. Laura wiped her forehead and her hands, twisted the handkerchief, and waited.

Then Mackenzie said very gently, "I have records here in my case. Will you take a look at them?"

"No. I won't dignify the subject by reading such stuff," Bud cried.

Inquiring of Laura, Mackenzie now took another path. "Wouldn't it ease your minds if you were to find out more about this?"

"Our minds are quite easy," Bud said. "Quite."

"Mine wouldn't be if I were you. There were only five newborns in that hospital during the days when your son and this other boy were there. Three out of the five were girls."

"Listen to me," Bud commanded. "There were other male infants in that hospital. Some baby from the sick ward could have been brought somehow to the nursery. It's not even common sense to pinpoint the other boy in the nursery, who happens to be ours."

"Your possibility is farfetched, Mr. Rice, but still I admit it's a possibility." Mackenzie paused. "So that's why we have to look into everything, look at everything. My clients say that the switch couldn't have taken place anywhere but at the hospital, since once they took their baby home, he was never out of their sight."

"That's another crooked story," Bud said.

"If so, it's a simple thing to set it straight. All you need do is have some blood tests made, both of you and of your son."

Bud exploded. "Blood tests! I'll be damned if we will. It's unconstitutional, an invasion of our privacy."

"No," Mackenzie said. "I could get a court order, Mr. Rice, but I'd rather not have to do that."

Nausea was rising to Laura's throat. If Bud would only tell the man to go! If she might only lie down and pull her thoughts together!

"Why the hell don't they sue the hospital?" demanded Bud. "And let other people alone."

"The hospital doesn't exist, as I told you. Anyway, they're not interested in damages. They only want to know what became of their child."

Laura was struck unbearably by full horror. Tears that must have been gathering and been bravely contained now gushed in force. She put her hands over her burning face and let them pour between her fingers.

"Look," Bud said roughly, "look what's happening to my wife. A family torn apart on a nice summer Saturday. Just like that!" He snapped his fingers. And taking Tom's photograph from the library table, he held it up. "This is our son. He's not going to know one thing about this rot, Mr. Mackenzie. Is that clear? It would destroy him, and I won't allow it."

Mackenzie said only, "He's a very handsome young man." He reopened the attaché case. "I have here a picture of Peter Crawfield."

"Keep it," Bud told him.

Mackenzie then held it up in full view. Unwillingly, Laura raised her eyes. A fair-haired youth with a delicate, narrow face looked back at her. The nose was short, the upper lip long, the chin was markedly cleft . . . The face was Timmy's.

"It's Timmy. Oh my God, it's Timmy," she moaned.

Bud stretched out his hand and took the picture. "It's not Timmy at all," he said gently. "I'll straighten this business out. Leave it to me."

Mackenzie said calmly, "I think you should get a lawyer, Mr. Rice. This isn't going to go away, you know."

"Damn right, I will. Fordyce and Fordyce are my lawyers. I'll sue those people in every court in the land if they don't let us alone. I suppose they'll want custody next, eh?" he sneered. "Jesus Christ!"

"There is no question of custody when a person is over eighteen."

Laura was thinking, Who are these people? What are they trying to do? My Tom belongs to me. Oh, dear God. I don't, won't, can't, believe this. Even if that boy looks like Timmy. A lot of boys look like Timmy.

Mackenzie was looking from one to the other. Bud was staring at the floor; his hands, hanging at his sides, were fists. In half an hour, he has grown old, Laura thought, and raising her head, met Mackenzie's sad brown gaze. He was sorry for them. He was a decent man. Somehow she trusted him.

"Who are these people?" she asked. "May we know?"

"Why, of course. They already know about you from the hospital records."

Bud jumped. "The hospital doesn't exist, you said."

"When it was sold, the records were transferred to Wilson General. The family is named Crawfield. They're the department store people. Arthur and Margaret Crawfield. They used to live here, but they sold this branch years back and kept the main store across from the state capitol. You've probably been in it."

Bud's eyebrows drew together, making a long, straight bloodred line across the bridge of his nose.

"Crawfield? You don't mean to tell me that they—they're not—"

Mackenzie gave him a long, calm look. "Not what? Jewish? Yes, they are."

"Well. Well. You not only bring an unbelievable story, that's bad enough, but you add insult to injury. Jews. It's disgraceful."

Bud was almost unable to enunciate. He fell back onto a chair. He will have a stroke, thought Laura, but I can't afford to come apart. And it seemed to her that in spite of everything, she would cope with this catastrophe. Somehow. And somehow, Tom must be shielded.

"You said, Mr. Mackenzie, that this—other boy—this Peter, was ill?"

Again she met a sorrowful brown gaze. "Yes, almost from birth. Or I should say, right from birth. He had cystic fibrosis."

Her heart was hammering again, racing, spinning in her chest. Cystic fibrosis. And that photo had—yes it had—looked like Timmy. Yet she managed to form words.

"And what became of him? I mean, how is he now?"

"He's dead, Mrs. Rice. He died three months ago."

CHAPTER

9

"I don't know how you manage," said Margaret Crawfield, "tearing back and forth across the state for the campaign and now for our affair on top of it. You must be exhausted."

"I like the activity," Mackenzie told her, smiling.

There was in Margaret a kind of peasant strength that pleased him. It was odd to apply the term "peasant" to a woman who was so fashionable, from the cut of her swinging thick black hair to the scarlet sandals on her feet, but she was sturdily constructed and had a look of endurance that was not urban. He always felt whenever he was in the Crawfields' house that he envied Arthur, and how good a thing it would be to marry. And yet he never had.

"So you were there yesterday," Arthur said a trifle impatiently. "And?"

"And as I told you over the telephone, I believe they may be the right people."

Margaret took that up quickly. "Why, Ralph? Circumstantial evidence? Because theirs was the only other male infant on the maternity floor?"

"That figures mightily, of course. But there's more. When I showed Peter's photo to Mrs. Rice, she was shocked. It was quite clear. And she told her husband that he looked like

Timmy. They have two sons, Tom and Timmy, you remember."

"Tom being the elder," Arthur said. "You saw his picture, you said. And?" he asked again.

"A rather handsome young man, I thought." Then, seeing how the two leaned forward on their chairs and how they tensed, Have I said too much? he asked himself. And he retreated quickly, "Of course, she may have imagined Peter's resemblance to her boy. Only the blood tests will tell anything certain, as you well know."

"But you said Mr. Rice objected, didn't you?"

"That doesn't matter. We can obtain an order if we must, although I rather think that won't be necessary. Mrs. Rice was quite willing."

"She sounds more reasonable," Margaret said.

"She is." And he recalled the moment when, in her struggle for control, she had put her hands over her face and then looked up at him—so hurt, like some frightened woods creature discovered in the moment before the crash of the gun.

Margaret pursued the subject. "What does she look like?"

He knew that the question stemmed from more than a woman's natural curiosity about another woman; it stemmed from Margaret's certainty that these were the people who had her child.

"Blond. Simply dressed," he said. "Refined. But please, Margaret, don't get your hopes up too high and too soon."

"What about him?" Arthur asked. "I have the impression you didn't like him."

Nothing escaped Arthur. He had the pale, indoor skin, and the sedentary body of the legendary scholar; his expression was acute. You had to be careful of your words, of every nuance and tone.

Have I already said too much? Ralph asked himself again. There would be no sense in telling the truth about Rice, that he was hot tempered, stubborn, anti-Semitic, and had made me angry. Suppose the Rices were, after all, not the ones who had the Crawfields' boy?

Yet Ralph was almost certain that they were.

"I neither liked nor disliked him," he replied. "It was too short an interview to learn much about anybody."

"Everything moves so slowly," Margaret complained. "All these months since Peter died, the investigation and the conferences, everything moving like an iceberg, inch by inch."

She made a sweeping gesture, upsetting the glass of ginger ale, which splintered on the porch floor. Exasperated with herself, she apologized. "Sorry. I'm not a very patient person."

Arthur contradicted her. "On the contrary, you are extremely patient. This situation is enough to make a saint frantic." And he stooped to pick up the fragments with a paper napkin.

Arthur talked like a professor. There was no affectation in this; it was merely his way of expressing himself. Yes, he should have been a professor, Ralph thought with fondness. And a curious, amusing contrast came to mind: Arthur Crawfield and Rice. Was it "Bud" she had called him? Then came another contrast: Bud and his wife. "Laura"—the sound of it was serene.

Arthur made a neat little bag out of the napkin and set it on the glass-topped end table with a caution. "Be careful. I'll get rid of it in a minute. What I have to ask you, Ralph, is, what comes next?"

"Next. I plan to call Mrs. Rice tomorrow and try to make an appointment at the hospital for blood tests. That failing, I'll need to—" He stopped, for the daughter of the house was just then coming across the twilit lawn.

"You may talk," Margaret said. "We haven't kept anything from Holly. Good heavens, she's going away to college in September. She's not a child."

"Who's not a child?" asked Holly. "Oh, you're here, Ralph. I've been out canvassing for you." And she dropped a kiss on his forehead.

"It's you who's not the child," he replied, "although it's hard for me to believe that only yesterday when I first met you, you were wheeling a sumptuous doll carriage down the street."

"I remember. It was one of Grandma's presents. They're always sumptuous."

"Ralph saw the parents of that other baby boy," Margaret said. "That's what we're talking about."

"I hope that other baby boy isn't the one we're looking for," Holly said with surprising vehemence. "There's a guy named Rice who goes to state U, and Allison's brother knows him. He's some sort of Nazi, a real horror."

A sudden stillness came upon the listeners. Ralph's gaze moved outward over the grass toward the low brown-stained wing of this peaceful house with its Japanese air; he saw disaster falling on it from the sky.

"Jews . . . Disgraceful . . . Insult and injury . . ." By such a parent, a seed like that might well have been sown.

"He writes for a rag of a paper," Holly said. "Far-right bigots."

When Ralph turned to her, he knew what recollection had suddenly flashed in his head: the eyes of the young man in the photograph that Rice had thrust at him. Heavy-lidded, wide-open, and unusually large, they had dominated the face. And now these same eyes glowed in Holly's face. Better-looking than either of her parents, neither dark as Margaret was nor sandy-haired like Arthur, she was distinctive. It was the eyes that made her so. He remembered such eyes.

Deeply troubled, he said to Holly, "Rice is a common enough name. I wouldn't jump to conclusions."

It seemed to him that he was hearing a long, communal sigh. The pressure on these people must be unbearable. And he looked at his watch, saying, "I'd best be going. I have a speech to prepare, half a night's worth of work. But I'll take care of your matter again in the morning."

"We're here. We'll wait," Arthur said soberly.

They watched Ralph's car go down the street and turn out of sight before going back into the house. During these last months all Margaret's hopes had rested in him, as if he were a conjurer who could pull truth out of the vacant air, or an electronic brain who would compute the truth, or a healer who by a touch would heal the wound.

She spoke briskly. "I do believe Ralph's on the right track, and he knows he is. He just doesn't want to stress it yet until he's certain. Yes, I do believe."

"What if he is, Mom? And what if it's the Rice that Allison's brother told about? What'll we do then?" asked Holly.

Arthur nodded gently, "Come, come. 'What if' never solved anything. We'll wait and see. Meanwhile, we'll get a good night's sleep."

CHAPTER

—— 10 ——

Joseph Fordyce of Fordyce and Fordyce was starting to lose patience with the case. He had been working on it, such as it was, because actually it was not at all complex, for more than two weeks. He had gone over hospital records, ordered new tests, examined two separate sets of reports, engaged one of the best-known pathologists in the area to check the reports, then engaged another pathologist to check on the first one; he had through main effort convinced Rice to submit to blood tests, and on some pretext to get his son to do the same. He had done all there was to do, and now that the matter was solved, he was tired of his client. He had less wearying matters to attend to than coping with Bud Rice's wild, shifting moods: courteous, heartbroken, cantankerous and overwrought, he was intolerable.

To be sure, this was a dreadful situation. How would he feel if suddenly he had been told that his twin daughters were not his? But somehow he felt more sorry for Laura Rice. He had always seen her when they met at dinner parties as a charmer, a thorough lady, yet never stiff or pompous. And so lovely, with that springtime air! Fordyce was not usually given to such poetic expression.

Now they were in an office somewhere at the bottom of a hospital, and Rice was badgering the nurse, the sole remnant of the staff that had been in the nursery when his boy was born.

"Okay," Bud said. "There were two other nurses there with you. Okay, so you don't know a thing about what might have happened, or whether anything did happen. I believe you. But what about those other two?"

The nurse was containing her anger. Her face was flushed. "Mr. Rice, I've told you, Maizie Neill died in a car accident, and Dot Grimm got married, moved to Hawaii, was divorced and remarried. I never heard from her after that. I don't even know what her name is. Listen, I've been over all this six times, and I don't know any more than what I've told you all, and I'm tired of it. I said to them and I'm saying to you, what reason would I or anybody else have had for mixing up your babies? I'm sick of the whole thing."

"Please, Bud," Laura said weakly. "I want to get home."

"Come on, Bud," said Fordyce. For God's sake, couldn't the man see that she was about to fall over? "I'll drive you home."

They went outside to Fordyce's car. Laura sat alone in the back. Through the rearview mirror he could see her; her eyes were closed, and she was breathing hard. She was sick, poor woman, and why not? Bud was, too, sick not with sorrow and shock alone, but with rage.

A Jewish kid in Bud Rice's family! It was almost comical.

"So you're saying there's not a doubt," Bud said.

"None."

"I don't believe it. I won't believe it."

For the tenth time, Fordyce tried patience. "Bud, you've had two reports explained to you by experts. The boy's blood matches the Crawfields'."

For a moment Bud was silent. Then he burst out, "It's their kind of rotten trickery! They did it, those people, that kind. They paid somebody to make the switch so they could get a better baby."

Fordyce lost patience. "If that's so, why would they have

taken the sick one and let you have the healthy one? Talk sense, at least. Talk logically."

Bud turned bright red. "Well, sorry, you're right. I'm not thinking straight." He slapped his fist into his palm. "Anyway, I don't believe it. Tom's the image of Laura's father. You know Tom, you've seen him often enough."

"I also know Timmy," Fordyce said dryly. "Doesn't that tell you anything?"

Bud gave a sob. Fordyce looked over and looked away. A bad, bad business. The man was gray; suit, eyes and face were the color of cracked earth in a long drought.

They rode on uptown, and no one spoke until at last Bud whispered, "Can we keep it out of the newspapers at least?"

"I'll try. I'll talk to them over at the *Sentinel*. But you know there will be gossip at the hospital, and it will spread. This is a rare case, a human-interest story, and if the Associated Press gets wind of it, there'll be no help. But I will try, Bud," said Fordyce, thinking of Laura and of the boy whose very identity was to be turned inside out.

The car turned up the hill and stopped. There, under dusty summer leafage, the fine old house stood in its simplicity and grace.

"Oh," cried Laura, "how ever are we going to tell Tom?"

In the hall Earl looked up from his doze on the cool floor and went back to sleep. Tom had left a note on the table.

Timmy and I gone biking. Back around five.

The sight of his familiar script, which seemed to lope across the paper in imitation of his very walk, was too much for Laura. Gone was her indignation, gone was her worry over his beliefs or his future place in the world, gone was everything but horror. This was the end, the abyss that had no bottom.

At the window she stood with her forehead pressed against the glass, her eyes too blurred to see anything outside but a green glare; her shoulders were shaking.

In back of her Bud paced. His heavy tread swayed the

prisms on the lamps so that they tinkled as he passed. He muttered and groaned.

"Look. Look at him."

She knew he was holding Tom's picture, but she did not turn.

"Intelligent, strong. His face shines. A perfect specimen of an American boy. And they tell me he's not ours. Christ, I won't believe it. I can't believe it. I want—we deserve one at least who isn't sick, God damn it, we do."

At that Laura did turn to stare with a look whose fierceness was so unmistakable that Bud cried out, "No, no, it's not that I don't love Timmy. You know better. But—but this one is my right arm, this one—" And he wept over the picture.

Pity for him mingled with revulsion over the words "one at least who isn't sick." But if that other one, Peter Crawfield, had stayed with them, then would there not have been two sick ones in this house? And what then would Bud have done?

So they stood, frozen in fearful expectation, like people waiting for the surgeon to come out of the operating room with news. I have to pull myself together, she thought. For three days now they had been in possession of incontrovertible facts, and for three days, tossing at night, wringing her hands and stifling tears in secret, she had been repeating to herself: I have to pull myself together. I need to talk to somebody. What if I lose my mind? It was so obvious that they both needed counsel and some support to endure this catastrophe, but Bud would have none of it.

"What will you do to Tom? Do you want to spread this crazy news through the city?" he had demanded.

"But it's bound to come out. The Crawfields will want—"

"Damn those bastards! I won't hear of them! The whole thing's a hoax, and I intend to get to the bottom of it. I don't want anyone snooping into this affair, no doctors, no ministers, nobody until I've settled it my way. My way, Laura."

There was no reasoning with him.

The screen door banged, and Tom appeared with baseball cap and mitt in hand.

"Hi. I left Timmy at the ice-cream store with his buddies. He'll be home in time for dinner. Hey, is anything the matter? You two look awful."

I can't say it, Laura thought. No, this is impossible. As well amputate a leg without anesthesia. No. No.

Tom's wide-open eyes opened wider in alarm. "What is it? Tell me."

Bud intervened before Laura could speak. "It's nothing, a little problem. Problems in business. They happen. You know how your mother —"

"No, Bud. This isn't right. Tom's bound to be told, and he must hear it from us."

"You have cancer," Tom said. "That's it, isn't it? Or something else, and you're afraid to tell me."

She summoned all her strength. She was pushing a rock uphill, she was gritting her teeth against some hideous pain. And she put her arm around Tom's shoulder.

"Come into the library. We'll sit on the sofa together, and I'll tell you."

Bud threw up his hands. "Let it be on your head, then. I can't go through with it. Oh Jesus!" he cried, and fled from the room.

She took Tom's hand in both of hers. "Listen to me," she began. Through some miracle her voice stayed steady. "I have to tell you — no, it's not that anyone is going to die, nothing like that. But it will shock you! Do you remember ever reading about any newborn babies being mixed up in the hospital and going to the wrong families?"

"Well, vaguely, I guess. It's hard to believe it can happen, though."

"Yes, but it can."

He looked straight into Laura's eyes, began to say something, paused, and then with difficulty, murmured, "You're telling me something. It's happened in our family."

"Yes," she whispered.

"It's Timmy. He isn't ours."

Her eyes had never left his. Such wonderful eyes, he had, so rarely beautiful, glimmering and deep as a lake at night.

"No," she said, "not Timmy."

The silence was long, long enough for a delivery truck to wheeze up the hill past the house, to shift gears and go beyond hearing.

"Me?" he asked, with that dark gaze still fixed on hers.

"Yes," she said, and bursting into tears, pulled his head down on her shoulder, kissed it over and over. "My boy. Oh, my little boy."

He said nothing, and she realized that he could not speak. When she felt a spot of dampness on her shoulder, she knew she was feeling his tears. And she raised his head, holding his face with its closed eyes and seeping tears between her cold, shaking hands.

"Hear me. Hear me, Tom. You're ours. You're my boy whom I nursed and loved from the first minute and still love and always will. Nothing else matters. Nothing."

He drew back to stare at her. "It's too crazy. It's not really true, is it? You're not really sure, are you? It's some weird mistake, isn't it?"

She wet her dry, parched lips and replied, "It's not a mistake."

"What does Dad say?"

The truth. Tell the whole truth. "It has crushed him. He won't believe it."

Tom suddenly went wild. "How did it happen?" he shouted. "Who are these—other people? Whoever they are, I don't want to know them. I won't have anything to do with them. I won't. Who are they?"

"Their name is Crawfield. When the nurses mixed up the babies, they got the one who belonged to us."

" 'The nurses mixed up.' I'd like to kill them, whoever they are. I'll track them down and kill them. A slight mistake—oh, just a small mistake, nothing to get excited about!" He stood confronting Laura. "My life, Mom! What's happened to my life! They've spoiled my life!"

"Darling, no. We aren't going to let it spoil your life. We're all in this together, and somehow we'll come to terms with the thing. We will."

"You said Dad doesn't believe it."

"It's that he doesn't want to, even though the proofs are all there. The blood tests."

"So that's why we all had our annual checkup so early."

"Yes."

"What did it show?"

Laura took a long breath. "That you were born to the Crawfields."

Tom groaned. Sweat shone on his forehead. After a long minute, he asked weakly, "And the other boy, the one who was born to you?"

"He died a few months ago. He had cystic fibrosis."

"My God."

Two of them, she thought, and suddenly saw again the face in the photograph that Ralph Mackenzie had shown to her, the wistful face of Timmy's brother. Those Crawfields—had they done the best for him, for her poor child? And yet, here stood Tom, more hers, really, than that other who was unknown. She was torn, riven in half.

"You must never let Timmy know what he died of, Tom. We must think of something else. A ruptured appendix, that's it. That's what he died of."

"Who are these Crawfields, anyway?"

"I only know what the lawyers told us. Mr. Fordyce has talked to theirs, who of all people happens to be Ralph Mackenzie, and he says they are very respectable people. They own that department store across from the capitol where we bought your raincoat last year after you lost yours." She hesitated. "I understand they have another child, a girl about seventeen." Hesitating again, she then plunged forward. "They are Jewish, Tom."

He was electrified. It seemed to Laura that his nerves had

jumped, first with astonishment, and next with outrage. Then he did a strange thing: He ran to the mirror that hung above the mantel to switch on a light and stare at himself.

"Me," he whispered. "Me. It isn't possible." He whirled upon Laura. "Look at me. Look. Do I look like one of them? Do I?"

She said gently, "They come in all sizes and shapes, the same as Protestants or Catholics. And none of them wears horns."

"Don't try to appease me. There's nothing you can say. I hate myself. I ought to put a noose around my neck and hang myself in the backyard. I despise myself," he shouted. "Why the hell don't I drop dead right now?"

"Don't say that. Oh darling, please, we want you alive."

But he had already raced out of the room. She heard him clattering up the stairs.

A moment later Bud came in holding a glass. "Brandy," he said. "I needed it. You've told him."

"Yes. Somebody had to do it."

He apologized. "I know I should have been here, too. But Laura, it's as if somebody had used a hammer on my brain."

He had gone white, a sickly green-white. It came to her that he might faint, or even have a heart attack.

"You know, I'm pretty tough. I can take a lot on my shoulders, but this is the worst. I'm ashamed to be falling apart while you're holding together."

"Holding together." When there was such a drumming in her head . . . And she had a wild thought: Am I possibly imagining things?

"Crawfield! God, what bitter medicine. Our Tom. A Jewish department store. God!"

In the yard Earl was barking a shrill welcome, which meant that Timmy had come back.

"Let's go upstairs and close our door," Bud said. "I don't want him to see me this way."

The late afternoon sun streamed into the bedroom. From the windows they watched Timmy put the bicycle in the shed, hug Earl, and walk toward the back door. He looked so small. He looked so vulnerable. And now he would have to know that his beloved brother, his hero, his model (I look just like Tom, don't I?) was not his brother.

They were both waiting, deliberating whether it was better to go in to Tom's room or to let him alone, when the bedroom door, which no one ever entered without knocking, burst open and Tim shouted, "Dad! Mom! I went to Tom's room, and he told me. He's crying so—"

Tom sobbed and punched the pillow. "Oh Mom, oh Dad, I want to die." His face contorted when Laura went to him. "But you're not my dad, not my mother."

She sat down on the bed and cradled his head. "We brought you to this house when you were three days old and cared for you. We love you. Just suppose you had been adopted. There's nothing awful about that, is there?"

"That's different. That's entirely different. These people didn't give me up for adoption. Now they'll want to see me. And I can't, I won't—"

Bud, forlorn at the foot of the bed, and Timmy, teary and openmouthed, stood silently. And Laura, still stroking Tom's head, asked, "Would you like to see Dr. Foster? Perhaps a talk with him will help you."

"No," Tom said bitterly, "with all respect to our minister, I don't need him. I can tell you right now what he'll say: 'God tests you. He never gives you any trouble too heavy for you to bear. You'll come out of this ordeal stronger and better than ever—' Bah! No, I don't want him. I don't want anybody."

Nevertheless, when they left Tom's room, they telephoned Dr. Downs, who never made house calls but probably would make an exception for this extraordinary situation, and could certainly be trusted to let no word about it slip.

Alone with Tom, he spent an hour and a half upstairs, while downstairs Laura tried to fix a little supper, which neither one wanted, for Bud and Timmy.

"I've given him a very mild sedative, enough to take the edge off his grief," the doctor reported. "He'll be all right, I'm confident. He's young and resilient. And then he added, "Poor boy. He has some image of how a 'real man' mustn't let his emotions show. He's embarrassed because he broke down. I tried to set him straight about that. I told him, when I was in Vietnam I saw many a brave man cry."

There was no refreshment, no sweet relief in sleep that night. Laura was tossed from one dream of frustration to another. With all her power, she ran from a pursuer and was yet unable to advance a step. She arrived at an airport without her ticket, raced home to ransack the house and could not find it. Late! Too late, she cried, and woke up to the awareness of Bud in a brandied sleep beside her and of Tom in his room alone. She had to make sure nothing had happened to Tom.

At his bedside she stood looking down at where he lay in a dim beam of light that came from the hall. It was queer to think that she had been angry at him only two days before. Her love for him was a knot in her chest, an ache that flowed through her flesh.

"Mom? I'm not asleep," he whispered. "Mom? Will they want me to leave this house?" He spoke quietly, and she was grateful that the sedative had taken hold. "I'm not going to leave you and Dad and Timmy. They can't make me."

She reassured him. "There's no question of that. You're over eighteen. You can do what you want."

"Will I ever have to meet those people, though? I can't do it."

She considered the matter practically. Naturally, they would want to see Tom. Even if he refused, they would contrive to see him. In their position, who wouldn't?

"You do owe them something," she said. "You know how you feel, but imagine their feelings, too."

"I don't care about their feelings. I have nothing in common with them, anyway."

"Because they're Jews, you mean? Just that?"

"That's enough."

"Mr. Fordyce spoke to their lawyer and both agree that you really must meet."

"I'm being tortured."

"No, I'll be with you. It won't be unbearable. Hard, but not unbearable."

"Well, in any case, I want Dad there, too."

"I don't know whether he'll do that, Tom. He's taking this harder than you are in some ways. He won't admit that all this is true, and that worries me because ultimately he'll have to admit it."

"I just don't want to meet those people," Tom repeated. "I'm sure you don't either."

She surprised herself by her own response, which needed a minute to take shape.

"Well, mostly I don't, yet in a certain sense I do. I'd like . . . I want to see what kind of home Peter had," she said, and heard the crack in her own voice.

"They named him 'Peter'?"

"Yes," she replied, thinking that it must cross Tom's mind that 'Peter' would have been *his* name if—

"Why?" Tom blurted. "It's all past, finished, what difference does it make where he lived? You never knew him."

Laura's chest was sore with pity. How could a boy of nineteen be expected to understand a person twice his age, a woman, a mother?

"Tom, Tommy—" she hadn't called him "Tommy" in years —"this has nothing to do with my loving you so much that there are no words for it."

He looked gravely back at her, nodded a little and said, "Mom, you won't mind? I'd like to be by myself now."

"Of course. We'll talk some more tomorrow."

Almost immediately, he telephoned Robbie. He thought he would start to howl if he couldn't confide, couldn't in some way impart his agony to a person who would understand it.

By her voice, he knew he had awakened her. "So late? What's up, Tom?"

"Just needed to talk to you." Then he knew this was a thing he couldn't talk about over the telephone. For this he would have to be in a quiet room behind a closed door with her arms around him. "Can I see you tomorrow?"

"Tommy darling, I tried to reach you earlier tonight to tell you, but nobody answered your phone."

True. They had all heard it ringing and had just let it ring.

"I wanted to tell you I'm going away till the first of next month."

Tom's heart sank. "Going away?"

"Yes. I'm so excited, wait till you hear! My chemistry professor reached me yesterday, he'd been trying to get me. I can hardly talk, it's so wonderful." She laughed. Her laugh always trilled up the scale. "There's a three-week summer course up in Iowa someplace that's supposed to be stupendous, some famous analytical chemist, you wouldn't know the name, I didn't, but anyway, Dr. Morgan says that there's even a little stipend for traveling expenses—" Breathless in her joy, she bubbled, "He had recommended Joe Miles for it, but last Monday Joe's father got sick and now he can't go, so Morgan called me instead. Isn't that fantastic?"

"It's wonderful. I'm proud of you." And he was proud. Beautiful and brainy she was. Analytical chemistry. He wished he was able to feel her enthusiasm right now.

"This will be great on my record. It should do a lot toward getting me some grant toward graduate school. With that and my waitress job I really do think I may make it."

"Good luck, darling. I'm glad for you. Oh, but I'll miss you."

"It's only for a few weeks. Are you okay, though? You sound dreary."

"I am dreary without you."

"Listen, get busy working for Jim. That'll take your mind off things for the time being. He's fighting hard. Did you read yesterday's speech! He really trounced Mackenzie. It was great!"

So the talk moved on, and after a while the sheer flow of it began to soothe him. When she hung up, he felt more calm. There was such strength in Robbie! She would be back soon, and her love would strengthen him.

CHAPTER

11

W̲e̲ are all nerves, a collection
of jitters, Margaret thought as, passing the hall mirror, she
caught sight of her twitching lip.

The rest of them were sitting in the living room waiting,
stiff as a congregation at a wedding or a funeral. Arthur, trying to read the morning paper, hadn't gotten through the first
page. Holly was doing a crossword puzzle at the game table.

"Do sit down and calm yourself," Arthur said, looking up.

"I'm quite calm. You'd be surprised how calm I am," Margaret replied.

"I would be surprised. You haven't stopped for breath.
Leave those flowers where they are, they'll do perfectly well,"
he said, for Margaret had shears in her hand to cut fresh
marigolds from the garden.

She laid the shears down. "It's only that I want things to
look right. The boy—Tom—" She stopped as the control that
had kept her going ever since this meeting had been arranged
began to wane.

And uncertain what to do with herself, she surveyed the
room, from the circular sofas to the splashing primal colors of
the abstract paintings, to the subdued mosaic of book bindings
on the floor-to-ceiling shelves. Everything that could be
dusted, polished, or vacuumed had been cared for.

Her thoughts went somersaulting. "Ralph says their house

is lovely, very old and full of antiques. He says the Paiges, her side, have been here since before the Revolution. It must be good to be rooted like that in a place where your people before you have always lived."

Arthur said quietly, " 'Before the Revolution' is a little over two hundred years ago. My grandparents lived in Germany in the same town since the expulsion from Spain in 1492."

"I wouldn't need to go back that far. I meant a place like those Confederate-style houses with high ceilings and double staircases."

"The Confederate past is not yours. Be happy with this brand-new house."

"Arthur, I am happy with it. I only meant—"

She closed her lips. They all were on the thin edge, ready to be pushed over. Now her gaze shifted to the dining room table, which was visible across the hall.

Arthur, following her gaze, assured her, "There's enough food for twenty, if that's what you're worried about."

"I know, but the drive is over a hundred miles, and they must have left early. They'll be hungry."

But maybe they wouldn't. After all, she knew nothing about them, about Tom or—or his mother. And again her mind went somersaulting. If I can get through this, I guess I can get through anything, she thought, bringing her mind back to rest. Think of the lunch: chicken salad, fruit, her mother's almond cookies . . .

"She sounded very nice on the telephone," she said, although she had already told the whole family ten times over about that call. "I would gladly have gone there, but I could see she preferred it this way. Her husband is very upset, she said."

"Upset!" Arthur grumbled. "Ralph finally got himself to admit the truth. Rice is in a fury because we're Jews."

"I know. So he's not coming. It'll be just she and the boy."

Margaret looked at her husband. Pain struggled on his face; she supposed it must be struggling on her own, too.

Holly, hearing the name, looked up from the puzzle. "And

he's supposed to be my brother," she said. "A redneck bigot. My brother." She was hot with outrage. "Can you believe it?"

"Holly, don't," Margaret warned.

"I can't help it. I'm sorry. But the things I've heard about that group at state U are so horrendously awful, that—"

"That'll do," Arthur commanded. "It's cruel to upset us any more than we already are. And don't say 'supposed to be.' He is your brother, and as such we must accept him and love him." His voice broke.

"All right, Dad. But all I can say is, this whole thing's insane. It makes me feel disloyal to Peter. My brother was Peter, not this Tom person."

"Holly, don't," Margaret said again.

Silence followed. The mantel clock, an antique with a man-in-the-moon on its face, gave a rattle and banged out the hour. Noon. They would be here any minute. And Margaret's eyes roved, moving from Holly's flute to Arthur's history books, to the photograph of Peter, and last to the photograph of Tom that Laura Rice had so thoughtfully sent last week. It was still in its cardboard folder, not yet framed. Whenever she looked at it, her legs went weak and she had to sit down.

I must remember, she thought, that Laura Rice feels everything that I am feeling, all my loss and sorrow, all my fear and anger. Yet more: She has had two sick children, and one of them, the one she never knew, is dead. Now she will never know him, while I at least have a chance to know mine, I hope. She will ask about Peter, and I suppose I shall have to tell her all of it, the rectal prolapse when he was two, the pneumonia, all the crises, and the death. How am I going to do it?

Holly, who had gotten up to stand at the window with the curtain pushed aside, reported, "There's a car coming slowly down the street as if they're looking for the number."

"Do get away from the window," Margaret admonished. "It's rude to peer out like that."

When the curtain fell, Holly peeked through the parting. "Yes, there they are. She's driving. It's a Mercedes. The husband didn't come. They're getting out of the car. They're coming up the steps. She's pretty, tall and blond. He—"

The doorbell rang.

They had left home shortly after nine o'clock, crawled through morning traffic, reached the highway, and were now headed eastward into the glare. Without explanation, Laura had taken the wheel; ordinarily, she gave Tom the macho pleasure of steering this fine car, but today she was too tense to be a passenger. She needed to concentrate on something, something other than their destination.

The red sun presaged a long heat wave. She had never thought in just this way of how one's view of the natural world depends upon mood. On a day of happiness, this red sun would be like a circus balloon hanging in the sky, but today it was a burning coal, ominous and sullen.

Her heart went out to Tom, who had been silent all the way, staring at the depressing interstate and the approaching city as strip malls, ten-screen movie theaters, and factory outlets with their fashionable shoddy wares flashed by.

Soon came the outskirts of the city, heralded by new, multi-storied office buildings, oblong glass boxes stood on end. They passed through the city, made a wrong turn and retraced the way, coming at last to a suburban quarter, it, too, so new that the trees were still saplings.

"We're almost there," Laura said. Her mouth was parched and her hands were clammy cold.

"We're going to regret this, Mom. It's a big mistake."

"If it is, there's nothing else we can do because we have no choice. You do understand that, Tom."

"Dad made his choice."

"Ah Tom," she answered sadly, "poor Dad is only fooling himself. You can't escape reality." She slowed the car. "Here it is, number seventeen. Here's our reality."

It was all blurred, a fog through which he walked half blinded and half deafened; yet penetrating sights and sounds emerged, only to fade again into the blur. Tom had read Dreiser's *American Tragedy* and had been stunned by the death house scenes in which a man doomed to the electric chair is yet aware of incidentals.

There was a room, large and bright, filled with a vague feel of trees and space beyond. All the walls held books. People stood in a semicircle, facing him. In the first moment he had a sense of crowding, of many people all staring at him, but when his eyes came quickly into focus, he was able to distinguish among them and saw that they were actually only three, a man and two women; and one of these was a young, pretty girl with big, astonished eyes and white frills around her neck, who looked dressed up, as if she were going to a party. Maybe she thinks this is a party, he thought angrily. I don't. The other woman ran to hug his mother; they rushed together, crying, as if they were old friends who had met again after many years. His mother had left him to face the others, alone and awkward with his arms dangling like some poor ape's in the zoo. It was humiliating.

And then the women, with little cries and exclamations, broke apart, fumbling for handkerchiefs. His mother turned toward him as if beseeching.

"This is Tom," she said.

The other woman was young, too. Her hair was thick and dark, her skin white as paper. She looked as if she were going to faint. Presumably she was his mother . . .

Bullshit! Dad said, *She's nothing of the sort.* But of course she was. He recognized himself in her. He felt sick. God, he hoped she wouldn't kiss him and cry over him. His heart thumped and there was a thumping in his ears. Nobody would believe this, he thought, it's so crazy. And wildly he looked behind him toward the front door, which had to be somewhere down that hall, but they had also made a turn into a little corridor — where? Where?

"Tom," the woman said. Her voice was low and trembling. "Tom, don't be afraid."

She did not touch him, did not even take a step toward him,

but retreated slightly as though she expected or feared his approach to her. She merely looked and looked, with such a strange expression that he winced and turned his head to scan the room again.

Everywhere were eyes, unnaturally enlarged, glistening and wet in every face. To each face a name was now attached. Arthur: a slight man with graying light hair. *My father,* Tom thought. *Never. Compare him with Bud. God, no.* Holly, the frilly girl. *I don't like the way you look at me,* he told her silently. *Okay, I don't like you, either.*

"I took a tranquilizer," Margaret said. "I remember when Arthur's father died, the rabbi told his mother not to take anything, that tears are healthier, and I agree, but not today. At a funeral, you are expected to cry, but today I thought it would be better if I were somewhat frozen, you know. And I'm not frozen, not at all, even with the pill."

Her tears spilled over, and Tom saw Laura take her hand. And he knew that Mom liked this woman. Queer. Everything was so queer.

For the first time Arthur spoke. "Margaret, Mrs. Rice is thinking of—"

" 'Laura,' " said Laura.

"Margaret, remember that Laura is here for—that Peter also—"

Margaret's hand flew to her mouth. "Oh, how dreadful of me! I'm not thinking. Of course . . . What can I do for you? Tell me. Would you—would you maybe want to see his room?"

"Please," murmured Laura.

When the two women went upstairs, a painful jealousy flared up in Tom. A sensation of aloneness overwhelmed him. It seemed to him, as he took a seat apart in a room which now suddenly appeared enormous, that he belonged nowhere. Who was he? Tom who?

The man's voice came from the end of a hollow tube miles away. "We have so much wanted to see you, Tom."

He looked up. This was supposed to be his father, this thin-set man all tremulous with emotion. If only he might answer with candor, "Well, I surely haven't wanted to see any of you." But Mom would never forgive him, so he merely nodded in reply. "We know how shocked you are. You needn't make conversation if you don't want to."

Conversation! He had absolutely nothing to say except: *Vanish. Cease to exist. Let me get out of here and never think of you again.* But he merely nodded once more.

There was silence. For no apparent reason, the girl changed chairs, jingling gold bracelets as she moved. Robbie said Jews liked jewelry, that the Jewish girls at college wore the best jewelry, and too much of it.

The silence continued. Clearly, Tom thought with satisfaction, these people are as uncomfortable as I am. Well, maybe not quite as much as I am.

"Holly, perhaps Tom would like a drink," the man suggested to the girl.

The girl stood up and addressed Tom. "Would you like lemonade or a Coke?"

"Nothing." And then remembering, "Nothing, thank you."

"Perhaps Tom would like to go outside."

They talked about him as though he weren't there. Possibly Arthur became aware of that, for he next asked Tom directly whether he had a dog.

"My brother has." Get that? My *brother.*

"Holly has a collie, a white collie. Take Tom outside to see Star, Holly."

Willingly, he got up and followed the girl. It would be easier to breathe outdoors, away from stares and questions. The girl was graceful, and her figure was as good as Robbie's. But they were enemies, he and this girl.

At the far end of the lawn a weeping willow drooped over a tiny pool where goldfish drifted. There in the shade the white collie lay asleep.

"He had his run this morning. He's tired," Holly said. The dog stood and raised his head for her to caress. "Good boy. Sweet boy."

Tom would have liked to stroke the dog. He couldn't imagine a family without a dog. But he thought of Earl at home and could not touch this one. Home. His throat ached with the word.

Holly, kneeling, looked up at him. "You don't like us." Her black eyes snapped.

"That's right, I don't."

"I know things about you."

What could she know? Big shot with the frill and the bracelets.

"I don't care the least what you know, or anything else about you."

The sliding glass door opened, and Arthur called, "I'm putting a pitcher of lemonade on the porch table if you want any. Then I'm going upstairs." He slid the door shut.

"Listen," Holly said. She spoke fiercely. "I don't want to talk to you any more than you want to talk to me, but I'm not going to hurt my parents' feelings. They've had enough hurts. I'll get a couple of magazines, we'll sit there pretending, and we won't have to say a word. Okay?"

"Okay with me," Tom said.

This was Peter's room. In one eager sweep, Laura encompassed it: posters, books, stereo, and linen curtains, beige with a fine red thread running through. Prominently displayed on a chest of drawers was a photograph of Peter; in very proper dress and with a serious expression, he stood before what appeared to be a series of long tubular objects, each one topped with an elaborate metal ornament. Here Laura paused.

A minute or two passed. Then Arthur spoke. "He was thirteen. That was his bar mitzvah. Do you know what that is?"

"I've read that it's something like a confirmation."

"Yes, something like. The words mean 'son of the commandment.' The boy now takes his place in the community as a responsible man, no longer a child. He knows the difference between right and wrong. He understands his heritage, handed down from the time of Moses on Mt. Sinai, father to son, to the son's son—"

Arthur stopped, turning away toward the window, hiding his face as he resumed. "He gave the most wonderful sermon that morning. People talked about it long afterward. He was an ecologist, you know, the founder of the ecology club at school, and that's what he talked about, how the Israelites came to the land of milk and honey, how they cherished the land that God had given, how we here today must care for this planet so that our children will have—" Again, unable to go on, Arthur stopped.

And Laura knew that he mourned for two, for the boy whom he had reared with love to do the family so proud, and for the other one as well, the stranger, flesh of his flesh, who now sat downstairs.

Margaret explained softly. "Those are the scrolls of the law in the background, the first five books of the Bible, of what you call the Old Testament. The ornaments are called crowns, to honor the scrolls, you might say."

"I see."

The familiar face, Timmy's face, juxtaposed with these curious objects, swam before Laura's eyes. It was all exotic, a colossal accident. The silence tingled.

"Tell me about the beginning," she said, "and then I will tell you about Tom. It's what we need to know."

Margaret sat down and began with a sigh. "He gave us problems from the start. He was a demanding infant, making fists when he cried, and he cried most of the time. But our first doctor said it was nothing, a lot of babies are like that."

Laura nodded. "They said the same about Timmy. You do know about Timmy, of course?"

"Yes. Ralph Mackenzie told us."

"And then?" Laura prompted.

"Then we moved here. Arthur's father had a stroke, and he needed Arthur to take over the business. He'd been working on a Ph.D. in literature, but he gave it up, although he still knows more than most professors do."

Arthur interrupted. "Laura wants to hear about Peter, not me."

"We went to another pediatrician, and another, while Peter lost weight, got pneumonia, recovered, improved, got sick again—" Margaret made a wide, hopeless gesture. "Then finally came the blow when we learned what was wrong. And then we went all over, to the famous places from Minnesota to Boston; up to the very last month, we were still asking, hoping to help our sweet boy. We went to a great teacher in New York, we—"

"No more, please," Laura said.

It was as if Margaret had not heard, or if she had, was unable to stop herself.

"I remember my first thought, the day we learned that he was not our biological child. The doctor, such a compassionate young man, was looking out the window while he talked to us; he was looking at the dogwood. And all I could think of was that somewhere there was another child of mine, and I wondered what he was, for surely he would be something like the people who had reared him, as Peter was like us. And I thought that probably he was vigorous and healthy."

"Yes," said Laura, "as you see." It was her turn now. "Our baby had been crying too much while we were in the hospital, or so I thought. But I knew nothing, after all. And when we got home, he was wonderful. I suppose we never appreciated what an easy baby he was until Timmy came." And she said almost wistfully, "What you've told me about Peter is the same as what I can tell you about Timmy."

What shall I say about Tom? she asked herself. They are waiting. She began. "Tom is a good son. It's impossible to sum up a life. A good son. A student. An athlete. He and his father —and Bud—are companions. Timmy goes everywhere with them. Tom takes care of him, he's wonderful with Timmy." The phrases came jerking out of her head in no particular order. "Naturally, after a year away at college, he's changed, grown more independent. He's always had friends. I'm telling this very badly."

The other two had been intent on each syllable. Margaret spoke first, almost tenderly.

"We, at least, never had to tell Peter. He died not knowing the truth about his birth. What would have been the use? But you have had to tell Tom." And Margaret shuddered.

"Of course this is unspeakably awful for Tom, anyway," Arthur said, "and added to it is the fact that we're Jewish."

Laura looked into the shrewd gray eyes. Obviously, Mackenzie had told them. But here, she recognized, was a steady, reasonable, grown-up man, not given to stubborn resistance or childish tempers. Now the eyes were waiting for an answer, so she gave it directly.

"Yes. It is so."

There was a collective sigh. Margaret's mascara had streaked her cheek, and she wiped it. Arthur blew his nose.

"Where do we go from here?" asked Laura.

"Sufficient unto the moment," Arthur said, "or something like that. Right now, we'll go back downstairs."

On the other side of the glass door sat Tom and Holly, far apart, both reading. They came in, when called, with sullen faces.

"You must all be hungry," Margaret said, making a brisk effort to lighten the atmosphere. "I've made a little lunch. You are hungry, I hope, Laura?"

"Not very." And almost shyly, Laura inquired, "Is Peter buried very far from here?"

"No. Just three or four miles. You want to see his grave."

"If I may. If it won't be too much."

"Of course not. We can go right now."

Oh, my God, Tom thought, a cemetery. Still it was better than being left behind with that girl, who had not wanted to go.

This day was a disaster, worse even than his imagining of it had been. And yet, in spite of jealousy and anger, he was sore with pity for Mom's flushed face and brittle speech; she was having trouble with words. He wished he could say, Come, let's get the hell out of here. He wished Robbie would hurry back. He needed her. To her, at least, he could talk sense.

The two women were talking, talking like crazy in the front seat. Laura was driving her own car, the two-and-a-half-seater, they always called it. From where he sat cramped in the back beside the man, he had a clear view of the women. He was curious and he was quick at sizing people up. This woman, this Margaret, was educated; you could tell by her speech. She was refined; her dress was simple, like Mom's, although more fashionable; he knew enough about women's clothes, Robbie having taught him, to recognize that. Well, why not, since they owned a department store? Her arm, which she had rested for a few minutes on the back of the seat, wore a narrow gold bracelet, and on her finger there was a green ring, a gleaming, dark stone, no doubt an emerald. He compared the faces, Mom's and the other's. The Other—for he had in these few minutes already begun in his mind to name her—had hair like his own and a nose that was slightly arched, like his own, and like the statues, too, of ancient Romans, Cicero and Caesar. There was no question that he resembled the Other more than he did Mom.

Mom, he cried silently, what have you done to me? And in rage, what are you doing, bringing me here?

And yet, it was not her fault. There was nothing she could have done to prevent it. He had to struggle against tears.

The car drove through a gate beneath an ironwork arch with the Star of David in the center. Oh my God, look where I am, he thought.

"It's a very small cemetery," remarked Laura.

"There aren't very many of us in the city," Margaret answered.

They got out of the car, walked on gravel paths, and stopped at a grave so recently dug that the ivy blanket was not yet grown over it.

"The stone will be set before the year is up," Margaret said.

The grave lay under a giant oak, and they stood quietly in

its shade, each with his private thoughts. *Timmy's brother,* was Tom's thought, and it was a bitter one.

"He loved music," Arthur said suddenly to Laura. "Ralph told us you are a pianist, so you must know that whenever we traveled to a big city where there was a great orchestra, he wanted to hear it. He knew the histories of the composers, he could distinguish among the styles of the conductors."

Soon they will be making a saint out of the fellow! A guy my own age, one day apart. The Other and her husband are holding hands. When they look over at me as if they expect me to smile, or maybe to cry, I look away. Mom, for heaven's sake, get me out of here . . .

The Other urged, "You people have come a long way. Let's go home if you're ready and have lunch."

"We should be getting back," Laura said.

"It's only a quarter past one. You have time to eat a little something first. Besides, my parents will be there, and they want to see — see everyone."

Back at the house there were *three more lined up to inspect me,* thought Tom as they faced him. There was Frieda, the grandmother with dyed hair and brown, wrinkled hands, an elderly version of her daughter. There was Albert, the grandfather, with a mustache and a thick foreign accent. And there was Cousin Melvin, nondescript except for a large nose. *That figures,* he thought, observing the man's nose.

Now came the repeat of the earlier encounter, the eyes, the old woman's tears, and the halting, uncertain speech of people dumbfounded by an unimaginable situation. Fortunately, Margaret rushed them all immediately to lunch.

"Holly and I finished a game of chess while you were gone," said Cousin Melvin to no one in particular. "Then she put the food out. Timed it just right."

The dining room was serene and spare. Everything in the room, from the oiled teakwood table, the ample matching sideboard, and the Chinese-style chairs, to the Japanese lantern sconces, was new. And over all the afternoon light poured in from a wall of windows.

Platters of chicken salad, potato salad, green salad, bowls of fruit, vegetables in aspic, plates of hot rolls and cake, stood on the sideboard. Laura was astonished. The woman must have worked hours to prepare such an array.

"Just help yourselves and sit wherever you want," Margaret said.

Laura sat down next to Tom, who had Cousin Melvin on his other side. She had no appetite; nevertheless, she filled her plate to make up for Tom, who was ostentatiously not eating.

"Tom," said Margaret, "won't you have anything at all to eat?"

"Thank you, no."

They were looking at him and trying not to, he knew. Did they think he didn't catch their quick, sly glances, peeking and peering? He ignored them, refusing to look up until they turned back to their plates and their manufactured conversation, after which it was his turn to investigate them.

He despised these people, the old man with the thick accent, the smartass girl with the bracelets, and the teary old woman, mourning.

"How we loved him! He was so patient with his illness. He never complained."

"Don't, Mama," said Margaret.

"He was such a kind boy, so happy here. I can't stand to look at that piano, his piano—"

"Don't, Mama, please."

The old lady blew her nose. "You're right. Forgive me, I shouldn't."

So *emotional*, Tom thought, with their sainted Peter, dragging Mom upstairs to look, and out to the cemetery . . . Fallen from outer space, these people are, to destroy my life. And I'm expected to sit here nicely, talk nicely, and eat their food. I will not talk to them. Will not.

And he looked at Arthur with contempt. He was a shrimp compared with Bud. I love my father! Tom cried inwardly, and was stricken with an actual pain in his chest. The outrage was unbearable.

In her very bones Margaret was sure she felt Tom's distress. His poor head must be spinning. Laura, this lovely woman, has been his mother, so what can I mean to him? Can he ever want to know us? He's been well cared for, well brought up. He pulled out her chair when she sat down, I noticed that. There is a tiny space between his two front teeth, the same as Holly has. Will we ever know him? Poor Tom. My own head is spinning.

This lunch was a mistake, Laura thought, we are all ill at ease. Tom was right. But they had meant well. They were good people; you saw that at once. The parents were gentle. The girl was bright and clear-eyed, a pretty little thing, so feminine in the ruffled collar, with her jingly charm bracelet. And the grandparents had great refinement; the old man, regardless of his German accent, spoke a remarkably eloquent English.

This is where my baby grew up, she thought. He sat in one of these chairs.

And she said as if musing, "When I saw that first photo of Peter I thought, He's Timmy's twin."

Tom was furious. He had to curb his tongue, on which the words lay ready to leap: No! Timmy is *my* brother, mine, do you hear? It's me he loves, it's I who taught him to pitch and to swim, I who take care of him, who know about medicines and the oxygen. I, do you hear?

And he gave Laura an anguished, furious look, which she did not see.

But Arthur saw it. She would walk a hard road over this, he knew, before it came to an end. And he watched her. A lovely Nordic type, she was. In old Europe she could have been a countess, delicate and elegant. The husband was different, a narrow-minded "good old boy," according to Ralph. In that case, Arthur reflected, there must be deeply conflicting influences over Tom. A handsome boy, but sullen. Of course this was unspeakable for him. Think of the bewilderment, the terror! Yet it seemed to Arthur that he saw real hatred in Tom, too. Pray God he was mistaken. He wanted to love this son.

Abruptly, there came a lull in the talk, as if nobody knew what else to manufacture. It was Albert who rushed to fill the deadly void, saying heartily, "Only a couple of months till November. They're running neck and neck, Ralph says."

"Ralph's got a real fight ahead," came from Melvin.

Albert responded, "He can manage. There's a lot of steel under the velvet. Ralph's tough."

Arthur explained to Laura, "Father means toughness in the right sense. Ralph's our longtime friend, we have reason to know him well, and I can tell you he's one of the finest human beings you'd want to meet."

Laura smiled. "I long ago made up my mind to vote for him. I first learned about him two or three years ago when I heard him speak, and I liked what I heard. I remember he talked very wisely about conservation of open spaces, about land use and land-grabbers."

"He's a country boy," Margaret explained, "and he wants to save some country spaces for the next generation."

"But he wants to save a lot more than that," Arthur added. "Good schools, good housing, and most important, a decent attitude, people caring about other people. Without that, the whole structure will go to hell. Ralph sees that."

Melvin snorted. "Tell it to Jim Johnson and his meatheads. Bunch of Ku Klux aborigines in disguise. But Jim himself is clever. Don't sell him short. He knows how to direct his appeal, especially to the young in the universities. Yes," he said hotly, "Ralph's got a real fight ahead. Tune in the television, and there's Johnson. Open a magazine—hell, you don't even have to open it, he was on the front cover of both news magazines last week, with his pretty-boy smile and his eight-hundred-dollar suit."

This was too much for Tom. It was too much to expect himself to stay silent, after he had resolved to sit like a stone through the ordeal of this outrageous day, among these people with whom he did not belong. And now this ugly big-nose, this loudmouth, dared to mock his betters. *Pretty boy!* And all Tom's fermenting fury burst out like a popped cork.

"I happen to know Jim Johnson personally, and I'll tell you that he's the best thing that ever happened to this state, to this country. You don't know what you're talking about."

Laura gasped. "Tom! What's gotten into you?" She looked around the table. "It isn't like Tom to be rude. I'm so surprised, I don't know what to say."

"I'm not surprised, Mrs. Rice." All heads turned to Holly, who then confronted Tom. "I told you I know things about you. You go around with a girl who makes dirty phone calls and leaves hate notes under people's doors in the dorms."

"That's a lie," Tom said.

"No, it isn't. My friend's brother told me there's a whole group of your kind down there. A lot of rotten bigots. You hate everybody but yourselves."

Dismayed, Laura was thinking again, We shouldn't have come. A wave of dizziness passed over her. This was hideous. The girl—so clearly a sister to Tom with that determined mouth and those vivid eyes—has probably read the nasty newspaper that he writes for. And she went hot with shame.

Margaret said, "Holly, stop. This is awful."

"Yes, it is, Mom." The girl's face was flushed, agitation had enlarged her pupils, but her voice was controlled. "Tom here is an anti-Semite. We might as well recognize it." And she demanded of him, "Isn't that so?"

He defended himself, "Where there's smoke, there's fire."

"I take that to mean that you think Hitler was justified, then."

No one was eating. In shocked silence, they had laid their forks down on their plates and were staring at Tom.

"To begin with, Hitler never did the things he was accused of doing. Most of this stuff is trumped-up propaganda."

"Oh, most of it." Holly was smooth as ice. "But what about the rest of it? Even if only a fraction of it, let us say for the sake of argument—an outrageous argument—should be true? What then?"

"It was a movement for social change in Germany, and unavoidably some people had to suffer."

"It's strange how the 'some' are mostly Jews in this kind of social change," said Cousin Melvin contemptuously. "Hitler, Stalin—well, we've been there before, haven't we? What's new? Same business as when your grandfather had to change his name from Krehfeld to Crawfield, Arthur. Be invisible. Tremble. Right?"

As he spread his hands wide, Melvin's elbow touched Tom, who shrank, thinking: *Krehfeld*, oh my God. Krehfeld. His whole body tingled with shame as though he were embarrassed before his very self. Then he drew another inch away from Melvin's intruding shoulder. I am not "Krehfeld," and I am not "Crawfield." Dammit, you fools, I am Thomas Paige Rice.

"Melvin, that's enough," Arthur said, frowning. "You know very well why the name had to be anglicized. My grandfather was peddling to farm wives back in the 1890s. Who of them would have known how to pronounce Krehfeld, I ask you?"

"If they'd wanted to buy his pins and needles, they'd have bought regardless of the name," retorted Melvin, "and they'd have despised him neither less nor more, just like Jim Johnson and his young admirer here. You're a foreigner who won't fit in. As for me, I'm still 'Krehfeld,' and be damned to anybody who doesn't like it" He shifted and turned face to face with Tom. "Yes, Tom Crawfield, you have a lot to learn about the world. 'Social change,' eh? 'People have to suffer,' eh? Well, I suggest you start by learning who you are, young Crawfield."

"My name is Tom Rice." Tom, starting to rise from the chair, was held back by Laura's gripping fingers.

It was Melvin who left the table, saying, "I know what I'd do if he were my child, my son, I can tell you that."

"But he isn't your son."

"Well, excuse me anyway, folks, and no hard feelings, I hope. I have to get back to the office."

When the front door closed behind Melvin, Margaret broke

the miserable stillness. "Sometimes Melvin can really be the bull in the china shop. I'm glad you said that, Arthur, because he's your cousin, not mine, and in-laws can't afford to speak their minds if they want to keep peace."

"Yes, peace," Frieda said bitterly.

Laura hung her head. No one in his right mind would have expected this meeting to be smooth, but here, here was disaster. And it was Tom who had made it.

Arthur folded his hands into a pyramid at his lips, pausing as if about to deliver a verdict. Three deep, parallel creases crossed his troubled forehead. After a minute, he rested his hands on the table, and when he spoke, he echoed Laura's thought.

"None of us expected this to be an easy day. But I don't think we expected it to be quite so stormy, either. Tom," he said solemnly, "this is a horror for you, as it would have been for Peter. I must tell you something, though. Peter had no prejudices. He wouldn't have been shocked to learn that his biological parents were Methodists."

Tom's face burned. His hands were sweating. The man was too moderate, too pious, with that mellifluous, tolerant tone put on to show how superior he was. Cousin Melvin, the big-nose, was easier to deal with, coming at you with two fists so that you could put your fists up, too.

Arthur continued, "Does what just happened here break our hearts? It does. Are our hopes destroyed? No. We can still hope, Tom, that events will open your eyes. But as I have said, we must be completely honest with each other. We have been told, Laura, that your husband will not come here to a Jew's house, so naturally we cannot go to your house, either."

Laura shook her head, fighting tears.

"This complicates what is already too complicated. Yet isn't there some way around it?" asked Arthur.

Finding voice, Laura replied, "Tom and I will come back again. Yes, Tom, you will."

Tom looked at her. The look said: Never. You will never get me back here.

As if a signal had been given, everyone now rose from the table. The plates were half full of melting Jell-O mold and crumbled rolls, a rejected mess. A splendid dessert stood untouched on the sideboard. The meeting was over, and there was no sense pretending that it was not.

At the front door Arthur took Laura's hand. "Please be sure that we will never try to come between Tom and you," he said with a sad smile. "What we would like so much is for us all to come together. Let us pray for it."

So they took their leave. Tom rested in his seat, pretending to be asleep. All the way home, no word was said. And Laura was baffled, sick at heart for him, for the Crawfield parents and for them all.

At home, alone with Bud, she had to give an account of the day.

He scolded, "I told you it was a bad, bad mistake. The boy didn't sleep all night, dreading it. Damn frauds! You fell for it and for that sweet-talking lawyer."

For perhaps the tenth time in the last few weeks, she tried reason. "Bud, it isn't a fraud. Blood tests don't lie, the DNA doesn't—"

"Bah! DNA. PZY. What, what the hell? A researcher gets a couple of ideas, the papers get hold of them, everybody takes them for gospel truth, and then a couple of years down the road we read, 'Well, maybe . . . The results show that conclusions were perhaps too hastily drawn, too soon.' Bah!"

"Bud, even leaving all that out, if you had been there, you would have seen the resemblances. The mother and the daughter and Tom—"

Bud's voice rose now in anger. "Resemblances! How many kinds of eyes, noses, and mouths can there be on this earth? Every one of us looks like a million other people. People see what they want to see or, in this case, what someone has told them they ought to see. No, Laura, keep that boy—*our* boy— out of this mess from now on. I've never given you an order but I'm giving you one now. Let Tom alone."

"I heard you talking," Tom said, standing in the doorway. "Dad's right. They're trying to pull me away from you, can't you see that, Mom?"

"Ah, no. Nobody could ever do that."

"I hate their guts, the whole lot of those Jews."

There was an ugly look on Tom's face, on the beloved face of her boy. And she said, almost pleading, "What is it that you hate so much? The label? If you had not been switched, you would have been brought up Jewish, and still you would be Tom, with the same skin and arms and legs and brain."

"Your mother," Bud said, putting his arm around Tom's shoulder, "will come to her senses about this fakery, I have every confidence. We'll just have to be patient till she does, that's all."

Timmy had followed Tom and now burst forth, "I wish those people would go back where they came from."

"Where is that?" asked Laura.

"Germany, Tom said."

She sighed. "To begin with, Arthur Crawfield and his parents were born here. As to their ancestors, you might remember that everybody on this continent got here from somewhere else. Even the Indians came from Asia across the Bering Strait. You know that, Timmy."

Timmy was silent for a moment. Then he muttered, "Their boy died of cystic fibrosis, Tom says."

Oh, Tom had been expressly told never to mention it! In all his agitation, he must have let it slip out.

Bud jumped at that. "You see? You see where this has led? Opened up a whole can of worms. Listen, Timmy," he explained, "it was an entirely different case. I know all about it. The damn fool lawyer did tell me that much. That boy had all sorts of complications, something wrong with his heart valve and—and diabetes besides, and—an entirely different case. You've got no trouble with your heart or anything else. Come on outside. Let's shoot some baskets."

From the window Laura watched the three at the basketball net, three males together, excluding her. She didn't mind that.

It was Bud's devastation that scared her. He was so hurt that he no longer thought or spoke with any sense. And this denial of the truth was dangerous.

Driving through Fairview Street, Laura was shocked to see a prominent For Sale sign on the old Blair house's front lawn. Why, they were letting themselves be driven out! It was wrong, wrong! And yet she had to ask yourself whether she would have the courage, the heart, to stay in that house if she herself had been under attack there on that awful night. She decided to ask Lou Foster, as soon as she reached home, what she might know about it.

"Yes," Lou said, "I heard. Not from the Edgewoods — they still won't talk to anybody — but from the real estate agent."

"What a shame. I wish there was something we could do."

"As a matter of fact there is. I was going to call you, you're next on my list. Some of us had a meeting after church, and we decided it would be a good idea to get up a petition in the congregation and in the neighborhood, asking the Edgewoods not to move. We'll tell them that we people welcome them, that we most vigorously condemn the terrible thing that was done, and we want them to stay. What do you think of that?"

"What do I think? Are you asking me whether I'm willing to sign it, for goodness' sake?"

"Not really." Lou laughed. "I kind of thought you would."

When she hung up, a thought came to her: What about Bud? It would be rather odd if her signature should go back without his, too. Well, she'd cross that bridge when she came to it.

Nevertheless, after the long scroll lined with names was delivered a few days later, she took it to her desk and unrolled it without saying anything, signed her name and sat there wondering how best to get through another fruitless argument.

"What's that?" Bud asked, the minute he entered the room.

When she told him, he grinned. His eyebrows went up, making a pair of shallow V's, and his cheeks rounded into a sheepish sort of grin.

"I guess I'll have to sign," he said. "I made a mess for you with Betty Lee, didn't I? So I'd better not make another mess at church."

"Especially since you go to church there yourself," she reminded him.

"Okay. I'll put my John Hancock down. What the hell, I don't live on Fairview, so it's no difference to me. I wonder what Ordway will say to it, though."

"Don't worry. If I know Lou Foster, he'll sign this too."

So Bud, very likely a good many others also, for the sake of appearances, did swallow the pill. A few days later, the For Sale sign disappeared from the Edgewoods' lawn. A few days after that, Lou Foster reported to Laura.

"I got a lovely letter from the family, thanking us all. They really opened their hearts. It made me cry to read it."

"I should go back and see Mrs. Edgewood," Laura told herself. "I'll do it one day next week. It will be a pleasure this time."

But then something intervened. A telephone call came from Ralph Mackenzie.

"If I'm intruding in your personal affairs, please tell me," he began. "I'm calling now not as a lawyer, since there's no need for lawyers anymore, but as a friend of the Crawfields'. And, I hope, of Tom's and yours."

"You're not intruding," Laura said.

"I would like to help if I can. Arthur tells me that the meeting went very badly."

"It did. It was far worse than I could have imagined. I had expected tears, of course, but this was rage. Tom—" She paused, not wanting to paint Tom black.

"I heard. Margaret's taking it very hard. She's such a strong, commonsense woman ordinarily, the family's always depended on her, and now, seeing her so crushed, they don't quite know what to do."

"Oh, has there ever been anything like this before?" cried Laura.

"Yes, as you know, there has, but very rarely. It's surprising that the newspapers haven't gotten hold of it this time."

"Mr. Fordyce has connections," Laura said.

"That's good. I don't think it would help Tom to have this affair spread all over the news."

"It's what I most dread. Tom's very, very troubled, too, Mr. Mackenzie. He's built a wall between himself and the subject. I can't even talk to him about it."

"Do you think I might?"

"It's not just Tom. It's more complicated than just Tom, not something I can put into one sentence, very complicated." She broke off.

"Suppose we take some time to talk about it, then. I'm in town for the day, and I could come to your house for an hour this afternoon, if you'd like."

"I don't think so. Tom works with Bud, but sometimes he comes home early."

Mackenzie interrupted. "I understand. Not a good idea. Perhaps at my campaign headquarters? Or, around the corner at the Hotel Phoenix? We might have a cup of coffee and see whether we can iron something out."

His very voice was reasonable, an assurance that here was a human being who would not lose his temper or shut his ears to whatever she had to say. There was comfort in that voice.

So, at four o'clock that afternoon, dressed in pale green linen with a white ribbon bow on the back of her head and feeling an unfamiliar lift of the spirit, she met Ralph Mackenzie at the Hotel Phoenix.

He greeted her. "You look as cool as mint. How do you manage in weather like this? I think I ought to tell you," he said immediately as they sat down in the coffee shop, "that all the Crawfields think you're wonderful. All of them, even Holly and the grandparents."

"I liked them, too, Mr. Mackenzie. Please tell them for me."

"I'm Ralph, please. And I will tell them. They're really remarkable people, Laura, very sensitive, very kind. I'd like somehow to ease their pain a little, if I can, and yours, too, and Tom's."

"Ah, Tom's! He has gotten himself all twisted up."

"Tell me about him."

She needed so much to relieve herself, and yet the story came reluctantly from her lips, for there had been no one, no friend or relative—even if the aunts had been home—to whom she would have exposed her disappointments. To Bud she owed a wife's loyalty, and to Tom's reputation she owed a mother's protection; surely he would grow away from his aberrations and be again the person she had so carefully reared? Even now, in speaking to this stranger, this man whom she felt to be honorable and decent, she was self-conscious. These, after all, were her people's own secrets that she was revealing: Bud's prejudices and Tom's fall from grace.

"I wonder sometimes whether Tom's neatness has something to do with his affiliations. I mean the kind of mind that craves perfect regimented order, like the Hitler Youth. You go back and back in your mind, trying to find out why and how. I am what I suppose you've been told and Bud is—well, Bud like many people has his prejudices. But Tom I don't understand," she finished.

"The Nazi youth leader, Baldur von Schirach, had an American mother whose great-grandfather had fought for the North in the Civil War. It was a book by Henry Ford that turned him into an anti-Semite when he was still in high school. He ate poison, you might say."

Laura was cold. Unconsciously, she warmed her hands around the coffee cup.

"The coffee's cold, too. You need a refill," Ralph said kindly.

He had been watching and listening without an interruption during her recital, nodding when she spoke of *The Independent Voice* and the night of the attack on the Edgewoods' house.

"I don't suppose you followed the news very carefully this past week," he said now, "or you'd know that the hoodlums who attacked that house were connected with the Johnson rally on the Andersons' lawn across the street. They got their timing wrong, that's all. The attack was supposed to be on the following night, the bungling fools. That kid, Greg Anderson, is a dangerous article. Somebody talked, so the police went on a search and found shotguns, pistols, and ammunition hidden in his room. They don't think his parents had any idea what he was really doing, nor even know now where he is. He skipped town the next day."

"Maybe I'm as blind as they were, maybe a complete fool for saying what I'm going to say, but I don't believe Tom ever was or could be involved in anything like that. Tom's all talk."

Ralph said gravely, "As Johnson is. All talk. Except that the talk and the words have a way of erupting in unexpected places, as Henry Ford's book led to Hitler's youth leader. The power of the word. That's why I entered this race for the state senate."

They were sitting by a window, and now as the sun came back through the sultry clouds, a stream of light fell on his head, turning from copper to red the wavy hair that he had tried without success to flatten down. Rufus, Laura thought. He is properly named: Ralph Rufus Mackenzie. His face was long and angular, like those westward-leaning faces on statues of trekking pioneers. And something touched her inside as, when a knife grazes a finger without penetrating, a tiny shock startles the whole body. Just weeks ago, the aunts had told of seeing him in Florida and of the way he reminded them of Francis Alcott. . . .

She said suddenly, "My aunts saw you in Florida last winter. They mentioned you at my house before I had met you. They said you reminded them of someone whom we all knew very well, and it's funny, but I had the same reaction myself just this minute."

He smiled. "Who was he? An old love of yours?"

"A childish crush. How did you ever guess?"

"I don't know. Sometimes I have a sixth sense. And besides, you have a very expressive face."

She had no idea why she said the next thing that came into

her head; maybe it was merely because she wanted to prolong the time.

"My aunts admired you, though they'd vote for Johnson if they could," she told him, laughing. "I don't think they understand Johnson, but they would vote for him just the same."

"Plenty of good people will. They're not alone."

"I want to see you get elected," she said.

"I want to get elected. I never especially wanted a political career. Yes, the prestige is pleasant, as well as the chance to do something important, but I don't crave either. I enjoy the law. I simply want to defeat Johnson. I must. Somebody has to stop such people."

He looked at her, she looked back, and for an instant something passed between them, some sense of trust, of curiosity, of—of what? She lowered her eyes to twist her bracelet, which had become caught in her sleeve.

"Well," Ralph said, "what are we going to do about the Crawfields and your Tom? They do so much want to see him again, Laura."

"Of course. If Peter were alive, I would race to the other end of the state this minute to see him."

"They hope that the second time will be better, and maybe it will."

"He won't go again, Ralph. And Bud abets him."

"Will you let me talk to him? Often an outsider can do more than a family member can."

"That's so." But truly, she had no hope.

"I have to be back here early next week. I'll phone, you'll tell me when to come to your house, and I'll do my best to enlighten Tom. If I'm successful, I'll get him to come with me to the Crawfields'. How does that sound?"

His smile appealed, and it was impossible for her to say No, it's useless, forget about it.

Instead, "It's worth a try," she said.

"What all this nice talk boils down to is another visit," Tom argued, "and then I suppose another and another." He turned to sarcasm. "Joint custody, I suppose. Well, I'm not three years old, and if I were, I wouldn't belong to those people, anyway."

Ralph's patience was to be admired. In his place, I would have given up by now, Laura thought. Yet he answered again, "All they want, Tom, is a visit every now and then in the hope that you will acknowledge them and care about them. That's all they want."

And Tom answered yet again, "I'm not interested in what they want. I'm telling you now, and I've told Mom, my father is the only one who's sticking with me. Yes, and Timmy, too. It's a pretty sad thing when your kid brother understands you better than your mother does."

Laura looked furtively at her wristwatch. It had taken some maneuvering to get Timmy out of the house, as well as to get Tom home in time for Ralph to catch him, all this before Bud should arrive. They had been talking for almost an hour; soon Bud would be here.

"Tom," she cried, "please. Just go once more. Mr. Mackenzie will go with you. You can see that he understands you, he'll be your friend there, you won't feel so alone. Just once more."

"Have a heart," said Ralph. "You can see that this means something to your mother."

"Why should she care so much? Why do you, Mom?"

It would have taken more self-analysis than she had already undergone during these past weeks, more eloquence than she was capable of, and more energy than was left her to explain adequately why she cared.

"It's because I cannot let you be so cruel," she said softly.

That woman, that poor couple, seeing their son for the first time since his birth, seeing his sullen face, hearing the dreadful things that he had said . . . Those poor people.

And then there was the hurt in her own heart, so raw when it was touched that, without willing to at all, she blurted, "I am thinking of Peter, too, how he lived there all his life, and I never knew. Why, he might even have gone into that store one of the times I went there. When I bought my green suit, I might have passed him, not knowing—" She had to cover her face with her hands.

Ralph coughed and shifted in the chair. Tom was silent.

Then Ralph said, "I can't stay much longer. It's up to you now, Tom."

Laura took her hands down and apologized. "I'm sorry. There's so much mixed up in this, a sense of justice and sorrow and maybe just being too tired to think straight. I don't know."

"It's up to you, Tom," repeated Ralph.

Tom stood. His cheeks were hot, and he had in his agitation rumpled his hair.

"All right. All right, I'll go. Say when." He did not look at Mackenzie as he spoke.

"Friday?"

"Friday." And Tom left the room.

Laura saw Ralph to the front door and beyond to the drive where his car was parked in the shade of an oak.

"Wonderful old trees," he said, pausing beside the car.

"My great-grandfather planted them. We have seven."

"And all healthy."

"They've been well cared for. Last year the tree surgeons filled two cavities pretty much the way a dentist fills a tooth."

Again, as he listened, paying attention, really listening, she had that sense of *recognition*. He was leaning against the car as if he wanted to linger, waiting for her to say more.

"It's funny how you get to love them," she said, meaning the trees. "You'd think they were alive."

"But they are alive."

"Of course. I meant—"

He smiled. "I know what you meant." He hesitated for a moment, saying next, "Your boy is torn in too many ways. I can't tell you how sorry I felt for him in there just now."

"I know. Between Bud who means well, and Johnson who—"

"Also thinks he means well. One of my father's favorite

sayings is, 'The road to hell is paved with good intentions.' It's trite, but true."

"But how can the terrible things that Tom said at the Crawfields' house be good intentions?"

"A philosophical question. We'll have to talk about it some other time." Ralph laughed. "Do you see it as a debate between Johnson and me?"

"Hardly."

Still he lingered, and she said spontaneously, "You were so wonderfully patient with him. I don't know how to thank you. And the Crawfields must be grateful to you, too."

"A situation like this is a challenge," he replied simply.

"You have plenty of challenges right now, so you must like them."

"I'll let you know better in November how much I like them."

"I wish I could help you get elected," she said.

"You can if you really want to. After things settle down for Tom and everybody, you might want to help at campaign headquarters in town. They're always in need of help."

"I would like that," Laura said. Suddenly remembering the time, she put out her hand. "It's late, and I've been keeping you."

"Not at all." He got into the car. "I'll fetch Tom on Friday."

For a long minute she stood at the front door, watching the car. It had almost reached the end of the road when, from the other direction, Bud's car appeared.

"Who was that?" he demanded.

"Ralph Mackenzie. He came to see Tom."

"To see Tom! What the hell did he want with Tom?"

"He asked him, and I asked him, to make one more visit to the Crawfields."

Bud threw up his hands. "Ah, Laura, I've asked you for God's sake to leave the boy alone. He's sick over this."

"I know he is. Who wouldn't be? His whole identity recast in another mold: Who am I? It's a nightmare in itself. But on top of that," she said, "on top of that, you deny the facts, you won't let him face the reality that he will sooner or later have to face. And then on top of that the Johnson business. Don't you see that Tom is poisoned? Johnson is spreading poisoned food through the whole community, and Tom has eaten it."

Bud brushed past her into the house. "Ah . . . you're mixing up our grief with politics. It makes no sense."

"I'm not doing it. They are mixed, and they make a vicious brew."

"Why? Because those frauds are Jews and Tom doesn't like Jews? It's not so unusual to dislike Jews." Bud laughed. "Hell, I need a drink." He poured a jigger of whiskey over ice. "Tom didn't say he'd go again, did he?"

She answered honestly, "Yes, it took some persuasion, but he finally agreed. Please don't talk him out of it, Bud."

"Can we drop the subject, Laura? It's been a long day. Long weeks." He stared out of the window. "Sometimes I think maybe it's true—oh damn, I don't know what to think—about that other kid, and if he was ours we never knew him, and it's all so damn sad. But then I think, no it's not true. Tom's the right one. He's ours, and they're driving him crazy. It's not fair. We were—we are—good parents, and why should this happen to our family?" Turning back to regard Laura, Bud frowned sadly, his forehead puckered, his eyes deeply ringed. "You look beat. I don't want you to lift a finger tonight. Let's go out for lobster or steak, whatever you want. Come on, let's cheer up if we can."

CHAPTER
—————— 12 ——————

On the Friday, in spite of his father's dissuasion, Tom left with Ralph Mackenzie. Resentment boiled in him; he knew himself well enough to understand that it was his mother's sorrow that had moved him; she was so soft, so close to him, that he had been unable to refuse her plea.

And at least he was being accompanied by a gentleman, a person to whom he could relate, a *Mackenzie*, not a *Krehfeld*, not one of those awful people who now claimed him as their own. At this reminder, he winced. A foreboding chill passed through his blood. What if Dad was wrong? What if he really was—was a Krehfeld? And again something within him, a dread voice, spoke as it had when he had taken a deep look at Margaret Crawfield, *You are and you'll have to acknowledge it.*

At that moment the car, on its way to the interstate, passed by the sign lettered RICE AND SON, all bold and glittering in the morning light. Then his heart swelled, and instinctively he sat up straighter in the seat. By God, he'd show them! He wasn't going to be worn down. *Rice and Son.* And Son.

Mackenzie, who had until now been silent, reached toward the radio and the stereo, asking Tom what he would like to hear.

"I assume you'd like music instead of a bunch of chitchat

between you and me. Unless of course there's something you want to say."

Tom was grateful for that. "Music," he said.

"What kind? Country, rock, or Mozart? You name it."

"I don't care. Whatever you want."

"Since you don't care, I choose Mozart."

Mom played all of the sonatas. It pleased Tom that he was able to recognize so many of them, but he said nothing, allowing the music to flow through him, trying not to think.

When finally toward midday they turned into the street, his fear came surging back. There was the house, number 17. Would he ever forget that door with the tubbed evergreens on either side? Or the heart-pounding walk from the car to that door?

"Ten minutes past twelve," Mackenzie said. "Good timing."

"I don't want lunch," Tom told him. "I won't eat here."

"You needn't. But Margaret's a good cook. So I'm going to enjoy myself."

Margaret opened the door. Behind her in the hall the family formed a phalanx: Arthur, Holly, the grandparents, and the white collie. Only Cousin Melvin was missing. In one quick glance, Tom saw all this.

And he took quick measure, too, of the atmosphere. Voices, faces, and body language were different from the last time. There was no outward anxiety; the greetings were cordial and unemotional, almost as if he were a casual guest, an afterthought whom Mackenzie had brought along with him. And he knew that this change must be the result of a careful strategy, the result of a conference between Mackenzie and the family. Clever indeed, he thought wryly.

Again there was a spread in the dining room. Did these people do nothing but eat?

"I had something on the road," he lied.

"You can come in and sit down anyway," Mackenzie said. "You can have a cup of coffee or not have one, as you like."

The man had a calm way of letting you know what he wanted. To resist would be to make himself conspicuous, Tom knew. He sat down next to Mackenzie with a vacant chair, the eighth chair, on his other side. That empty space felt good.

The table talk, all about the campaign, its personalities and finances, was of no particular interest to him. No attempt was made to draw him into the talk; indeed, no one seemed to be paying any attention to him. Since they were not looking in his direction, it became possible for him to look in theirs and to reassess his previous judgments.

Holly was even prettier than he had remembered. Dressed as she now was in jeans and T-shirt, he could really see her shape. A little taller and a little heavier than Robbie, she still curved in the proper ways, Robbie's ways. And she had spectacular hair, glossy, black with red lights or blue lights as she moved, or as the light moved.

The old lady, Frieda, seemed not as old as he had thought, perhaps because today her eyes were not red-rimmed by tears. She was quiet and barely noticeable. The old man with the bushy gray mustache was inoffensive except when he opened his mouth to emit his guttural, accented English. These people were unimportant. And Tom's eyes shifted past them to the head of the table, where Arthur sat, and to the foot, where Margaret sat.

She caught his glance, looked away, and without saying anything, got up and put before him a cup of coffee and an ample, double-sized slice of coconut cake. It had been a long time since breakfast, and he was starved, yet had she asked him whether he wanted any dessert, he would have refused. As it was, he ate it all. Then he thought about her gesture. It was the kind of thing Mom did, treating her husband and sons regardless of their ages as if they were little boys, while at the same time guarding their adult dignity. He had for a long time been aware of this nuance, the subtlety of a loving woman. In this instant now, he suddenly saw Margaret as a *person*, and it terrified him.

Arthur was talking. He had removed his glasses so that his eyes became again the focal point of his face. They were earnest eyes, quite stern as he made some forceful point in reply to Mackenzie, stern eyes in a face gone momentarily stern. This man would make a forceful enemy. There was no weakness in him; why had he thought there was? Because he was small in contrast to Dad? Napoleon had been small. And suddenly, seeing Arthur also as a *person*, he was terrified again.

As on the first time, he felt trapped. It was as if a vise were steadily, inexorably closing in upon him. If he could have risen and run from this house, if he had not been more than a hundred miles from home with practically nothing in his pocket, he would have done it.

"Shall we sit outside for a while?" asked Margaret. "There's a breeze. Fall's coming."

Fall. Back to school. Back to Robbie.

They were on the terrace where he and Holly had sat sulking apart that other time. A green-and-white-striped awning had been let down, and the dog, who had been sleeping out in the sun, came to lie down again under the awning.

"Star," said Arthur, "did you know that Holly took him from the animal shelter? She's been a volunteer there ever since junior high."

The remark, addressed ostensibly to Mackenzie, was meant for Tom, he knew, for surely Mackenzie must long ago have been told about Star.

"His owner died and none of the relatives wanted him. That's how he got to the shelter."

The dog, hearing his name, got up and stretched. Then he walked over and put his nose on Tom's knee, making it necessary for Tom to give some sort of response. Without speaking then, he stroked the silky head.

"Didn't you say you have a dog?" asked Arthur.

"I said my brother has." *My brother.*

"That must be what attracts him."

Tom kept smoothing Star's head. He was not going to be drawn into conversation. He was here, and for the second time, too. Wasn't that enough for them? No, blood was what they wanted, his blood. And he did not look up from Star's head.

No one spoke. Mourning doves crooned at the bird-feeder, agitating the silence. He thought of the trite expression "The silence rang." But it *did* ring. And he knew that they were all waiting for him to speak. Mackenzie ought to help him out by saying something, anything. He was furious with Mackenzie.

Arthur said, "Tom, you haven't spoken a word. You can't keep this up. It's unnatural. Surely you have something to say to us. Say it, then, no matter what it is."

Hadn't they heard enough from him? They knew where he stood. And now they were asking for more.

"Arthur, it's too hard," Margaret objected. "Let's not force things. Tom will speak when he's ready."

But Arthur persisted. "No. Let us be free with one another. It's the only way. We've been talking about Ralph's campaign, and you said you're for Johnson. Will you tell us more about it?"

The man was positively looking for trouble. Very well, let him find it. All the doubts about himself, the rage, self-pity, and fear that were balled up within Tom now burst apart and the shrapnel scattered.

"All right, I'll say what I think. You won't like it, but since you asked for it — I think Jim Johnson is the most honest man I've ever met next to my father. And a lot of people who won't always admit it because in certain circles the things he says are not acceptable, a lot of them know in their hearts that he is right."

"Right about being a Nazi?" Holly asked.

"That's not so."

"He admitted that he had been once."

"Yes, had been. When he was a kid, somebody inveigled him into joining the American Nazis, but he didn't stay there. As soon as he learned what they were, he got out. Jim's too smart for that."

"It all depends," Arthur said quietly, "on what you mean by 'smart.' A wolf in sheep's clothing is smart, too."

The old man, Albert, spoke up. "The man is a danger not

just to blacks and Jews. In the end he and his kind are a danger to everybody. People should realize that."

"Well, sir, you need to open your mind." Tom was dignified now, and cold, remembering that Bud had once advised him never to lose his temper in argument, for that was to show weakness. "You need to hear another point of view. Jim speaks for middle America, the real America, like my ancestors. The Rices arrived here before 1700. They came down over the Blue Ridge Mountains, they fought through the French and Indian Wars. Later, during the Revolution, Elijah Rice served under Marion the Swamp Fox and was decorated for bravery and—"

"And your great-uncle on my side, young man, received the Kaiser's Iron Cross for bravery and wounds at the battle of the Marne. Some years later he was shoved into a gas oven at Auschwitz." The old man, with furiously burning eyes, stood up to face Tom.

"Papa, please," implored Margaret.

But the old man still stood, swaying a little on unsure legs. "I remember you said it was propaganda, that there was no Holocaust. Here, look." And he rolled up the sleeves of his gingham sport shirt. "Look." He thrust his arm in front of Tom. "What do you see?"

"Papa, please," Margaret cried again.

"No, Margaret. These are things he must be told, so I'm telling them. This is the number they tattooed on me. I was in Auschwitz, too, but I was one of the lucky ones, if you can call it that, because I was still alive when the war ended. Don't turn your eyes away. It's important for you to see these things while some of us are still alive to show what liars your Jim Johnsons are. What did he say about propaganda? Turning crematoria into ovens? That there never were any ovens? Well, take me to him, I'll shove this number into his face. How does he dare, how can he—"

"Papa," Margaret said, "Tom was talking about the American Revolution, and this is—"

"No, Margaret. You want me to stop this unpleasant story, but I won't. It's important. It's necessary."

The gray mustache quivered, and the old voice cracked. In the face of this undignified emotionalism, Tom felt a certain calm superiority.

"Yes, Tom, I want you to know who you are. We left Germany before the war, my wife and I. I had another wife—her family had been in Germany for a thousand years, a thousand years, mind you—and a child, before Frieda. I married Frieda much later, after I came to this country. That's why I'm so much older than she." He paused and wiped his forehead. "Ah, what's the use. I think maybe I'm saying too much after all."

Mackenzie said firmly, "You should go on. You were right when you said it is necessary. Go on, Albert."

"Where was I? Oh yes, my wife and the little girl were in the south of France. Then the Nazis came, and the Vichy government, and we knew we had to move on. We thought of crossing the Pyrenees into Spain, then Lisbon, where we would wait in safety for some visa to anywhere in the world away from Europe. You hired a guide and went on foot across the mountains, a long, hard, dangerous trip. Guides could betray you, and German patrols lay in ambush. Nevertheless, we started out in a party of eight, people we had met along the way, and we would have gotten through if it had not been for my wife's miscarriage. I have to sit down," Albert said abruptly.

It relieved Tom not to have the man standing above him, blocking the view of middle space. There had been no place to which he could direct his gaze, since the dog had moved away, except the old man's chest. Now, while a volley of words continued, he looked out to the lawn.

"I'll make it short. As soon as my wife was able to walk well enough, though not well enough to cross a mountain range, we returned to the place in Toulouse where we had been hiding. What's the use of even trying to describe our days there? Huddled in a room, afraid to go out on the streets except for a quick foray to get food. So? So they caught us and interned us, women and children in one camp, men in another. After that came the long train to Auschwitz. I never saw them again. They died, my wife and our little Lotte. I lived. That's all."

"You're wearing yourself out," Frieda said. "It's not good for you to relive all that, not worth it."

"But it's good for Tom. It's worth it for Tom. Now I want him to hear your story."

Frieda was reluctant, and in Tom's opinion, that was to her credit. Who wanted to stand there or sit there and spill his guts out to a stranger? For I am a stranger, he said to himself, a stranger to them and their sadness. Of course, it's terribly sad about his wife and the little girl. And it has to be true, he couldn't have made it up, there are the numbers on his arm, he wasn't lying, his eyes were wet. Still, there has to be more to it, there has to be a reason why all this happened. When you read Hitler's book, you get the other side of the story, loud and clear. Anyway, what has it all got to do with me?

Frieda was hastening through her narrative. "I was born here after my parents escaped. My father was a young doctor in Germany when the troubles began. He had just married my mother. The two of them went to Italy, where he learned Italian and got a license to practice. Then came Mussolini; so they fled again, this time to New York, where he had to learn a second new language and start all over. But for me, life was easy, I was an American child. I grew up, married Albert, we had Margaret, and when she married Arthur, we came here to be near them. That's all. A short story."

"But far from simple," Mackenzie observed, and looked meaningfully toward Tom.

Again Tom had the feeling that the entire performance this day had been rehearsed. They were trying to rope him in, to make him one of them. But he wasn't one of them. The very thought made him sick. These people were victims, always beaten, always losing . . .

And he had a vision of them down through the years ahead, continually reaching for him by letter, telephone, and in person. He would be asked again and again to come back here. Mom would plead with him to go. Dad would defend his refusal, and the home that had been calm would be destroyed by quarreling. Worse yet, the news about this horror would leak out. The world was not so big that such a thing could remain hidden forever. AMAZING BABY SWITCH would scream out of the headlines in those papers that they sell at the supermarket checkout counter. . . . He felt breathless, stifled.

"Well, have you any thoughts about what you've heard?" asked Arthur.

"Not many."

"A few thoughts, then. I would like to hear your few thoughts."

He would not look at Arthur, but kept his gaze upon the lawn and on the trees through which the wind was briskly moving. It reassured him to see that air was circulating, that he was not going to be smothered.

Patiently, Arthur repeated, "Your thoughts?"

Tom forced himself to come to. "I'm sorry the little girl died. All of them. It was sad."

"They were your people. Did you feel that?"

"No, I'm not Jewish. I'm a Methodist."

"You're perfectly free to be a Methodist, but they were still your people."

"No."

"Well, let's allow for the moment that they weren't. Should anyone at all write the things that appear in that paper for which you write? Should anyone?"

"I got hold of a copy," Holly said. "It has your name on the masthead. Your disgraceful name."

"Holly!" warned Margaret.

So that was what they had been leading up to.

"Your church doesn't agree with the ugly lies in that paper."

The man hung on like a bulldog with its teeth in someone's leg. And Tom flared up.

"Look, I came here because you wanted me to. I didn't come to defend myself. I didn't expect to be attacked."

Margaret said softly, "It's only that we want you to accept us as we are, Tom."

She was sitting in a wicker chair close to his, and now impulsively, she laid her hand over his hand, pressing it so hard that he turned to her in astonishment. Her expression was so intense that it frightened him. It repelled him. This was the first time she had touched him, and he had an awful thought, shocking himself with the awareness that, in spite of Bud's denials, this was the woman within whose body he had come to life. It had never crossed his mind to think of Mom in that way; if it had, he would have shrunk from the thought as from an obscenity. And now this woman, this strange woman—

He jerked his hand away. Everyone saw him. The gesture was unmistakable.

"I just want to be let alone, now and forever. It's a free country, isn't it? Why won't you let me alone?"

Margaret stood up trembling, and Holly put her arms around her.

"Today was my mistake," said Mackenzie, "I hoped it would be otherwise. God knows, I don't want to make things harder for you people."

"Or for Tom," Margaret amended.

"Well," said Mackenzie. "Well. Suppose we call it a day. Tom, let's go."

Tom was still not feeling well. It was still an effort to breathe. Mackenzie was angry, and would have plenty to tell Mom, no doubt about it. The affair was a mess. He had stupidly allowed them to make him lose his cool. So now, through civility, he had to try to retrieve it.

"I did not intend to be offensive," he said stiffly. "Please excuse me if I was."

"Oh, Tom," said Margaret, still holding Holly.

Arthur went to the door with them. "Thank you for everything," he said to Mackenzie, and shook his hand.

"Another time it will be better," he told Tom, and did not touch him.

As they drove away, Arthur was still standing at the door watching them go. On his face was the same stern, grieving gaze.

They went a mile or two before Mackenzie spoke, saying dryly, "Didn't go so well, did it?"

"What made you think it would?"

"I don't know. I sort of hoped."

They drove another short way before Mackenzie spoke again. "You hurt them, you know."

Tom knew well how much he had, especially when he had rejected Margaret's hand. He hadn't really meant to do that. It had been automatic, something he couldn't help. So he shouldn't be condemned for it.

"They wouldn't let me be. You heard how he forced answers out of me. Then he didn't like my answers."

"They weren't very likable."

"To you, and them."

"I don't understand. Your mom says you're softhearted. Yet I saw that you were annoyed with Albert's terrible story. I don't understand."

"I was only annoyed because they tried to connect me with their misfortune. These—Jews—are losers, and I'm not one of them."

"No, you're wrong. They're not losers, they're victors. People who can survive such horrors are victors."

"But first they're victims, and there's a reason. I could give you some literature on the subject and you'd see why."

"You're talking nonsense, evil nonsense. Someday you'll find that out."

Mackenzie spoke sharply. It was too bad. There were a hundred miles to go sitting next to a man who didn't like him. When he put on a tape, Beethoven this time, he didn't ask for Tom's preference.

A neighbor from across the street was standing at the front door looking up and down the road when they arrived at the house. Mackenzie had barely stopped the car, when she ran to it, crying frantically, "Tom, Tom! Where's your mother?"

"I don't know. What's the matter?"

"It's Timmy. He's awfully sick, the worst I've ever seen, worse than three years ago, remember Labor Day weekend when you had to rush him to the hospital? He couldn't get his breath, and the pain in his chest was that bad, remember—"

Tom's heart had begun to race. "Yes, yes. Where is he?"

"I called your father and he said it would take too long for him to come get him at home, so he asked me to take him to the hospital. And your father said he'd meet us in the emergency room." The woman was almost sobbing. "Your mother left first thing this morning, I saw her leave but I don't know where she went, she never stays away the whole day shopping! Oh, I wish I knew where she went!"

"Get back in the car, Tom," Mackenzie said, for Tom had jumped out. "Come on, I'll drive you to the hospital."

They rode for a few blocks, while Tom, turning away from Mackenzie, looked out of the side window. Mackenzie saw him gulp, his Adam's apple bobbing and all the color draining out of his face.

"This is a tough day for you. I'm really sorry, Tom," Mackenzie said gently.

"Thank you."

Suddenly Tom began to talk. "Three years ago, you heard, they didn't think he would live. He was choking . . . God, if you've ever seen anybody trying to get air . . . He turns dark blue. All his life . . . He goes a few years, and we think it's over . . . No, we don't really think it, we know better."

The terse words came rapidly as of their own volition, as if Tom couldn't stop talking if he wanted to, Mackenzie thought.

"He's such a good kid, they think he doesn't know he'll die young, but he does know . . . Sometimes I think, it's funny, if he were a healthy kid, he'd have been a pest. What seventh-grader wants a kindergarten brother to be in his way all the time? But he's been so sick, I've worried as far back as I can remember."

This hardly seemed to be the same person who had so callously dismissed those other people only a few hours ago.

"My parents," Tom said. "If Timmy dies this time—"

"It will be terrible," Mackenzie said quietly, adding as they arrived at the hospital, "If there is any way I can help, Tom, please let me know. And I mean that."

Tom dashed up the steps. Halfway to the entrance, he turned around to call, "Thank you for the ride. Thank you."

Mackenzie drove slowly down the street, not quite sure where he was going. The entire drama was unrolling before his eyes, a repeat of that other boy's life and death. Once more he saw a mother grieving and the despairing father walking up and down the room, up and down. This time, though, his picture was not of Margaret's round cheeks wet with tears, but of Laura's bowed, fair head. And he was intensely moved.

His desk at the office must be piled with correspondence after this whole day away, and to be prudent, he should really go back to it. On the other hand, the local campaign headquarters was only a five-minute drive away. It would be prudent also to find out what was going on there. Yet he knew he had another reason, for had she not said something about helping with the campaign? *Fool,* he said aloud. So Mrs. Rice attracts you. Mrs. Rice is not one of the married women— what's the percentage?—who play around. That, of course, is one of the reasons she is so alluring. *Fool,* he repeated, and stopped the car under the banner MACKENZIE FOR THE SENATE.

The front room was lively. Computers, telephones, and volunteers were working at full capacity. He walked about, questioning and greeting, while his eyes roved, seeking. Then, quite casually, he strolled toward the back room, the mail room, and pausing in the doorway, recognized her by her slender back and her hair, held this day by a loose, dark red silk bow.

Hearing him, she turned and smiled, saying gaily, "I'm as good as my word, you see. I've sent a thousand flyers out today." Then, as if she had this moment recalled the occasion, anxiety wiped out the smile.

"How did it go?"

One calamity at a time is enough for her, he told himself. And so, evading the question, he replied, "Not too badly. But—" And again, as once before, there came to him that image of the deer raising its trustful gaze toward the place where the gun waited. "But they're looking for you. Timmy isn't feeling well. I drove Tom to the hospital. Your husband's there. I really don't know any more," he said, while his heart sank.

At once, she swept up her purse and car keys, saying, "Thank you for taking Tom. How kind you are!"

"Are you sure you can drive?"

"Yes. You see, we always know this will come again. We've learned to plan how we'll behave." She spoke steadily.

"There's no doubt in my mind about your behavior."

"But I have to think of Bud and, especially of Tom. He's had so much . . ." And now her voice did trail away.

Ralph followed her to the door and watched her out of sight. And he recalled the night, not long ago, when lying awake and allowing his mind to wander without aim, he had counted the times and estimated the minutes he had spent with her. They were very few, perhaps three hours' worth all told. It was strange that they seemed like so many more.

You entered the hospital at the side where ambulances came and went. You rushed through the bustle of the waiting room, crowded with white uniforms, bloody bandages, stretchers, and haggard relatives. As always, you felt a shock of surprise that all this commotion should produce so little noise. An ominous quiet, that was it. Waiting. Waiting. Afraid to make a sound. Half whispering, you inquire and are directed, as you knew you would be, to the curtained cubicle where the patient lies.

Bud and Tom and two youthful doctors were standing over Timmy. Laura grasped Timmy's hand.

"Darling, Mom's here."

His eyes recognized her. She knew that the pain in his chest was too sharp to permit speech, that he was struggling for breath, that he was terrified. His wheeze was frightful; you could imagine that his lungs were being torn like a piece of cloth and, like cloth, were shrieking.

"Darling, you're going to be fine. You've been through this before, so you know. And you've been so brave each time."

To this his eyes did not respond, but closed instead. His poor damp, sweating head rolled to the side. He was turning blue.

She saw the two young men glance at each other. It seemed to her that the glances were deeply meaningful. She saw by a change on Bud's face that he had caught the glances, too; his eyebrows rose in a question that he must know she was not able to answer. They two, the parents, were in a strange country whose language they did not begin to comprehend.

The white coats moved quickly now, speaking in curt phrases.

"Oxygen."

A nurse came running. Oxygen gushed from the wall above Timmy's head. Then a white-coated woman, authoritative, came running.

"Blood gases, now. Right now. Hurry up, Vanderbeck, will you?" She turned to the nurse. "Then rush the sample upstairs. And I mean rush."

They took blood from Timmy's arm, arterial blood, that much Laura knew, as it spurted forcibly into the tube. The boy shuddered. Feeling his pain, she winced. More people came into the cubicle, shouldering Bud and Laura to the side. Tom left; perhaps he knew that he, like his parents, was superfluous here, or perhaps the sight of the blood had been too much for him. Numbly, only half comprehending, Bud and Laura watched.

"Look at the color," said the one called Vanderbeck, as he held up the tube. "The lungs aren't getting enough oxygen."

Another man pushed the curtain aside and entered, panting like someone who is running late, and immediately demanded,

"What's the white blood cell count? Have you done the venipuncture?"

A strap was bound around Timmy's other arm. Now there were four doctors and two nurses crowded around him. Next came a technician, wheeling an X-ray machine.

"Do you mind?" somebody asked Bud and Laura. "We need the space."

When they stepped out, the curtain fell behind them. Their boy was in the hands of strangers who didn't even know his name. And yet these strangers, tense, competent, and anxious, were trying to save him.

Tom hovered with them in the corridor. They were all three in this situation, but not of it. What, after all, did they really understand of the bewildering bustle behind those curtains?

Somebody came out with the X-ray plate and raced away with it.

A young man holding a paper cup embedded in crushed ice called over his shoulder, "Be right back. Just running this blood down to the lab."

Mingled voices seemed to mumble and rise. Laura strained to hear.

"Carbon dioxide is up."

"Just as I thought."

"Get the IV. Water and sodium chloride to rehydrate. Hurry."

Now appeared the familiar face of Dr. Sprague, summoned from a crowded office—it was always crowded—to this emergency.

"Doctor," Bud began, but Sprague, barely nodding, brushed past him.

"What's the evaluation?" They could hear Sprague's brisk demand, then other voices, and then Sprague's again. "We have a real problem here. I assume you've examined the sputum?"

"Yes, it's bloody. He came in totally dehydrated, heart racing, fever one hundred two."

"Get another sputum up to the lab. And I need a pulmonary

man. No delay. Whoever can get here fastest, say in sixty seconds. O'Toole, if he's in town, or young Alan Cohen."

Dr. Sprague's peremptory orders were comforting. He was familiar, and he was in charge. But his words, when he came to Laura and Bud, were not comforting.

"Frankly, I'm worried about an infection. The pain is all over his chest, so it's probably an abscess. Pneumonia and/or an abscess. Well, you people have been here before, so I guess I don't have to say much."

Neither Bud nor Laura replied. And Sprague paused, as if he were weighing the need to explain against the pain that explanation would bring with it.

"We'll have to load him up with antibiotics. Where's that resident with the reports? I phoned my orders in—oh, there you are." Impatiently, he waited as the young man came to report.

"It's definitely a streptococcus infection, Doctor. Lots of polyps and gram-positive cocci."

Frowning, Sprague shook his head. "Okay. Let's get him up to ICU. I want him in isolation, of course. Keep the oxygen going. Keep checking. I'll wait until O'Toole gets here. Vanderbeck," he called, parting the curtain. "Who called O'Toole? What? Oh, thanks." And turning back to Bud and Laura, he reported, "Dr. O'Toole's out of town until tomorrow afternoon. He left Alan Cohen to cover for him, and Cohen's on his way here now. We'll have Timmy upstairs by the time he gets here."

Sprague must have read something in Bud's eyes, or perhaps, Laura thought, in the curl of Bud's lip, because his answer was a reprimand.

"If O'Toole lets anyone cover for him, you can bet that man's the best. Cohen is from Harvard Medical School, with a fellowship in chest diseases at Cornell, and on top of that, he's got heart. What else do you want?"

The curtain parted, and a moment later, Timmy was brought out on a gurney. His eyes were shut; he lay so still as he trundled away past his parents, that Laura was overcome by the certain presence of death.

Dr. Sprague's tone changed. Very gently, he said, "I'll be working with the chest expert, I'll be in touch with you anytime around the clock. You know that. We've got to see your Timmy through this thing."

"Thank you, Doctor," Laura said.

And Bud repeated thickly, "Thank you, Doctor." But he knew as well as she did that their boy was dying.

Days and nights moved through a time split into four-hour segments. Every fourth hour they were admitted to the isolation cubicle where Timmy fought for life. Silently, scarcely whispering—for what was there to say?—they stood looking down at the small face, the pale eyelids delicate as shells, the pale lips around which, as light fell, the faintest down was visible. And the hands, the sight of those helpless hands, was unbearable for Laura. Long ago, a hundred years ago it seemed now, when Timmy was three years old, they had shown her the slight curving, "clubbing," of his fingers, the first, almost invisible signs of oxygen deficiency, and she could never look at his hands without remembering.

Through the silence came a steady beep from the wall monitor, the heartbeat transmitted through the wires attached to Timmy's chest. All the machines! At regular intervals a pulmonary therapist brought another one to force air and medications through the mouth into the lungs. Laura's eyes and ears were alert to the rhythms of machines.

The fever stayed high. New X rays showed that a part of one lung had collapsed. In the waiting room where Bud and Laura, and often Tom as well, sat holding unread magazines, Dr. O'Toole came once or twice each day to report.

"It's a large abscess, and pneumonia has developed, as of course—" He broke off. "What can I tell you? It's a repeat, only somewhat—"

"Somewhat worse." Bud and Laura spoke together.

"Yes. But we're pouring in the antibiotics, monitoring the

blood gases, watching the white blood cell count, doing everything—" And he broke off again.

When he had gone, the three just looked at each other.
Then it came to Laura that there was something else, something that, because of this agony, had actually been forgotten.
But now it came flooding back, that other agony, and she put
her arms around Tom.

"Go home and rest," she told him. "Take the car. We'll get a
taxi when we're ready."

"No. I want to be here near my brother."

"You have to go home. Earl's been locked up all day. And if
anything's happened to that dog when—when Timmy comes
home—so go now, Tom. Please go."

He lay outside on his father's steamer chair with Earl lying
beside his feet on the footrest. He had fed the dog, and, too
mentally tired to care about preparing any food for himself,
had eaten an orange, a banana, and a roll, then had come out
here and lain down to wait for the first stars. No doubt he was
only one of countless millions who, from the beginning of
time, had drawn from the constellations, the circling fires in
the night, a sense of calm. No doubt it was a cliché for man to
reflect on his own insignificance before such grand mysteries.
But it's true, Tom thought, and that's why it's a cliché.

"So look," he said aloud, causing Earl to look up into his
face, "I came here, I didn't ask to come, I'll be here a little
while, I'll leave, and what will it have mattered? So I don't
even know who I really am or where I belong, so Timmy will
probably die, so my heart's breaking and who the hell cares?
Why should I care? I don't care. I don't give a damn whether
I wake tomorrow morning or not."

The dog crept up onto his lap and licked his arm. "Take it
easy," he murmured, half to himself and half to Earl. "Take it
easy." Tears stung, and he closed his eyes. Just drift. Just
sleep. Maybe with luck you won't wake up.

He dreamed, and although the dream had all the power of

reality, it also in some strange, unfathomable way flashed seconds in which he knew that he was dreaming.

Timmy lies in a coffin under a blanket of red flowers. *I planted those last year,* Mom cries. *Take them away, they'll smother him!* And Margaret Crawfield is weeping; she is approaching Tom, looming larger and larger, expanding like a balloon, so that her face becomes enormous, so close that he sees her dark, separated lashes, a small brown mole on the side of her nose, and a pearl in her earlobe under the glossy fall of her hair. *Who are you to cry?* Bud shouts to her. *He's not your son!* Who isn't her son? Timmy? Tom? And that man Arthur stands apart with a smile in his all-knowing eyes, an eerie smile. *I see through everyone,* it says. Tom shudders and takes the flowers that Mom is tearing from the coffin; his arms are filled and he can hold no more, so that they spill onto the ground. *Mom, don't,* he begs. *Mom, stop.* And at the same time, he is a little boy in a big store among tall people, crowding. *I'll be right back in a second,* Mom says. *Stay here. Don't go,* he begs in his terror. *Mom, don't leave me,* he begs.

He awoke in a sweat, but was stiff and cold. It was quite dark. The telephone was ringing in the house. He sprang up and stumbled on the steps. If it was from the hospital . . . If it was Timmy . . .

"Hello! Hello!" he shouted.

"It's me. It's Robbie. Where have you been? I've tried day and night all week to get you."

"It's Timmy. He's in the hospital, and we're there all the time."

"Oh, Tom. Is it very bad again?"

"Yes, very. We don't know—don't know what's going to happen."

"Oh. How terrible for you all!"

Sympathy was the worst. You wanted it, you needed it, and still it tore you up.

"I'll call you as soon as we know anything," he said.

"You won't reach me. There's no phone in my room. I'll keep phoning you from downstairs. It's absolutely marvelous here, I'm learning so much. But this is no time to talk about that. Tom, Tom, I miss you."

A rush of yearning rose and clutched his throat so that he could hardly speak.

"God, I wish you were here. I'm going upstairs to bed, a cold bed without you. And I'm so cold already that I'm shivering."

"Nerves do that. But honey, it won't be long. Only the week after next. Until then—oh Tom, I'll be praying with all my heart. I feel for Timmy as if he were my own brother, even though I've never even seen him. I feel for him because he's yours. Don't forget that he's recovered every other time before this."

"I'll try."

"I have to go now. Good night, honey. Get some sleep, if you can."

When he replaced the receiver, he stood a moment feeling the faintest smile start to shape itself on his lips. Neither one of his two gigantic burdens had been in the least alleviated, and yet, in these few minutes, his mood had changed; he no longer felt himself to be without significance under the stars, a piece of matter whose disintegration meant nothing.

It was her spirit that had revived him, plain as day. Her warm, husky voice had done it alone, a reminder of her cheerful strength. Almost, it seemed, that Robbie's will might force Timmy to live. And as for the—the Crawfield business—how she would scoff! He could see her throw her head back in scornful laughter. *What gall! What a roaring, stupid joke!* she would say. *Who do they think they are to come up with a scurvy scheme like that?*

And he wished that the new semester were starting tomorrow. She would have her new room ready. There would be white curtains with ruffles and heaven only knew what other little knickknacks in the room, along with the usual pile of stuffed animals on the bed. It was funny, and part of his delight in her, that a girl who got honors in analytical chemistry could also fuss over ruffled pillows and black lace nightgowns.

Suddenly he recalled having seen in the hospital's gift shop a big white polar bear with an absurdly lovable face, furry and soft. Robbie would love it. Tomorrow, no matter what else happened, he would buy it for her.

"We've got to keep cupping," said Dr. O'Toole, curving his hands as he slapped Timmy's back. "Let me turn you over, son, so I can do your front. We've got to break up that mucus in your lungs."

Timmy gave a faint smile. Breathing was still a struggle, and he did little talking, but now, at the end of the first week, his fever had broken, his temperature was almost normal, and he was ready to be moved out of intensive care to a private room.

"I want to emphasize how important it is to be careful about cupping," O'Toole warned Laura. "You absolutely must keep it up long after he's at home."

So they really believed he would be coming home . . . Another battle won, she thought, although not the war. No, not the war. She was giddy after a week with no more than two or three hours' sleep at night, and so tired. So tired. Alarm shook her, and she cried anxiously, "Was I not doing it enough? Is that why this happened?"

"No, no, you've done everything right. That had nothing to do with it."

"It was tennis," Timmy murmured. "My fault."

"Nonsense." The doctor's tone was hearty. "Nobody's fault. Except," he continued, modifying his tone, "that you do know your rules about getting yourself too hot or too tired."

Timmy nodded. When his eyes met Laura's, she understood. He had been playing in the heat, had been losing the set, and hadn't wanted to call it quits because he would have looked like a sure loser. It was the story of his life.

When the doctor was finished, she walked out into the hall with him.

"He's going to make it this time," said O'Toole. "Today is the first day I feel it's safe to say that." He looked sharply at

Laura. "It's been a terrible week for you and your husband. How is he?"

"He's been a wreck. I made him go to work this morning because on top of this awful worry, he's been worrying about the business, too. He's had a double load, poor man."

"You're a good woman, and he's a lucky man. I hope he knows it."

She had often remarked that age has a privilege: Elderly men and women can afford to speak with a bluntness that young people seldom attempt.

"He does," she replied.

"Well, good. Now it's time for you to take care of yourself. Try to get some sleep, and try to get out for a couple of hours, out of the house and away from this hospital. Timmy's going to sleep all afternoon, anyway."

She had no idea what she might do, but the advice was probably sound, so she drove home prepared to try a nap, when the telephone rang.

"Hello, Laura? This is Margaret, Margaret Crawfield. I won't keep you, I only called to ask about your boy. Ralph told us what happened, and we're so sorry."

"Thank you, we think, we're pretty sure, he's on the mend. Very slowly and with our fingers crossed. But you know all about that."

"Yes, we do. Well, please let us know whether there's anything we can do."

The telephone clicked, leaving a vacancy: she had not asked during these last days about that second visit to the Crawfields, and of course Tom had said nothing either.

She lay down on the sofa in the big dressing room that had once held her grandmother's voluminous wardrobe. Dr. O'Toole had given her a good deal of relief this morning, relief that should have eased the way toward badly needed sleep, but somehow it had not done so. Wide-awake, she followed the pattern of birds that flew across the white-and-green toile wallpaper. So Ralph had told the Crawfields about Timmy. Ralph. Not Mackenzie, as until now she had thought of him.

And suddenly she had a vivid recall of that afternoon in the coffee shop, a recall of her sense of him, of his quick comprehension, and of an odd moment in which a curious, knowing glance had passed between them . . .

Really, really, he had been so kind, had taken so much trouble to smooth their way through a terrible, rough passage.

It was just then that the telephone rang again.

"I was concerned about your boy," Ralph said.

"Timmy? Thank God, he's leaving the ICU. Things are looking much, much better. Last week this time—"

"I know. I could tell by Tom's face how bad it must have been. Did he tell you I've phoned a few times?"

"He didn't tell me. It's not like him to forget."

"Don't say anything about it. Tom can have no love for me. I've plagued him to do something he hated to do."

"Then the visit was a total failure again? These last days I never got around to thinking about it."

"Yes. The others tried, but Tom wasn't willing, so I guess you'd call it a failure."

"If I only knew what to do!"

"Maybe we should talk about it. Yes, I'm sure we should. Are you by any chance free this afternoon?"

Laura hesitated. "Well, but I have to have an early dinner and then go back to the hospital."

"I only meant a couple of minutes at the Phoenix coffee shop. I plan to stop in at campaign headquarters, anyway."

Truly, she needed help with Tom . . . "All right. We'll meet there. What time?"

"Is four all right? And don't meet me. I'll circle around and pick you up at your house. I'm going to be in that part of town."

This is wrong. Well, if not wrong, not exactly right, either. But no, don't be ridiculous! It's no *assignation*, for heaven's sake! It's important to know what's happening to Tom and to all concerned in this bizarre predicament. Since there's no talking about it with Bud, who has both blinded and deafened himself to the subject, to meet this way is the best that can be done. So it's right. Of course, it's right.

She bathed and used Gardenia body powder and perfume. The day was dim, which would make white linen seem tacky; instead she put on a blouse and skirt of blue-gray silk, a muted color to blend with the day, and then brightened the whole with a coral-flowered scarf.

"I like those colors," Ralph observed when she got into the car.

"Thank you."

"I'm so glad to know that your boy's come out of the woods."

"Thank you."

Suddenly, she felt awkward and knew she sounded prim, she to whom conversation came easily, she of whose social graces Bud was so proud, often so embarrassingly boastful. Her hands had folded themselves in her lap as if she were an unpopular girl waiting to be asked for a dance, or a patient in a dentist's waiting room. And loosening her hands, she managed to think up a bright comment about Johnson's latest speech, at which Ralph laughed, and so the air was cleared.

At the Phoenix, they took the same table and began the same topic.

"No, it didn't go well," Ralph said ruefully, "not at all. Laura, this is the saddest business I've ever had to deal with, and I'm no stranger to tragedy."

"Margaret telephoned my house while I was out today."

"Yes, she told me she was going to ask about Timmy. But I'm sure she hoped, too, that Tom might answer the phone. Arthur tells me she's in anguish over Tom. She's lost weight and can't sleep."

"I'll call her back tonight. But I can't force him to accept them. I've tried, and I've only made him angry at me."

Ralph said thoughtfully, "Maybe none of us should try anything just now, but just sort of lie back and see what develops. If Tom should lose touch with you, he'd be left in limbo. No doubt that's where he already feels he is."

"He has his father."

Ralph corrected her gently. "He needs his mother, too."

His mother. The woman who telephones, who is in "anguish" . . . Bitterness rose in Laura, a bitterness that she could almost taste. Here were two women who, if they were not the women they were, could quite naturally come to hate each other and leave the son, the object of their struggle, hating them both as well.

She swallowed hard, saying, "I know. But fortunately, he and his father are unusually close."

"In their politics, too, I imagine," Ralph said surprisingly.

"Yes, they're both Johnson men, although actually, Bud isn't much interested in politics."

Ralph smiled. "The love of politics has to be in the blood. Some might say it's a disease of the blood."

The conversation was circling, almost warily searching for a direction, a straight line. Sensing that, she waited.

And Ralph said, "I guess I ran for every office in school and college. Won some and lost some. Funny thing is, Arthur Crawfield was my opponent a lot of the time, and we were best friends through it all."

"You grew up together?"

"Yes, and stayed together when we both moved downstate. Then I went with my present firm and came back here, but we still manage to see each other often." He said seriously, "They're very special people, Laura."

Tom's parents. This, then, was the straight line that Ralph had found. She wanted to follow it, to know more, while at the same time she didn't want to know more. But it was expected of her to respond.

"Tell me about them, please," she said.

"Naturally, I know more about Arthur. He's a brain, for one thing, the kind of brain who becomes a department head at Harvard or someplace, one of those 'name' teachers who live on to be ninety and still have people fighting to get into their classes. He really would have loved that life, but when the family needed him in the business, he gave it up, came home, and has never spoken one word of complaint as far as I know. So now he runs a department store, and very efficiently, too."

"That's a rather touching story."

"It could be sad, but Arthur's not given to sadness. Somebody had to take care of a business that had been built out of sweat. You heard how it started, like most of the great American department stores, with a Jewish immigrant peddling through the countryside. Well, the father died, there was a widow, there were three sisters, two still in college and the third a young widow herself with four babies and no inheritance from her husband. So Arthur took over."

"And Margaret?" she asked.

"Oh, Margaret is all heart. She's not cerebral, like Arthur but she's smart in her own way. I always think of them as the rare, perfect match. He and I were at somebody's house one night when they met. There was a crowd, and we were having a good time. And suddenly, Margaret walked in. He couldn't take his eyes from her. You could almost feel the thing that sprang to life between them in the first minute. It was like a current—extraordinary. They were married six months later." Reminiscing, Ralph looked off into the middle distance. "I always think that's the way I want to be married, that way or not at all. I want to feel: 'This is the one, the only one, and if I can't have her, then I'll go on the way I am.' I do believe that's the right way to be married. Perhaps I'm absurdly romantic. Do you think I am?"

She was remembering that she, too, had wanted it to be like that, a purity, without compromise. The only one. And that way or not at all.

"I certainly don't think you're absurd," she answered quietly.

"I'm glad you don't. Arthur and Margaret don't think I am, either."

There was an instant's pause then, during which their eyes met and shifted as Ralph raised his cup.

"I'm drinking too much coffee, and I know it. This campaign's bad for the health. Late nights, rubber chicken banquets, coffee. But I'm afraid I'll survive."

"How's it going? I've quite lost touch this week. A world war could have started for all I knew."

"We're still ahead, but according to the polls, our lead's shrunk a bit. Johnson is a formidable opponent, let me tell you. He's an orator, and he's good-looking. The women go for him."

"It depends on the woman. A matter of taste."

That smug, tidy face belonged in an ad for male cosmetics, while the face on the other side of this table, this long Lincoln face with the strong nose and the fine, bright, kind, intelligent eyes was—well, one wouldn't, or at any rate she wouldn't, be apt to forget it.

And she said abruptly, "If all keeps going well, as soon as Timmy's home again, as soon as I can, I want to go back and help you win this election."

"You wear many hats. Mother and politician and pianist and what else?"

She noticed that he had not put "wife" on the list. And before she could answer, he continued, "I just recently learned about your music. One of my partners heard you play at somebody's party, and he was impressed. 'Marvelous' was his word."

"No, I'm not 'marvelous.' I am 'very good.' Good enough to teach talented pupils, but no more than that. However, I'm happy with it. I look forward to September, when lessons begin."

Again there was a pause, a meeting of the eyes and a turning away. And Ralph spoke quickly, as if to fill the gap.

"Tell me how you got started and where you trained."

Time pulled at Laura: the house, the dinner, the hospital, all waited. With a slight move of the wrist, she was able to see her watch. Half an hour had gone by. Another fifteen minutes, she told herself, and not a minute more.

And so she began the simple story of the first lessons and

the extravagant piano provided by the dear, extravagant aunts, and the advanced classes, the whole, straight story.

Then Ralph told his own tale.

"For a while at college, I was very serious about the classical guitar. I even went to Spain one summer to study at the source. I had the craziest teacher, eccentric, comical, and wise. He was a master of flamenco music, an addict. And he made an addict out of me. It's like fire in the blood."

So they talked on. It surprised each to discover in the other a person who truly knew something about music besides the usual lip service that is paid to this greatest of the arts by those who want to seem as if they know something about it.

"You've never been abroad?" asked Ralph. And when she said that she had not, he counseled, "You ought to go. You must go, in fact. To hear Mozart in Salzburg or Beethoven in Vienna—ah well, you see, I am a romantic after all. Can't get away from it."

She smiled. "But not an absurd one."

Her wrists were resting on the table. Light flashed on her wristwatch and startled her. The few minutes had turned into an hour and a half.

"Do you know what time it is?" she cried.

"I'm sorry. It's my fault. Come. I'll have you home in ten minutes."

A quietness came over them on the way, a quietness so abruptly marked, so deep, that Laura had to break it.

"We wanted to solve Tom's problem, and we haven't done it at all."

"Time will have to solve it, Laura, for good or ill. It always does. But it's Tom who has to make a decision. No one can do it for him."

"For good or ill," she repeated. "Which do you think it will be, honestly?"

"I have no idea, none at all." Ralph gave her a shrewd look. "But I do know this. It will be hard for you, either way. The more Tom leans toward you, the greater will be the Crawfields' pressure on him, and he'll be taking that hard. But if, by some chance which I find almost impossible to envision, he should ever go in their direction, why then — I don't need to say any more."

She did not answer. To lose her Tom, the vigorous, chuckling baby boy, the eight-year-old scamp, the high school scholar, the son who writes poems for her birthday, even the young man who writes for that scurrilous paper—

She said mournfully, "If only there might be some middle way."

"That's what we have to hope for."

When the car stopped in the driveway, an aberrant thought almost formed itself into words on her tongue: When shall I see you again? You are so sane, such a *man*. I need to see you again. And immediately came chastisement: *You are a fool, Laura Rice, a big damn fool. What can you be thinking of?*

"I hope," Ralph said, "I shall find you working away the next time I drop in at headquarters. That will mean that Timmy's doing fine." He laughed. "To say nothing of the fact that I want all the help I can get." And as she moved out of the car, he added, "I'm sorry we didn't solve Tom's problem, Laura. But will you remember me to him anyway?"

"I will. And thank you for everything, for trying and for being a friend."

She was inserting the key in the lock when the door opened and Bud faced her. "For Christ's sake, where've you been? Who's that who brought you home?"

"Ralph Mackenzie."

"Ralph Mackenzie! What's going on here, Laura? What is this?"

"Going on?" As she walked toward the kitchen, he stood in her way. But she pushed past, saying, "Nothing's 'going on.' I worked at the campaign. You know I'm against Johnson. I haven't made a secret of it. Now I'll have something on the table in fifteen minutes so we can get back to the hospital."

"Yes, we do have a sick son, don't we? But, of course, Mackenzie's campaign is more important."

"That's not fair, Bud! I was with Timmy from half-past

eight this morning until half-past one. It was Dr. O'Toole who told me I must get out for a few hours, now that Timmy's so much better."

Bud stood in the kitchen doorway while she put out the cold supper that had been prepared in the morning. Whenever she turned, she felt his eyes on her back. Guilty thoughts produced a flush that was hot on her neck.

"How did you get downtown? Your car's in the garage," he demanded.

"Ralph telephoned to inquire about Timmy, which was very kind, I thought, and when I mentioned something about going to work a bit on the campaign, he offered to give me a lift. Since he was to be in the neighborhood anyway," she amended.

"You're blushing red as a beet. Is this guy making a play for you? Is that it?"

"If I'm blushing, it's because your remark is so idiotic."

The lie now burned all the way to her forehead. Yet it wasn't altogether a lie, was it? Really, this is much ado about nothing, she thought, and said, "Ralph has been a friend to us, Bud."

"Such a helpful friend. A real friend of the family."

"Don't sneer. He truly is. He's taken a lot of trouble to help Tom."

"Tom doesn't need his help. And we don't need any more friends, Mackenzies or Crawfields with their phone calls and presents. Bastards, all of them."

"What presents are you talking about?"

"Tom got a package, a book from him, a big book on astronomy. How the bastard knew Tom was interested in astronomy, I don't know, unless maybe the kid mentioned it when he was at their house. Anyway, Tom was too upset to talk about it. He went up to his room and left the thing on the library table."

The book, still lying in its wrappings, was magnificent, a thousand pages of narrative, drawings, diagrams, and splendid photographs. Beside it was a gift card inscribed simply, *From Margaret and Arthur, who hope you will enjoy it.*

From Margaret and Arthur, to their own son. Surrounded by crumpled paper, the book was a sorrowful symbol; it seemed discarded, dead at birth. Objects take on the mood of the viewer.

"The nerve of them," said Bud. "What do they think, that they can buy his affection? If my son wants a book, I guess I can provide it for him."

And picking it up, he let it drop on the floor upside down, so that the binding split of its weight.

"Oh!" cried Laura, "you've ruined it. You're no better than a vandal. How can you be like this?"

"Why not? Tom doesn't want the thing. Throw it out, or give it away. I'll buy him another one if he wants me to."

She said nothing. Anger boiled within her, but it was less important to vent the anger than to get the supper over with and go to the hospital. They ate in silence.

Day by day, almost hour by hour, Timmy returned to life. In the middle of the second week, he got out of bed with the intravenous pole attached and walked very, very slowly down the hall. Next, he was detached from the pole, and to keep his legs moving, was allowed to walk all the way to the sunroom at the end of the hall. Finally, he began to get cranky, which was a sure sign of improvement.

"It's boring here," he complained. "I'm sick of it. I haven't seen any of the guys, and I'm worried about Earl."

Dr. O'Toole winked at the parents.

"I want you here a few days more so we can watch you. The guys will be just as glad to see you next Monday as they would be today."

"Well, I'm still worried about Earl."

"Who's he?"

"My dog."

O'Toole winked again. "I'm sure your parents are taking

good care of him. After all, they brought you and your brother up pretty well."

"Actually, it's Tom who's been responsible for Earl," Laura explained. "He's had his run every day, Timmy, and every-thing he needs."

When Timmy was sick, she forgot that he was eleven; she saw him as a little, little boy and tended to talk to him accordingly.

"And when you do go home," cautioned O'Toole, "you tell the guys and Earl to sit in the yard with you and do nothing but sit for a whole week. After that, you may start with a short walk in the cool of the early morning or the evening. I do not want to see you back here in the hospital ever again, Mr. Timothy Rice. Hear?"

Laura smiled, going along with the mock severity, the *game*, the *play*. For someday, as they all knew well, although they could not know when, he would be back in a hospital just as Peter Crawfield, his brother, had been before him.

In Timmy's room on the table by his bed, the medicines stood in a row as they had always stood beside a glass and a pitcher of water. Oxygen was at the ready in the far corner by the windows as it had always been. Nothing had changed. And yet it would take time, a long time, to fall back into the familiar order of the house.

Laura reflected: We have come back from a far, dangerous journey. A soldier returning from brutality and terror must have these feelings, too. There was a tension among them all, revealed in sudden bursts of laughter when nothing particularly funny had been said, revealed in quick glances that met behind Timmy's back, revealed by unspoken questions on each other's faces, Laura's, Bud's, and Tom's.

Wan and tired now although he had been clamoring to go home, Timmy lay outside on one or another of the large chairs, moving from shade to sun and back again. He read, dozed, listened to his Walkman, and talked to Earl, who, after chasing a squirrel, always returned to his place at Timmy's feet.

Toward the end of the week after the air had cooled, he went for his first walk. He would not admit it, but the effort was obviously exhausting, and he needed no persuasion to go directly to bed. The others, hearing his intermittent cough, were restless.

Tom worried. "Are you sure I should go out tonight? You might need me."

"No, go," urged Laura. "We'll get you at Eddie's house if we should need you, but we won't need you. Go."

"The kid's a prince," Bud said when the front door closed behind Tom. "Do you realize how faithful he's been from the first minute in the emergency room right up till now?"

"I realize."

She wanted to ask but did not: And do you realize that he is being torn in two?

"Character," said Bud. "Quality. It's in the blood. Well, he's got good blood on both sides, yours and mine. Staunch people."

A long sigh struggled up from the region of Laura's heart and was stifled, unheard.

Bud went on cheerfully, "Eddie must have a couple of girls over. For all we know, our Tom's got a girl right here in the neighborhood. I hope he has. This is his time. Nineteen! I'm not too old to remember what it felt like. That one in the photo on his desk isn't bad-looking at all." He chuckled. "Have you noticed?"

"I noticed."

One of the girls who wrote the venomous trash in that paper. The photograph had stood in its place all year, so it must be serious. She, too, was not too old to remember what it felt like to be nineteen . . . This time the sigh escaped.

"You're tired," Bud said kindly, "and I am too. It'll take a while to recover from what we've been through. Let's go on up."

Timmy called good night when he heard them in the up-stairs hall.

"Good night, Mom. Good night, Dad."

The voice had the nasal tone that often went with his partic-ular illness. Its every nuance and catch was too familiar, as were every modulation and variation of his wheezing cough. How many nights had they not lain between sleep and wake-fulness, estimating the strength and duration of the cough, asking themselves and each other whether this was the "nor-mal" chronic cough or something dangerously acute!

With every muscle tense they lay stretched out beside each other, listening, listening, until the last cough died and the house was still.

"He's okay," Bud said. "He's fallen asleep. Poor guy. God knows what his next few years will bring. Years when he ought to be playing ball and chasing girls. Poor little guy."

This litany was also familiar. Bud saw no future for Timmy. There was no space in his vast, tragic disappointment for the slightest word of hope that Laura might speak. Having learned that, she rarely uttered one. Now, as he put his arm around her, she said nothing, but merely waited for what she knew was to come next.

Sex could be comfort. Some, when beset with troubles, lose all desire, while others find reassurance and escape through its delights. It depends, she supposed, on personality, or mood, or one's particular hormones. *And on the partner.*

Now Bud desired her. No innovative lover, his routine was unchanging; simply it was the vigorous demand of a healthy male. He was satisfied with himself, and because he was lov-ing and because she was a healthy female, she, too, had long been satisfied. Besides, she had really never thought very much about it. . . .

His hands moved through her hair, spreading it over the pillow. As his mouth came upon hers, his body sank its full weight on her, and he settled into the merging that was to give all pleasure. His repetitious murmurings were meant to excite and to arouse erotic fantasies, which generally they managed to do. But tonight, her response was mechanical. It was flat. Disordered, fleeting thoughts absorbed her; what he was doing to her body seemed of a sudden to have no connection with her *self*. It had no significance, no reality.

Something was happening to her. A profound change was taking place.

When he had reached the climax, he turned over and, as was his way, fell almost instantly asleep. For a while she lay staring up at the ceiling. This summer night was a white one, so that the room was only half dark and she could even discern the line where the wall met the ceiling with a thick band of plaster foliage. Bud's shoulder heaved in a strong arc, like a whale's back. He breathed lightly, never offending with a snore. From his warm, clean skin there came the astringent fragrance of good soap.

It was a pity that all of a sudden she had no feeling for him. None at all. Even her anger was dead.

It was past midnight, long after Tom's footsteps whispered on the stair carpet, when she got out of bed and went downstairs. The house, the beloved house, oppressed her, and she went outside. The sky was still white so that the black treetops formed a pattern on it. In the center of the lawn, on the dew-wet grass, she sat down with her arms around her knees. No thoughts came. There was only blankness and deep loneliness. A small wind, swishing sadly through the trees, deepened the loneliness. She was lost on a mountaintop, abandoned in the desert, on the ocean, in a forest— And yet, behind the holly hedge, now grown twenty feet high, there rose the chimney of the old Alcott house.

She covered her face and cried. Great sobs came out of her chest and whimpered in her throat. Her tears fell, warm and slippery, on her fingers; she let them fall unchecked and unwiped.

Two weeks ago, there had been reason aplenty for tears, while pacing and sitting and pacing through the antiseptic-smelling corridors. But she had controlled her tears then. So why not now?

After a while, though, they ceased, and she was relieved. She was also ashamed.

"There is no excuse to be like this," she said firmly. "Get up now, Laura. Go about your business. God knows, you have business enough to take care of."

In the morning she had errands downtown, at the bank, the dentist's, and a shop to exchange Tom's sweater. These brought her at last into the vicinity of the Hotel Phoenix, around the corner from which were the headquarters of the Mackenzie senatorial campaign. Having promised both Ralph and herself that she would volunteer again as soon as Timmy came home, she decided that there was no better time to start than right now. And she walked briskly around the corner with a feeling of good purpose. The woman who had sat weeping on the grass the night before would not have recognized her.

Mackenzie's party had leased a store; through the wide windows a whirl of activity could be seen. For a moment she paused to look in, not knowing why she paused. Then it occurred to her that if Ralph was there, he might think she had come to see him. But that was absurd. Had they not agreed that she would help his campaign? She was a concerned citizen, only one of dozens of women in this city who aided their favorite candidates. He was a fine man, an attractive man who had made extraordinary efforts on behalf of his friends the Crawfields, and in doing so had incidentally been very kind to Tom. That was all he was.

All, except that he admired and was attracted to Tom's mother. But what of it? Thank goodness she was attractive enough to be admired! What of it?

You're acting like a high school girl, she scolded, becoming aware that she had been standing in the doorway for several minutes. But suppose somebody was to see her hesitating there, as if she were disoriented, suppose Ralph was to drive up and see her; suppose he was actually inside right now, wondering what was the matter with her?

She fled. Clutching Tom's sweater, she almost ran and almost tripped in her high heels. She frightened herself. Her mind was doing tricks. *If you play with fire, you get burned,* warned Aunt Cecile. And it was true. You had only to read the newspapers or watch television to learn the ways in which people burned themselves. Stay out of this campaign. Stay away from Ralph Mackenzie . . .

Across from the parking lot was a row of stores, among them a music store, from which now sounded the raucous voices, the tom-tom beat of teenagers' music, reminding her that she had offered to buy some CDs for Timmy. And she went inside, made her selection, started out the door, and went back to ask about recordings of classical guitar.

"Segovia? Bream? We've got a few of each, and we'll order if you want anything that we haven't got. Are you looking for something in particular?"

"No, I'm not at all familiar with the guitar."

"But you most surely have one of the country's largest collections of piano soloists." The man smiled. "Not giving up the piano for the guitar, are you?"

Laura smiled back, thinking, It's funny how we feel compelled to fill every moment with these friendly, joking, meaningless remarks; we all do it.

"Hardly. I was just talking to somebody the other day and got the idea that I'd like to hear some guitar music."

And that was true. Why, only a while ago, she had heard a flute recording on the car radio and gone right out to buy a James Galway selection. This time it was the guitar, that's all.

At home that afternoon she took out a disk: Segovia playing "Granada" and "Sevilla." The room was cool and shadowed by the sycamore, now that the sun had gone around the side of the house. Through this coolness the music flashed; it danced and sang; one could imagine water rippling through a Moorish garden, a red-flounced, whirling skirt, castanets, a pleading serenade.

"Like fire in the blood," he had said.

So it was. Laura lay back on the chair and shut her eyes.

The back door closed with a bang, and Bud came in wiping his forehead.

"Whew! It's a sizzler out there. What the deuce is this racket? I could hear it out on the back steps."

"I like it," she said, and got up to press the "stop" button.

"You didn't have to do that. Did I say shut it off? If you like it, have it. I don't have to like it. Gee, you live here, too."

Immediately, she felt ashamed. "Never mind," she said. "Not important. Where's Tom?"

"Coming in. The place was busy today, a madhouse. You wouldn't think so in this weather. Tom worked like a horse. I told him I wish I could get a few more men like him. How's Timmy been?"

"Quiet. He read, and then a couple of the boys came over to play board games. No coughing, or very little. I'll have dinner before you're through washing up."

When the telephone rang, Laura took it in the kitchen. A voice, now familiar, spoke her name.

"Laura? I hope Timmy is feeling better?"

"Thank you, he is. Margaret?"

"Oh, I'm sorry. I'm a little nervous, I guess. Yes, it's Margaret. Margaret Crawfield."

It seemed to Laura that her heart actually did sink a few inches. This voice, like a living presence in her kitchen, came to remind, to warn that it was now *attached* to this home and family, forever attached, and never to go away. God, if those people would only go away!

Yet the voice was tremulous and appealing. "Is this a bad time for you? Am I interrupting anything?"

"No, no, it's all right. And so good of you to ask again about Timmy."

"Well, we know it must have been very bad. Ralph didn't need to describe what was happening. We knew it all."

"Yes," Laura said weakly. *My other son. Peter Crawfield, my other son.*

"Ralph said he had called a few times and spoken to Tom. Do you think—well, to tell you the truth, I hoped it might be

Tom who'd answer the phone just now. Do you think—will you ask him to talk to me? Is he at home?"

Laura knew without asking that he would not talk to her. It would be easier to say that he was not at home, but she also knew that she could not do that.

"I'll call him," she answered.

The other must have detected some hesitancy, because she hurried in explanation. "We sent him a book on astronomy. Arthur thought maybe that might be a talking point. I don't know—"

And Laura, thinking, she is close to tears, as am I, said quickly, "Hold on. I'll try to find him."

Tom and Bud were in the library standing near the telephone.

"Don't bother to ask," Bud said. "I know who it is. I picked up the phone the same time you did."

Defiance was written on Tom's lips, sucked into a thin line, and on his pose, arms folded across his chest, feet apart.

If only that woman would give up, Laura thought once again.

Yet she pleaded, "Please. It's only a few words, Tom. You can't keep evading this. Something's got to give."

"Let that woman give," Bud said. "Damn pushy persistence. It's typical. Jews never give up."

"Put yourself in her place, Bud," Laura said quietly. "Have some mercy."

"Mercy! For a pair of impostors who've shoved themselves into our lives with a pack of slick lies so they can take Tom away from us? If murder weren't illegal, I know damn well what I'd do. I'd get my shotgun and—and—" Having reached the top of a crescendo, he paused.

Appalled, Laura warned, "You're shouting! She can hear you. Shut the door, Timmy."

The boy, hearing the commotion, had come running downstairs and now demanded to know what the trouble was.

Tom told him. "It's those people. She wants me to talk to

her, and I don't want to. Mom wants me to, but I won't. I'm sorry, Mom, but I can't. You don't understand. I can't."

Laura put her hand on his shoulder and looked up—how tall he was!—into his angry, sad, fearful face. "Tom dear, I do understand, much more than you think. We're all in this together, so we have to understand each other."

"We're not all in this together," Bud shouted again. "I'm not. Listen, Laura. If you want to let yourself be dragged into it and be hoodwinked by these crooks, that's your problem. But count me out, and count Tom out, too."

She turned now to her husband. Stubborn, stupid . . . But Bud was hardly a stupid man. Bud was merely blinded. Hatred had blinded him. If the Crawfields were Methodists, would he be acting this way? No. He would certainly resist, and he would be heartbroken, as she herself was, but he would not be in just this kind of intractable *rage*. She knew that surely.

Still quietly, she said, "Bud, when will you face the truth? This woman gave birth to Tom. She—"

"God damn it, Laura! I've heard enough of these lies. Lies! I've been patient with your sentimental tears, I've accepted our differences, you a softie and I a practical man who's gone out ready to fight the world and protect you so that you might rear the children, give your little piano lessons and—"

Timmy had stuck his fingers into his ears. "I'm sick of this!" he cried. "Everybody's fighting all the time. We never used to fight until those people, those Craw-Craw—whatever their name is—came around to mess us up. I hate them. I wish they'd all die."

At the other end of the telephone, Margaret was still waiting. It was no use, she had to be told. So Laura went to the kitchen to tell her.

"I'm sorry, Margaret. He will not talk to you. I've tried. I've done my best. I don't know what else to do. He's nineteen. He can do whatever he wants."

Once started, her feelings, her words were all jumbled; resentment at the fates for creating a situation that threatened so many innocents, despair over Tom's personal suffering—and over his bigotry, too—all these mingled with the ache over dead Peter, whom she had never known, Peter Crawfield, reciting at a bar mitzvah and buried under the Star of David, all these, and her aching pity for Margaret, along with her wish that Margaret would simply depart for Australia and vanish.

"I don't know what else to do," she repeated. "What's to become of us all?" And almost sharply she added, "You must see by now that it's no use. It would be easier for us all if you could just let Tom alone."

There was a moment's silence. Then in a broken voice came a reply. "Maybe I'll write him a letter. But I won't call up anymore. I heard—I could hear—I don't want to make things harder for you."

The telephone clicked off. For a few minutes, Laura sat before it waiting for mental order to return. She reflected upon the tides and ebbs of life; when only days ago they had stood in unity at Timmy's bed, the only thing in all the world that had mattered was that boy's life or death, yet now that he was restored to them, all their other troubles came surging back unchanged.

Nothing much happened during the next day or two. Yet nothing is constant, she thought. Secretly, slowly, things move. They get better or they get worse. You have only to wait.

Timmy, whose activity was still limited, hung around and, quite unlike himself, sulked. He worried that Tom would have to leave them, as though the hateful Crawfields could some-how conjure up some evil magic and snatch him away. In vain, Laura reasoned with him, and finally, in sheer weariness, gave up.

Overnight mail brought a letter from Margaret for Tom. It was a long one, handwritten, but he never got to the end of it.

"That's cruel, Tom," Laura said when he threw it into the trash can. "Can't you at least read what she has to say?"

Tom's face was red and he turned away without answering, but Bud answered for him.

"Tom and I have been talking about this on our way to work. And Laura, you have to let him alone. Those bastards have to let him alone. Damn their souls!"

This time it was Laura who turned away.

Gloom descended on the sunny old house. It was as if something heavy were lying on its roof, and on Laura's shoulders, too, a feel of frozen winter, dark and still. If only I had somebody to talk to, she thought. Perhaps if the aunts had been home, she would have called on them, but they were on the other side of the world. Friends, and she had many, were out of the question, since the family's trouble was, by Bud's and Tom's wishes, never to be revealed to anyone, ever. Ever.

The only possible person was Ralph Mackenzie, and she hoped, she waited for him to call. Yet when he did not call, she was, paradoxically, relieved. Life was already too complicated. . . .

A new anger, different from any that had ever gone before, lay between herself and Bud. Flashes passed through her whirling mind, visions of living without him, and these flashes shocked her. For, in spite of what he was doing now, had he not been good to her? And the boys loved him so! It was true that he didn't and never had truly *known* her, but then perhaps she didn't really know herself, at least not lately. She only knew, as on that night when Timmy had come home, that some deep change had taken place within her.

CHAPTER
——— 13 ———

Tom turned from left side to right, stretched out flat, then lay on his stomach and flipped back, straightened the pillow, and was wretched. At last, despairing of sleep, he got up, switched the light on, and took Margaret Crawfield's letter from the desk where Mom had put it after retrieving it from the trash can. And again, he scanned it. The sentences were abrupt, written, it was plain to see, by a person in a state of some agitation.

. . . so happy when you were born . . . wanted a boy so much . . . named you Peter after your great-grandfather . . . a scholar, so admired . . . you can see you look like Holly . . . no matter what anyone says . . . common sense . . . a new phase in life . . . an open mind . . ."

He read on, flipping through five pages filled with pleadings, assurances of love, and appeals to reason. The writing was certainly skillful, and the writer was persuasive. But she would never be convincing, because he refused to be convinced. He would always refuse.

I don't want you, he cried silently. Can't you understand that I don't? Yes, I believe it's all true. I was born to you, DNA doesn't lie and I do look like you, too. God damn it, I've studied my face, and I know. But it's too late. You can't come barging into my life like this to tell me I'm a Crawfield. I'm not a Jew! Never. And as long as I don't feel I am, and as long as nobody knows about this mess, I'm really not. I'm Tom Rice. That's who I've been all my life, and that's who I'm going to remain. So go away, Margaret Crawfield, will you? Go away and let me be.

He tore the letter into little pieces, threw them away and sat for a while just staring at the wall. Then his eyes lighted on Robbie's picture, an enlargement of a snapshot he had made at college last winter. Dressed in a big red sweater, she was perched on a low stone wall; on her head was a knitted cap with a pom-pom, and on her face, a bright laugh. He remembered that he had just been telling jokes and so had caught the laugh.

He felt such longing for her! Some people would say that at nineteen he wasn't ready for the "real thing," that he'd have "a dozen girls" before he was through. The workmen, talking over their lunchboxes, had already given him some kidding when, in a rash moment, he'd hinted about Robbie. But history told reverently of the pioneers, teenage married couples with babies who came south over the Natchez Trace or who went west over the Oregon Trail. For that matter, how old had Mom been when she married Dad?

He was still sitting there when Bud came into the room.

"What's wrong, Son? I had to go to the bathroom, and I saw your light."

"Nothing much. Couldn't seem to fall asleep, that's all."

Bud glanced at Robbie's picture and back at Tom. "Sometimes," he said slowly, "sometimes too many things creep up on you at once, and it seems as if you'll never be able to carry the load. But you'll carry it. You'll be back at school with your girl—she is at school with you, I take it?"

Tom nodded.

"And about this other affair, well, you—and me—we'll all get through that, too. We got through the last couple of weeks with Timmy, didn't we? And this is just one more hurdle to jump over."

Tom closed his eyes to blink away a rising wetness. The

unexpected visit in the middle of the night, the kindness, made him fill up.

"But listen. This house still feels like a funeral parlor, and right now it would do you a lot of good to get out of it more often. I have to go tomorrow night on some business, and I've been thinking anyway that it's time I took you with me. How about it? You're a man now, and I want to bring you with me on a man's business. You and I think alike on most things, don't we? Father and son. How about it?" Bud repeated, laying his warm hand on Tom's shoulder.

It felt so good to hear the words "father and son." "Yeah, Dad, I'd like to go."

When Bud left, Tom turned off the light. Father and son, he thought as he lay down. Bud had really steadied him. And now at last, he was able to sleep.

Bud drove home the next night in a small company van, a four-wheel drive with muddy fenders, explaining that they were going to the country and this was a country car.

Timmy asked, "How about me? Am I invited?"

"Not this time. You need rest, and we'll be home too late for you. Hop in, Tom."

The sinking red sun cast a hot glow over the familiar streets and glittered on the windows of familiar houses as they passed through their suburb, crossed the interstate on an overpass, and headed northward on a two-lane blacktop road. Tom asked where they were going.

"You'll see." Bud reached over and slapped Tom's knee. "You're my boy, aren't you?"

"Of course I am, Dad."

"I'm going to trust you with some very important information tonight."

"What is it?"

"Never mind. You'll see."

"How far are we going?"

"About twenty-five, thirty miles. Out to the sticks, the real country, where I grew up. Right near my home place, where our family's roots were planted two hundred fifty years ago.

That's a long time. Makes for deep roots. Not a whole lot of people these days can say that. Well, I guess you've heard me say it often enough, though. But you have to admit it's something to be proud of. Two hundred fifty years."

For some absolutely crazy reason, a recollection of that emotional old man, Albert, ranting about "a thousand years in Germany" popped into Tom's head. He wished to God that such thoughts would stop popping, those and dreams like the one he'd had a few nights ago: Margaret Crawfield had stood over him saying something horrible about his having lived nine months with her. Horrible. A nightmare.

The van jolted over holes so deep that they bounced in their seats.

Bud laughed. "Rattles your teeth, doesn't it? Must be mighty hard on a haywagon, these holes."

"Guess so," Tom mumbled.

The gray thoughts, like wisps of cloud, were still trailing, going nowhere. The dusk, gray too, now that the last pink streaks of afterglow were gone, hung over drab, impoverished fields among which lay, far apart, an occasional scattering of meager bungalows.

"You're awfully quiet. Must be the first time in your life you ever went five minutes without opening your mouth." When this teasing brought no response, Bud changed his tone. "Ah Tom, I know you're all worked up. And no wonder. Those tricky sons of bitches won't let you alone. But I'm going to put a stop to them, you'll see. Monday morning first thing I'm going to call Fordyce and tell him to muzzle those bastards once and for all. What the hell do I have a first-class lawyer for? He knows how to get after those bastards. So let him do it, and be quick about it. He knows. 'Crawfield'! 'Crawvitsky' is more like it!"

"There's nothing that Mr. Fordyce can do, Dad. He told you so. I heard him."

"Oh, that blood business. Why, any crook can cook up stuff like that, pay somebody, phony it up. Why, do you really believe it all, Tom? I know your mother does, but she's just scared, poor woman, so shocked that there's no fight left in her. But do you really believe it, Tom?"

"Dad, we've gone over this too often. I can't think of anything more to say."

"There's plenty to say. If you want to sit back and believe a lot of crap, that's one thing. But I don't want to, and I won't."

"Dad, you just said it yourself: You won't. You don't want to believe it. But you're too quick and smart not to see that it's true, all the same."

Tom swallowed something in his throat, a lump or a sob. He felt such tenderness. Surely Dad was able to put two and two together: Timmy's sickness and Peter Crawfield's. He felt such pity for him.

"It's because you love me," he said. "I understand."

"Yeah," Bud said roughly. "Yeah. I love you, all right."

They rode on. There was a hot stinging in Tom's eyes, and he kept them closed until it subsided. Shifting in discomfort, stretching his arm to rest on the back of the seat, he jumped and cried out.

"For Pete's sake, Earl's in the back. I just felt his cold nose, and for a second I thought it was a snake."

Bud groaned. "The little bugger must have jumped in while we were in the house. Now what'll we do? Timmy's probably tearing up the neighborhood looking for him right now."

"There's got to be a phone somewhere."

"Okay. There's a little jerkwater town at the next crossroads where we turn."

Earl was scratching to get into the front seat. Tom leaned over and lifted him onto his lap, where he settled himself in luxury. Fingering the shaggy hair, hugging the small, warm body, Tom imagined that he knew how Timmy got such comfort from a dog.

"Hasn't changed at all," Bud remarked as they approached the center of a town, whose nearness was heralded by a store with a Coca-Cola sign and a gas pump in front of it.

Two rows of unpainted houses, each with a front veranda, faced each other on either side of the road. Lights were on in all the back kitchens. Pickup trucks were parked, while in a few of the yards, near a shed, either behind or at the side of the house, lay a rusting wreck. At the four corners stood a wooden church, also in need of paint. Bud stopped between a beer joint and a garage.

"Toss-up. I'll try the garage first."

Tom waited. The silence here was oppressive. It was like a dead place with no one walking—but what would they be walking toward? A pickup passed, going too fast at a cross-roads, its radio blasting. And when it had gone, the silence closed back, a stillness as tight as a woolen muffler around one's neck. It was queer to think of Bud growing up in a place like this, Bud who went out in the Mercedes to address the Chamber of Commerce, Bud who wore a white carnation in his buttonhole when he passed the plate at the Memorial Methodist Church on Summerhill Avenue.

Somebody dropped a metal object inside the garage, making a clang and clatter, which were followed by a dirty curse, an answering curse, and a slammed door that blocked out sounds. After that, abruptly, as if to make purposeful contrast, rose a surging choir of crickets.

And from a place like this, Dad had gone away and married the beautiful young woman—for Mom was beautiful in her bridal photograph and was still beautiful—who lived in the old Paige house with the fine British library and could play for sheer pleasure a Beethoven sonata on the piano.

Bud's cheerful voice broke into these reflections. "Okay. I set Timmy's mind at rest. The poor guy was beside himself."

About to climb back into the front seat, he suddenly changed his mind, saying, "Wait a minute. I might as well do it now. Come back here and let me show you something."

A grocery carton filled with canned goods and cereal boxes lay on the backseat. Bud started to empty it.

"Here, give me a hand. Just lay this stuff on the floor."

Wondering, Tom helped remove the groceries. From the bottom of the box where it had been concealed, Bud withdrew what appeared to be a length of white cloth.

"Got to keep this out of sight," he explained. "You never know when you might get stopped or something. You have a fender-bender and some cop goes searching the car for drugs. Not that I blame him, but we people have to be careful. Especially a man in my position."

"I don't understand. What is this about?"

Bud laid the folded material in Tom's arms. There was a red circular insignia on the cloth, but in the dim light, Tom was not able to read its lettering. And he asked again what this was.

"You have no idea?"

Perhaps—perhaps he did have the glimmer of an idea. But it was so absolutely wild, so fantastically extreme to associate in any way with Mr. Homer Thomas Rice that he was embarrassed, for fear of seeming ridiculous, to tell it. So he shook his head.

"Son, I told you before we started out that I was going to admit you to a solemn secret You're old enough, wise enough, and trustworthy enough to hold it secret." Bud's voice grew deeper, even hushed, even here on this deserted roadside. "Tom, it's the Ku Klux Klan."

A cold thrill trembled up Tom's spine. All at the same time he was feeling a shock of disbelief, some troubling distaste, a good deal of excitement, curiosity, and a sense of adventure. Also a considerable fear . . .

"I never guessed," he said.

Bud laughed. "That was the general idea. I keep all this stuff hidden in my locker at the office. Come on, we have to get started. I'll tell you about it on the way."

Tom kept taking surreptitious glances at Bud's profile. It made no sense that Bud should suddenly look different, and yet it was true that he did. There was an image now in the eye of Tom's mind, an incredible image of Bud in a white robe with a tall peaked witch's hat, performing some occult rite before a burning cross. They were on the way right now to such a place. His heart began to pound.

"How long have you—" he began.

"I was a young man, about the time you were born. But I've been interested in it unofficially since I was a child. I had an uncle, my great-uncle actually, who used to tell me things, things he wasn't supposed to tell. He was a great talker. Everybody knew Henry could never keep a secret. Either he trusted me, or as I said, he just didn't know how to keep his mouth shut. By the way, I'm telling you because you can keep your mouth shut. And I mean completely, Tom. No word even to Timmy, hear?"

"I hear." Certainly not to Timmy, Tom thought. And he asked, "What about Mom?" Surely Mom wouldn't know about this.

"For God's sake, you know better than that. Your mother would disown me, I swear; she's so against what the Klan stands for." Bud sighed. "I wish I could talk openly to her—there are women auxiliaries in the Klan, you know—but it's impossible. She and those aunts of hers, good women, smart women, still don't see what's happening in the world around them. Yes, I wish I could be frank with her, bless her. This is the only thing I've ever kept from her." Bud sighed again. "Well, to get back to Uncle Henry. He used to tell stories about rallies back in the twenties, with concerts and picnics where they'd sign up new members by the hundreds. Once he smuggled me to a spot where I could watch a meeting. They had a burning cross, it must have been a hundred feet high. There was an electric feeling in the air, the whole mass of people united. I never forgot it."

Tom became aware that the cold fingers were still running up and down his spine. It was the way he had felt that night on Fairview, when the mob, screaming like banshees, had assaulted the house where the blacks lived. Could it have been the Klan's work that night? He had an eerie feeling, a sense of unreality now, about Bud's words, about the box on the backseat, and the lonely road curving through aisles of live oaks a hundred years old or more, with the moss hanging from them like the long gray hair of an old mad woman. And he hugged Earl closer to his chest.

Bud was reminiscing. "My dad was a preacher, as you know, but a lot of his folks picked cotton not far from here. Gosh, how my dad hated the Pope!" He gave his familiar chuckle. "Well, times change, and these days we don't hate the Pope all that much anymore. But Jews—that hasn't changed. Or blacks—my God, that never will."

Two needs warred in Tom: the need, born of fear, to hear no more, and the need at the same time to know the whole story.

"What—what is it that you actually do?" he asked, stammering a little.

"I personally? I'm the Grand of a Province. But I expect to be promoted soon to be Grand of a Dominion. The Empire is divided into five Departments. It's like a pyramid right up to the Grand Wizard at the top. All very well organized. Disciplined," Bud said proudly. "Interested, are you?"

"Oh, yes." Anybody would be interested in something so mysterious.

"You haven't asked about purposes or goals, but I suppose that's because you already know. It's not too different, after all, from the sort of things you write about in that newspaper of yours. In a sense, we're the fountainhead. Our ideas trickle down as they've trickled down to you already. Someday the trickle will be a mighty stream. Yes," Bud said, "yes, you'd be surprised at some of the names I could give you—but of course I can't—of prominent men who belong with us. That's to say nothing about millions of sympathizers, people who see how our way of life is threatened and who have the guts to join up with us. Because it takes guts. With the media and the FBI snooping, you're always on guard. You have to be. Why, look at Jim Johnson himself! He used to belong, you've heard that, but he's got to disavow us now if he wants to get elected. He has to condemn us. In a gingerly way, he has to skirt around the issues, never saying all of what he really thinks. But his heart's in the right place, Jim's is, and he's our man."

Our man. And with a little thrill, Tom recalled that day with Robbie and Jim Johnson, recalled the fine, educated manner, the frank, friendly attitude, the simple—was it too much to say "elegance"? — the simple elegance of his ideas. *Our way of life.* Contrasted to those *Crawfields,* to the homely, emotional old man with his tears, tears of the cast-out people whom nobody wanted, consider Jim Johnson's confident, optimistic smile. A winner's smile. If Jim Johnson belonged with these people where they were going tonight, it had to be all right. And Bud — Bud wasn't a man to make mistakes, either. Bud was a doer. He knew what he was about.

It will be all right, Tom thought. There's no reason to fear. And a soothing relief poured through him from head to foot.

"We're almost there," Bud said, "so I'll hurry and finish what I have to say for now. Tonight I want you to stand back and observe. I think you're in for a grand thrill. Then, if I'm not mistaken, you'll want to join us. It's not easy to be accepted. You have to be worthy, you know. They do a thorough investigation of your connections and family and of your antecedents. But given my position, they'll be no problem."

The soothing relief drained away as quickly as it had poured in. Very softly, Tom asked, "Antecedents? What if —"

Bud did not allow him to finish. "That crap again? I told you, forget it, Tom. I mean that. Forget that lying crap."

But if it was to leak out, not right now but a year from now or ten years from now, what horrors would result! All his life, this threat was to hang over him. He was marked. And his hatred of the Crawfields was like the taste of rot in his mouth.

They had turned off the road onto a dirt lane bordering a swamp. In the eerie black-and-silver night, you could discern the knobby knees of cypress roots rising out of the water, where surely water moccasins lurked and slithered. On the dry side of the lane great tree trunks were covered with wisteria, twisting and gnarled as a rope-veined arm. The hot, wet air seeped under the thinnest cotton cloth and clung to the skin.

Then, unexpectedly, the lane came to an end, and a wide space opened up before them. It was an enormous field, almost half of it taken up by rows of parked cars. Between them and the towering cross at the other end of the field, men in

white robes were gathered as if waiting to proceed somewhere. A curious, churchlike silence hung over the scene.

"We're late," Bud whispered. "Help me with the box.
Hurry."

Together, they unloaded the groceries. Bud put on the robe
and a tall pointed hat that covered his face except for two eye
holes. The hat added a foot to his height, and his eyes glittered
through the holes. He had been transformed.

"You can join the rest of the spectators as soon as we form
our circle," he said.

Tom watched him move off to join the robed group and
become indistinguishable from the mass. He was trying to
analyze his own vacillating feelings: his anger because of his
personal uncertainties, the return of his fear, and, too, the
comforting reassurance that Jim Johnson approved of what
was happening here.

Now the hooded men were forming into a line of march,
two by two. Each carried a lighted torch in his left hand. With
even tread, their feet soundless on the grass, they approached
the cross. There was an ominous quality to this united movement, and yet there was also something ridiculous about it
that gave rise to a nervous titter in Tom's throat, a titter
swiftly stifled as he became aware of the security guards who
stood about. These men, unrobed, were most visibly equipped
with knives and handcuffs. No doubt they were invisibly
armed with revolvers, too.

Many spectators were walking toward the circle that was
now spread before the cross. But filled as he was with this
confusion of excitement and uneasiness, he stayed at the out-
ermost fringe of the crowd. To see Bud—Dad—up there laying his torch at the foot of the cross was unreal. Yet it was
fascinating. And he stood quite still watching until the final
torch had been laid down and the fire had raced up the length
of the cross to light the sky.

Far to the front at the base of the cross, a leader took his
place, said a long prayer while all heads were bowed, then
gave a stiff-armed Nazi salute and began to speak.

"This cross burns for freedom, our freedom," he was saying, when Tom was abruptly distracted by, of all things, the sight of Earl racing toward the distant circle. One of the van's doors, not properly shut, had obviously swung open and now here was Earl running, quite certainly in search of Bud. It would disturb the ceremony to run after him, and anyway, Tom thought with some amusement, his nose will pick Bud out of the crowd. Disguised or not, there's no way to fool a dog's nose.

"—the struggle against foreign elements who are sucking our strength, the heritage that is ours." In combat against rising wind, the speaker had begun to shout. "International bankers, parasites, and swindlers, do we need them?"

From the listeners there came in response a furious "No!"

Surprised, Tom thought, Dad has studied business administration and he must know that, especially now in this new global economy, we do need international bankers. If some of them should be crooked, a lot of other people are crooked, too: doctors, lawyers, teachers, car salesmen, politicians, anybody. So what does that prove? Nothing, except that some people have always been dishonest. No doubt, though, Dad would excuse the speaker. He would say that no movement can be one hundred percent correct all the time and that you have to make allowances for oratory.

So Tom listened to the oratory, thinking that he himself, or Robbie, could have written all these words and done it more fluently, too. Yet these words were far more extreme, far more bloody, than anything he had ever even thought of! He felt his shocked heart racing, and something pulsing in his throat.

"Our brave ancestors shed their blood to make this country what it is, and if we have to shed more to keep it for ourselves, out of the hands of undesirables, we'll do it."

Another roar of approval went up as the words flowed on.

"We must prepare! We must have guns and know how to use them without hesitation. No more false, hypocritical mercy, no excuses. The enemy surrounds us, and—"

Clouds driven by the strengthening wind were darkening

the field and eclipsing the stars. Tom, looking upward, caught a glimpse of the Milky Way, and his thoughts were distracted from the booming voice, now grown too repetitious to hold his attention. How vast it was, this thick stream of stars, compared with the little earth on which he stood! And how small it was compared with the far galaxies beyond it, the unknown world so far past the reach of even our most powerful instruments! There is so much to know, he thought. We are only at the beginning.

People were singing. The melody was "Home, Sweet Home"; only the words were unfamiliar.

> "We all will stand together, forever and for aye,
>   home, home, country and home.
> Klansmen, we'll live and die for our country and home.
> Klansmen, we —"

It came as anything totally unexpected comes, incomprehensible as a gunshot or the strike of lightning on a summer afternoon. It came with a mad roar and a rush of air. It was gone before, seconds afterward, anyone realized that a powerful car had sped out of the dark lane and plowed through the circle at the cross. It tore a diagonal path across the field, and on screeching tires, disappeared at the far end before anyone could possibly identify it. Left behind was a momentary silence, followed by screaming bedlam.

For fully half a minute, Tom stood stunned. Moving clouds had passed away from the moon so that in the new flood of light, he saw men throwing off robes and hoods; he saw men lying on the ground, saw people running, some of them fleeing to the parked cars and others gathering around the injured — injured or dead. Then he also ran.

"Not Dad! Oh, please God, not Dad."

He looked wildly about for Bud, crying, "Who? Where?" into strange faces who did not answer.

There were three inert bodies. He was afraid, paralyzed, his legs not willing to move toward them and his eyes not willing to look at them. Their hoods had been removed, exposing the faces to the greenish light of the moon. And finally he made himself look because he knew. He simply knew.

The first was an unknown. The second, to his horror, was Rod Pitt, the genial general manager of Rice and Son. The third had a bloody head and a broken body, its legs twisted the wrong way, its arms a pulp . . . Tom fell down howling.

"Jesus!" someone said. "That's his kid."

How long he lay there he never knew, but it could not have been very long because the police and ambulances had not yet arrived. He came out of a faint to find himself half hidden in a thicket behind the last rank of parked cars near Bud's van. Two men raised him to a sitting-up position and held a glass to his lips.

"Drink it," one said. "You need it."

His liquor was beer and a very occasional mixed drink; he was unused to anything so strong, and it almost blew him apart. But it cleared his head. The full reality of what had happened came surging back, and he began quietly to sob. Then suddenly, as a thought struck him, he cried out, "Are you sure he's dead? Maybe he's just badly hurt, and they can—"

"No, son. No, your dad is dead. Three dead," the man said grimly, "and seven with broken bones, but they'll be all right. Somebody went to call for ambulances."

Tom whimpered, "Who did this? Who?"

"Some bastard. Went like a bat out of hell. Threw a cardboard message on the ground. Said, 'Die, you scum.' But never mind, kid. We'll have our day. When we get him we'll string him up. Your dad would be the first to say that. Remember it. Remember him and stick with us. You'll see. We'll have our day, and it won't be too goddamn long before we have it."

And now, like the fire that had swept up the cross, a terrible, vengeful rage swept through Tom. If he could have gotten hold of the men who did that to his dad, to Bud, who, not an hour ago, had put his hand, his hand that was always so warm, on his son's shoulder and told him how he loved him — oh, if he could get hold of that rotten creature! Tom's fists clenched and his jaw clenched, even while his cheeks were still wet with his tears.

The rage burst out of him. "Son of a bitch! I want to tear his heart out!"

Both men nodded, and one said, "You've got plenty of company. Stay mad. It'll do you good once you get over your first grieving. Then you can put your shoulder to the wheel for the cause. Bud Rice's boy will carry on Bud Rice's work. Stand tall. Be proud. He'd want you to."

Tom got to his feet. "You're right," he said quietly. "You're right, and I will."

Looking around, he saw that most of the cars had departed. A few men near the now smoldering remains of the cross were standing guard over the injured and the dead. And he waited uncertainly, not knowing what he was supposed to do.

One of the men took command. "Let's get him out of here before the cops come with a million questions. Suppose you take Bud's van and drive him home. He's in no condition to drive himself."

"Yes, I can," Tom protested. "I can drive."

"No, kid. Do as we say. Get in."

"I want to stay at least till they take — take my dad away." Again his voice broke.

"No, kid. Get in."

He thought of something else. "There was a dog. My brother's little dog."

"Was that yours? A little gray mutt? He was there close to Bud. We threw his body into the bushes."

"You threw it away? But I want it! I have to bring it home."

"You don't want it. It's crushed."

"Yes, I do. I do," Tom wailed.

The man shrugged. "Okay. Go bring it to him, Phil, will

you, while I turn the van around and get us the hell away from here?"

They laid the small heap of blood-clotted fur on the front seat between Tom and the driver.

"This it? This your dog?"

"Yes, that's Earl."

Tom picked him up and held him close on his lap. The red collar was intact, the fine new collar that Timmy had bought with his Christmas money.

About five or six miles down the road they passed three police cars and three ambulances going in the opposite direction.

"Reporters can't be far behind," grumbled the driver. "Newspaper bastards will have a field day with this."

In a few minutes from now, Bud will be carried down this road. They will take him somewhere. To the hospital first, most probably, there to be pronounced officially dead so they can keep records and sign papers. The last of Bud. Never to hear his voice again: *Come on, guys, let's have a catch.* This will kill Timmy. How are we going to tell him? The kid's so frail. How am I going to tell Mom? Oh God, oh Christ, how did this happen? I swear to God I'll spend my life finding out who did it, and I'll kill him. Torture him first.

So Tom sat with his fierce, bitter thoughts and the little dead dog held tight. The engine hummed. The cricket choir sang through the silence.

Laura, in her pink bathrobe, was on the big lounge chair in the bedroom reading when the doorbell rang. She wondered, since it was past nine o'clock, who it could possibly be. Cautiously, she went down and opened the door a few inches with the chain on.

"Police, ma'am. Are you Mrs. Rice?"

She went cold. Through the crack in the doorway she was able to see the uniform and in the driveway the car with flashing lights."

"Yes," she said. "Come in."

He entered the hall and stood there, halting, with his cap in his hand. Very young, younger than Laura, he was as frightened as she.

"There's been an accident," he began. "There was a driver's license with the name of Homer Rice. That is, there was no car, just the license. Is—was—he your husband?"

She stared at him, thinking, He doesn't know what he's saying.

In the same instant, apparently, he realized that he was not making sense, so he added gently, "What I meant was, there was a meeting out in the country, out near Ramsey, and it seems that a wild car drove through, ran over some people, and—I wasn't there, so I only know what I was told."

There was, fortunately, a row of chairs in the hall, for her knees would not have carried her any farther.

"Homer Rice. My husband. Is he—" And she set her dry lips.

"The report is—he's dead, ma'am." The young man caught her arm as she swayed. "Is there—are you alone in the house? Is there anybody to call?"

She thought: I am watching this. I have seen it before. In the movies the woman's face goes dead, she is still and calm, a zombie who can't quite believe what has happened.

She said stiffly, "If you will call my friend who lives ten minutes away, she'll come." And she gave Betty Lee's number. Her best friend Betty Lee would come. "The telephone's in there. No, I'll just sit here."

Bud. A meeting near Ramsey. A car. Bud is dead. How queer. No, of course it's not true. It's somebody's stupid mistake. The wrong name. The wrong place.

Then something struck her, and she screamed, "Tom! Tom!" rose from the chair and sank back with her hand on her heart.

The policeman came running. "Let me get your doctor. You shouldn't be here like this. You—"

She stared up at him, crying wildly, imploring him, "Where's my son? What happened to Tom?"

"I don't know, ma'am. Nobody said anything. Only Mr. Homer Rice. Nothing about any Tom. I'm sure they would have if—"

Yes, of course they would have. They wouldn't have sent the man here with only one name to report if there had been two. Would they? Would they? She gripped the arms of the chair and straightened her back. She whispered out loud.

"Hold on. Don't make a spectacle of yourself. You have to wait. Something awful happens, and people have to wait until something else can be done about it. That's all it is. Wait, Laura."

Then as she saw the anxious expression on the young man's face (he thinks I'm about to go mad), she fell silent, holding her gaze toward the photographs opposite, the ones of her father in uniform and of her mother who waited at home, not knowing as each day's sun rose, whether he was still alive.

When the doorbell rang, the officer answered, and she heard him murmuring in the vestibule to Betty Lee, so that when Betty Lee rushed to her, it was unnecessary to say a word, only to hold on to the strong shoulder.

"You can leave us, Officer," Betty Lee told him. "I'm here." And she told Laura to drink brandy. "I know you hate it, but even a thimbleful will help. Take my word."

"They say Bud is dead. I don't know what to do. Betty Lee, I don't know what to do."

"You need somebody here to tell you what happened, if it's happened. You need somebody."

Then it came to Laura: Fordyce would find out for her. He knew everyone. He wouldn't like being called at home, but no matter.

"Our lawyer, Mr. Fordyce. His number's in the book. Will you call him for me? I can't seem to move off this chair. My legs have gone all strange. They won't hold me."

She heard wheels on the ground. A motor came up the rise, chugging like Bud's van, and this time her legs did hold her as far as the kitchen door, where she fell upon Tom as he came in weeping at sight of her, sobbing in unintelligible gasps as she sobbed, too, and clasped him.

"Tom! Tom!"

"Oh Mom, what they did to him! If you could see—oh Jesus, what they did! But it was fast, so fast that I know he couldn't have been scared, because he couldn't have known it was coming. Like a knife in the back, the dirty bastards. They wouldn't harm anybody, all those people, only a little while before they'd been praying in front of the cross, imagine it! And then the dirty, murdering bastards—"

It took five minutes to quiet this hysteria. Now, because Tom was alive, because he needed her, Laura's legs began sturdily to hold her again, and her thoughts began to function.

In the library, as though the presence of a thousand books had some quieting effect, Tom spoke coherently. When Laura asked what kind of meeting it had been, he answered with only a trace of hesitation or reluctance.

"It was a gathering of the Ku Klux Klan. Dad was a member. I never knew that until he told me in the car on the way there."

"The Ku Klux Klan!"

"Yes." At Laura's exclamation, Tom raised his head with elevated chin, in a movement either of pride or of defiance. "He didn't want you to know because he said you wouldn't approve."

So you could live all these years with a person and not know a thing as fundamental as this . . .

"He held high office," Tom said, "and he was about to be promoted. He'd been a member since the time I was born."

The boy was not ashamed. There was an ignited spark in his wet eyes. And a shudder of fearful dismay shook through Laura.

"I plan to spend the rest of my life getting even. They killed my father." And Tom clenched his fists. "He knew what he was talking about when he told me that enemies are everywhere. Little did he know they were coming after him. That very minute, they were on their way, while we were riding along minding our own business and he was telling me how he loved me." Tom's voice rose loud and cracking.

"What's the matter?" asked Timmy. "You woke me up. What's the matter, Tom? You're crying."

Tom sprang up and grabbed his brother into a tight hug. "Timmy, you've got to be brave. We've both got to be. We've lost our father, lost Dad."

"What do you mean 'lost'? Is he dead?"

"He's dead, Timmy. We were at an outdoor meeting, there was a crowd and then a kill-and-run driver came through as fast as a bullet and ran right over people. Oh God, it was the worst thing I ever saw!"

Tom sobbed again, Timmy screamed, and Laura put her hands over her face to shut out the sight. And the three stayed huddled in the dim, lamp-lit room.

When Fordyce arrived, he was as efficient as always, quick to get the expected commiseration over with and to come to the point.

"I collected the reports by car phone on the way here. There are no suspects and not likely to be any found. There are three dead. Homer, your manager Pitt, and, to my astonishment, Luther Tyson, of all people, from the Merchants and Providence Trust. I would never have guessed it in a million years. The Ku Klux Klan! Not that I would have guessed it about Homer, either," Fordyce added with his nose wrinkled in disdain.

Much as Laura otherwise disliked the man's habitual cold arrogance, she could hardly fault him for his disdain of the Ku Klux Klan and for anyone, for any "gentleman" who would identify himself with it. Besides, she knew Fordyce hadn't thought much of Bud lately; he had scarcely tried to hide his exasperation with him because of his conduct in the Crawfield affair.

Tom spoke up. "Dad held an important office. He was soon to be the Grand of a Dominion."

Fordyce did not answer, but addressing Laura instead, asked whether she had known about Bud's membership.

Tom answered for her. "Dad said he didn't tell Mom because he knew she wouldn't approve. She doesn't—didn't—even approve of his supporting Johnson for the senate."

Fordyce gave him an angry look. "Suppose you let your mother speak for herself," he said.

This harshness, slight as it was, brought fresh tears to Laura's eyes; she was abruptly conscious of herself, a pitiable figure, disheveled in her dressing gown, an instant widow with a frail, sick boy and a defiant one. She could read the pity in Fordyce's eyes.

"Tom," she said firmly, "don't interrupt, please. I am at sea, and Mr. Fordyce has come here to the rescue."

Fordyce looked grateful. "So you were not aware at all."

"Not at all. He always said he had almost no interest in politics."

Fordyce nodded. "This will cause some stir in the business community. I'm afraid a lot of respectable people are going to come under suspicion. When a man in Tyson's position hides under a robe and hood, it makes you wonder. Well," he said briskly, "that's none of your concern tonight, is it? I was wondering, is there anybody you'd like me to inform? Save you the task? Your aunts, of course."

"No, I'm not going to send a cable to Egypt or wherever they might be now and frighten the life out of them. To say nothing of spoiling their once-in-a-lifetime trip."

"You'll make your own—arrangements, then? I suppose you'll want it at Foster's church?"

"Yes, Bud was an active member." How can that have been? It made no sense, mixing the Klan with a church that stood for everything directly opposite.

"I'll be happy to call him for you. I go to church at the other end of town, but I know Foster well. We were at prep school at the same time, he a year behind me. As a matter of fact, I think I should call him right now. It might help you to have a talk with him tonight."

"Thank you. I'd like that."

Tom and Timmy also needed a kind, strong voice. Timmy

looked like a forlorn young bird, sitting there with his wide mouth, Bud's mouth, hanging open.

In spite of his courtesy, there was no comfort in Fordyce's flat, brief sentences. No doubt he would prefer to wash his hands of clients like us, Laura thought. This was the second time in weeks that the Rices had given him work he would much rather not do.

At that moment, Timmy burst forth with a cry so piercing that everyone jumped.

"What happened to Earl? Tom, is Earl dead, too?"

"Earl?" asked Fordyce.

"His dog." And Laura turned a questioning look toward Tom, who made a helpless gesture.

"He was standing with Dad."

"So they killed him, too?" Timmy shrieked.

"Yes." Tom's arm drew Timmy close. "I brought him home. I thought you might want to bury him in the backyard."

Timmy wrested himself away, demanding, "Where is he? I want to see him."

Betty Lee, who had come running in from the kitchen, interposed. "No, you don't, honey. I looked, and I think you should remember him as he was."

But Timmy was already brushing past her. Laura heard the backdoor slam, Tom's and Betty Lee's protests, and last, Timmy's anxious wail at the sight of Earl's body, which Tom had apparently left where the van was parked.

Frightened, Laura murmured, "He's still weak, just out of the hospital. This is too much for him."

"You have your hands full."

The remark was banal and Fordyce regretted it immediately. But he was no good at this sort of thing, uncomfortable with what one might call "human interest" problems. He was a lawyer's lawyer, adept at the unraveling of knots, and would be helpful in the crisis that would inevitably occur at Rice and Son. With Pitt dead, there'd be no one left to manage it.

He was glad, though, that he had at least been able to keep the Crawfield matter out of the newspapers, so far, anyway. It was all she needed, to have that affair leaked to the world! Poor woman. He was relieved when the bell rang and Foster arrived.

At midnight Laura and Tom were still in the library with the minister. The doctor, whom Foster consulted over the telephone, had recommended hot milk for Timmy and bed rest at once. Against his will, Betty Lee had managed to get him to bed and he was now asleep.

"I remember you in Sunday school when you were in first grade," Foster told Tom. He was by now so weary that even his voice was weak. "Why ever do you think that you can stand out in my mind from so many other children after all this time? Well, for one thing, because you were such a bright little boy, and for another I suppose, because I knew your parents so well. They were involved, always involved, in the community."

"That's what makes no sense!" Laura cried yet again. "How Bud could be—and to think that his father was a preacher, too!"

"The religion that Bud grew up with is not yours and not mine," Foster said quietly. "It was fire and brimstone, mostly. Those were narrow lives in narrow places."

"But to have dissembled all these years!" And she clasped her hands together as if beseeching an explanation from Foster.

"That's not uncommon, Laura, unfortunately."

Tom had been fidgeting, trying to control himself in the minister's presence. Now he gave in to anger.

"You talk, both of you, as if Dad had been some sort of monster. How can you talk that way about him? You, especially, Mom. I can't believe the things I'm hearing you say."

"I never said he was a monster. He was my husband. But the things he obviously believed in—guns, blood, hate—those things are monstrous. To hate another human being because he's not quite like you, when he has as much right to live on earth as you have!"

"He hasn't. That's hogwash. People aren't equal, and one man is not as good as another."

Dr. Foster interrupted. "When you were in Sunday school, we didn't teach you anything like that, Tom. And I, too, have read some of the Klan's program, supposedly written in God's name, and it's heresy, that's what it really is. I'm astonished that you don't see it, Tom," he finished.

"I didn't say I believe in the Klan." He felt naked in the chair with those two pairs of sorrowful eyes judging him. He felt martyred for Bud's sake. My father, he thought, and continued, "But some kinds of people *are* better than others. I'll stand by that. And those people who killed my father—" His anger flowed into a rage. "I'm going to find out who did that and torture him to death."

Foster said quietly, "I understand. Yes, I do. But that would solve nothing except to add more pain to your life."

Laura grimaced. Pain, she thought. And Foster doesn't even know about Tom's real pain.

Tom got up. "Excuse me, but I can't talk anymore, and I'm going upstairs. Good night, Mom. Good night, Dr. Foster."

Laura and Foster exchanged hopeless glances. There was nothing more to say, and so Foster left, and Laura went to lock all the doors for the night.

At the kitchen door, feeling a sudden need for space and air, she stepped outside, and if it had not been for the light streaming out from the kitchen, would have stumbled over a box that lay on the step. What was left of Earl, a nauseous mess of entrails and fur, lay on a neatly arranged square of flowered cretonne, the remnant of some old slipcovers that had been stored in the attic. No doubt this was Betty Lee's kind work in preparation for the burial in the morning. Poor Timmy. Oh, poor Timmy, she thought.

And then came horror. The dog had been next to Bud when it happened. So then, Bud, too, had been mangled, mutilated . . . This was the picture in Tom's head, the picture that would be in his head always, always to the end of his days.

She retched, vomited, cried and vomited into the bushes

behind the garage. Then, shaken, she stood for a minute or two looking up into the sky, into the magnificence that so inspired Tom. But the indifferent, endless glitter refused to answer any questions or to console her spirit, and she went back into the house.

The night wore on. It was curious how her thoughts kept running in random, zigzag directions like chipmunks in foolish chase across the grass. And yet, perhaps there was a pattern to such a chase; you had to watch it for long enough to see the repeat in the design. She stretched her arm across the bed; the sheet, which should have been warmed by Bud's body, was smooth and cool; he would never sleep here again. How strange to think that last night when he lay down he had no way of knowing that he would never rest here again!

He had been good to her. Without ever truly knowing her, he had been good. And she remembered how he had wanted her, how he had made himself fit into this house and family, he, the ambitious young man so eager to please. Yet all the time he had had that other life, that mean, ugly life of an underworld. A secret mistress would be easier to accept.

Stiff and straight, lying like a corpse herself, she stared up at the ceiling. If this death—terrible word—had not happened, what would have come next? Would I have stayed with him forever? she asked herself. If he had not died, but she had somehow discovered his connection with the Klan, could she possibly have stayed under the same roof with such a man? She did not think it possible. But if everything had gone on as it had been during those few weeks since they had learned about Tom and Peter—Peter Crawfield, who was the image of Timmy, my Peter—what then would she have done?

Erratic thoughts leapt, making parallels. She'd had a lace dress long ago, a precious white lace dress, an extravagance that Aunt Cecile had "made" her buy. Over and over, she had tended that dress as it wore out, knotting the first loose threads, catching the next tiny rent, mending and hiding the splits one after the other, wearing the dress as long as the fabric could be decently held together, until eventually there came a tear too wide to be bound up, and the dress had to go. Perhaps her life with Bud had been like that and had been destined to end even without his death.

But the boys! How they loved him! Plenty of women these days wouldn't let that stand in the way of divorce, she knew that well. Plenty of women would, though, and did, not because they were martyrs, but because they were mothers. And Laura Rice was one of those.

These were futile maunderings. And yet, futile or not, there now came a stab of guilt, as if the presence in her thoughts of Ralph Mackenzie could have been in some way connected with Bud's death. That was crazy, of course. Death always gives rise to irrational thoughts on the part of the survivors, especially when they are not as grief-stricken as people expect them to be. She had read that many times.

Poor Bud.

She must have fallen asleep toward dawn because the sun was high when she was awakened by the sound of voices in the yard. From the bedroom window the view was clear all the way to the boundary hedge near the old Alcott house. There, under a redbud tree, the boys were burying Earl. Between them stood Betty Lee. And how to look into the face of this lady who had been serving Bud Rice all these years? She had either stayed in the house all night or come back early. She was holding a little clutch of flowers. Timmy was evidently speaking, perhaps saying a prayer; Tom shoveled earth over the tiny grave and Timmy laid the flowers on it.

"Oh God, help them," Laura whispered. What was going to happen to her boys, each of them with a rare, special burden of his own?

After her shower, she stood undecided at the clothes closet. She owned nothing black except a silk dinner dress; something would have to be ordered for the funeral. All her clothes were bright except those that were white, so white would have to do, a cotton skirt and sweater.

The boys were finishing breakfast when she came downstairs. They were wearing dark blue pants and starched white shirts. Tom gave her a sharp look.

"No black?" His tone reproved her.

"I have nothing. White is summer mourning, anyway."

"I'm going downtown to get black ties for Timmy and me."

"That's a good idea. Charge them at Benninger's. I have to phone for something black for myself," she said, feeling the need to explain. She, the mother, explaining to Tom. He was forcing guilt upon her.

Betty Lee said, "I put the *Sentinel* and the *Courier* on the back veranda for you to read. I figured you wouldn't want to be seen from the street this morning. Reporters will be coming."

"To the house? Oh, do you think so?"

"Sure as shooting." Betty Lee's mouth was grim. "Wait till you read the papers."

She sat down to read. There were headlines: PROMINENT COMMUNITY LEADERS MOWED DOWN AT KLAN RALLY; TYSON, RICE, AND PITT KILLED IN KLAN ROBES. There were subheadings: *No Clue to Driver of Death Car; Luther Tyson, Prominent Supporter of Jim Johnson.*

Down the column went Laura's eyes, and the letters rose from the page as if they were coming to life. The scene of the horror took color: the orange-red burning cross, the dark, the moonlight, the headlights of the ambulances and the police cars, figures running to and fro, the injured writhing on the grass, the gory dead.

She skimmed the first paper and made an exchange with Tom to read disjointed words and phrases. *Homer Rice, a well-known figure in the civic life of the city . . . the old firm of Paige and Rice . . . three generations . . . prominent family . . . survived by wife Laura and two sons, Thomas and Timothy.*

She skimmed the indignant editorials. *The respectable navy blue suit, the proper collar and tie, the affable manners and correct opinions disguising the real man who, in robe and mask, waits with his kin at night in secret to spread this evil disease . . .*

She was numb. Flexing her legs and hands, it actually

seemed to her that they were chilled, as though the blood had ceased to flow through them.

Jim Johnson can disclaim the Klan a hundred times over, but if his aims are so different from its, it behooves him to explain why so many of its members are also his supporters.

"Have you read all this?" Laura asked.

"Yes, I've read it," Tom replied.

"And?"

"And it's not worth the paper it's written on."

She got up to avoid any more words with him and went inside. The doorbell had begun to ring as she had known it would; friends and neighbors would be coming to bring food, offer whatever help she might need—and also, now that they had read the news, to satisfy their very natural curiosity.

Reporters came with photographers, who caught her on the front veranda, trying to answer with as much coolness as she could muster a clamor of questions.

"Are you then saying, Mrs. Rice, that you actually knew nothing about your husband's connection to the KKK?"

"I am saying just that."

"How is that possible, Mrs. Rice?"

"It's possible because he never told me."

"And why do you suppose that was?"

"Because he knew," Laura said patiently, "that I would have been horrified. He respected me enough not to want that to happen."

One of the neighbors from down the street, losing patience with a string of reporters, told Laura to go back into the house, and shouted at them.

"Have you no decency? Go away and let the poor woman alone."

Flowers arrived with notes of sympathy. Telephone calls came from people whom Laura had not seen in years, some of them men and women who had been at school with her or with Bud. Toward evening there came a call from Ralph Mackenzie.

In his direct and simple way, he asked only, "How can I help you?"

"I can't think of anything now, but I will call you if I do."

"I've heard from Margaret and Arthur. If they can be of any help—" And he corrected himself. "I'm sorry. I shouldn't be mentioning it. This isn't the time."

"You can speak out to me, Ralph."

"No, it really isn't the time. Well, all right. They're concerned about Tom. The paper they read said he was there, and they're wondering whether that was true."

"Yes, Tom was there. He'd gone along with Bud."

"Well," Ralph said.

"Tell them I feel just as bad about that as they possibly can feel. But tell them that Tom's otherwise all right, not to worry. Oh, here he is now."

"I'll hang up, Laura. Just remember where I am if you need me."

"I suppose that was Mackenzie," Tom said.

She turned to face a thin, bitter mouth and hard eyes. "Yes, a condolence call, like all the others."

"Like all the others," he repeated.

She followed him outdoors to where he had sat down at his usual place on the steps. An unopened book lay beside him. His eyebrows rested on his knees, and his head was in his hands. For a moment she stood unspeaking; the air was too thick with sorrow, the cicadas' drill too loud, the oak leaves too dreary and dusty in the heat, to collect any thoughts.

Tom raised his head. "Who's not to worry about me? Those Crawfields, I suppose."

"Yes, they care about you, Tom. They care very much."

"They have no right to. I'm nothing to them. They're nothing to me."

She laid her hand lightly on his hand, asking, "Tom, tell me, is there anything at all that I can do for you?"

The reply was so low that she barely heard it. "Nothing. Nothing."

She left him sitting there. The rage that had been firing him had used itself up, leaving a residue of caustic ash.

That Mackenzie, a meddling do-gooder if there ever was one! He probably had his eye on Mom, too. And those others who "care about you, Tom." Never. Never. A long struggle lay ahead, perhaps a lifelong struggle, unless he were to leave here and disappear on some other continent. Now that Bud was gone, there was no one to stand up with him or for him. Mom had not the faintest comprehension of his feelings, and Timmy was still a little guy, eleven years old, for heaven's sake, with a hell of a problem of his own.

If only Robbie were here! He wouldn't even need many words; once the first few bare facts were told, she'd grasp his meaning and take him into her arms with that hot, vigorous little body, hard yet pliable as rubber, the lips so soft, the hair slippery as silk spread over the pillow, the scent of flowers, the— If only she were here!

CHAPTER

—— 14 ——

Lugubrious chords descended from the organ loft, and a mournful purple light flickered through stained-glass windows as the sun went in and storm clouds gathered. All this was appropriate to the occasion, Laura reflected, as were her gloved hands resting on the lap of her black linen suit. Correct as he had been, Bud would approve the fine decorum of his sons in their dark suits and black ties; he would be pleased at the large and distinguished assembly here to say their farewells. How many of these people had come out of sympathy, and how many had come because it was an "event," she had no way of knowing, nor did it really matter.

She still felt numb. She still had that odd sensation of being at the same time outside of herself, observing the event and observing her own numb demeanor. Her eyes roved upward to the top of the windows, which were now quite dark. It would be raining by the time they reached the cemetery. Her eyes roved to the coffin, directly in front of her. They had asked her whether she wanted a "last look" before it was closed, but Dr. Foster had advised against that, no doubt because the body was so mutilated; hadn't Tom said something about the face? So there Bud lay under a sheaf of carnations with everything ended, everything: ball games with Timmy and Tom, Chamber of Commerce meetings, Rice and Son, along with the sinister robe and hood. Laura shivered.

Dr. Foster was giving a remarkable performance, a feat to tax the most ingenious sermonizer. On the one hand it was imperative to condemn, while on the other it was humane to recall with praise.

"We must view each life with compassion. No life is perfect. We can be loving parents and responsible citizens, and at the same time we can stray into dark places. The powerful forces, inner or outer or both together, that lead us into these are many and complex. It is not for us here to analyze Homer Rice, but rather to remember him as the friend he was, and to pray. Pray for him, for the man who killed him, and for us all."

Heads were bowed, while a soft murmuring accompanied the mellow voice. Timmy and Tom wiped their eyes. The organ played a recessional while the coffin was carried down the aisle between the ranks of men and women standing in respect. The next stop was the cemetery.

Bud always hated funerals, Laura remembered. He feared death, possibly more than most people did. She remembered that, too. Poor Bud.

On the way back home the rain was a torrent, so that the long black car had to crawl. She sat silently with her sons. There was, after all, nothing much to say, she thought again, perhaps for the hundredth time. Or maybe there was too much to say, so much that it seemed too discouraging to begin.

Tom said, "Mackenzie was in church. I saw him in the back row when we were going out."

"I didn't see him." Surely he needn't have come, but he had wanted to, and she was touched. A little lump came to her throat; in another second her eyes would be wet. She said quickly, "That was nice of him."

"I hate him," Tom answered.

Complications. There were too many. The windshield wiper raced from side to side, unable to cope with the rain. The car moved through the city toward the familiar home, now be-

come so strange, a hostile place filled with all these complications. And why? Why me, why us?

The question was: Where is my direction? In the first days
after the funeral, Laura went from her desk to Bud's, aim-
lessly sorting papers, bank statements, letters of condolence,
and a printout from the laboratory proving that Tom was a
Crawfield.

She leapt from the chair as if she had been shot. And, indeed, a wild thought had shot through her head: Just let us
get away from here. Away from Crawfields and the KKK, we
can get back the peace we had, my boys and I. With eyes
closed, she twirled the great globe and put out a finger. Someone must have tilted the globe so that her finger landed on
Patagonia, that vast, barren stretch at the tip of South America on the route to the South Pole.

"Well, that figures," she said aloud, "on a par with the rest
of our luck this awful year."

Then the telephone rang. Bud's secretary, Mrs. Fallon,
hated to bother her at such a time, but really, it was important.

"Nobody's running things, Mrs. Rice. The orders aren't going out, and five of the men reported sick this morning.
They're taking advantage, of course. But they'll be in later this
week to collect their wages, you can be sure." Mrs. Fallon,
who was a responsible woman, was much worried. "That
large project of Salsberg Brothers, those condos out on Route
Nine, you know?"

Laura had heard some mention of it, but little else. She only
knew that Bud had been jubilant over the order.

"Well, they've canceled. They're going elsewhere for their
supplies. They're Jewish, and with this stuff about the KKK,
well, you can imagine. And the MacDonald job fell through,
too. One of the typists there told me that the old man Mac-
Donald felt uncomfortable about dealing with Rice anymore.
So there we are, Mrs. Rice. I can't tell you how I feel for you
and the boys, Tom especially. He's such a fine young man.

The men all like him here. It's too bad he's not old enough to take over."

"Well, I'll think. I'll get some advice. I'll do what I can. And thank you," Laura said.

She sighed. If the aunts were still young enough and willing besides, there would be no problem. But they had been businesswomen since girlhood, while I—well, I have been a good mother and not-quite-first-rate pianist. What do I know about cement and two-by-fours?

Betty Lee came in, whispering that there was a visitor. "Mrs. Edgewood would like to see you if it's convenient. That's the black family who had all the trouble last month, you remember?"

Indeed Laura remembered. And wondering what the purpose of this visit could possibly be, she went to the room still known as the "front parlor." Mrs. Edgewood, holding a bouquet of roses, extended them to Laura.

"I always think that when you're really down, flowers can lift you up a couple of inches. They've always done it for me, at least, and I hope these will do it for you."

"They're lovely, and it's so kind of you. Won't you sit down?"

Mrs. Edgewood, complying, sat on the edge of a chair. She was nervous and frankly said so.

"I was nervous about coming here. You were so good to come to my house after that attack on us, and I wasn't nice to you. We almost slammed the door in your face."

Laura smiled. "It wasn't quite as bad as that."

"Yes, it was. I was punishing you for what other people did to us, and that was wrong of me."

"I understand it. You had been through a terrible ordeal."

"Yes, and you're going through one now. Ever since all that came out in the papers, I've been thinking, and I said to my husband, how hard it must be for a woman like you, what a blow, to find out—" And seeing the brightening film in Laura's eyes, she turned her gaze considerately away, continuing, "I had to get this off my chest. I couldn't treat you the way we're so often treated, all of us taking the blame whenever one of us misbehaves. It's not your fault that your husband—oh, but I've said too much. I'm sorry."

"It's all right. I know what you're trying to tell me, and I appreciate it, truly." This woman was genuine. She was among those few who had come to this house without a trace of morbid curiosity. "Let me put these wonderful roses in water and get some tea," Laura said. "I'll only be a minute."

"No, another time, if I may. I didn't come on a social call. You need to rest, not to entertain people right now." At the door Mrs. Edgewood remembered something. "You said once you would take my daughter as a pupil. Will you be going back to work, and will you still take her if you do?"

"Yes, to both. I'll be glad to. Just give me a few weeks to straighten myself out."

When the door closed after the visitor, Laura put her face down into the roses; the petals were tender, cool against her flushed cheeks and beating temples. Then she went to fill a vase for them, set them on the table in the library, and stood undecided over what to do next. Perhaps she should go to the piano. There was always solace in music.

Straighten things out, she had said. But how, with Tom so sullen, Timmy so scared, and the business on which this household depended now seemingly about to fall apart?

Somebody was at the front door again. If Earl had been here, he would have heard the footsteps long before they reached the door. His little body would have been shaken with excitement from his soprano bark to his scruffy tail. And she went to open the door.

"Hello," Ralph said. "You haven't called me, and I thought I wouldn't wait any longer." In the hallway he stood looking down at her with a quizzical, half-rueful smile. "You promised to ask me for help, and you mustn't tell me that you don't need any because I won't believe it."

"All right, I won't say it. Come sit in here. It's cool."

She felt a queer embarrassment. He was so bright with the light on his copper-colored hair and the sweetness of his smile, too bright and alive and easy to be engulfed by the mood of this house. So she was loath to speak, and she said so.

"Right now the problems seem insoluble. So why let them spoil a summer day? I'd rather hear what's happening in your campaign."

"The campaign is tough, we're working hard, we're hopeful because one has to be hopeful, and that's that. As for you, Laura, nothing's insoluble."

"Except death."

"Even that. You solve it by accepting it, your own death or somebody else's."

When she turned her head, she beheld Bud in a leather frame; seated in full dignity on a Queen Anne armchair, he had importance. Everywhere in this house, the faces of the family's dead looked back at you.

"It can be disillusioning," she said, the thought slipping out unbidden.

"Yes."

The syllable was gravely spoken, and she knew that he had caught her meaning.

"There's no one to run the business. The Klan—" she said, cutting into the word with a chisel, "the Klan has taken Bud and Pitt. Now there's no one."

"Perhaps it can be sold."

"Perhaps— Oh!" she cried. "Do you know what I did a little while ago? I spun the globe around, closed my eyes, and put out my hand. I said to myself, The place I touch is where we're going, the boys and I." And making a wry face, she told him that the place had been Patagonia.

"Plenty of empty space there. Desert and sage and rocks and wind."

"You talk as if you'd seen it."

"I did. I was curious, so one year I just decided to go and have a look."

"I knew somebody once who had that kind of curiosity. From India he went to Nepal and Tibet. That was years ago, when almost nobody went there."

Frowning a little, she paused. It occurred to her that she had mentioned Francis to Ralph one time before, yet she wasn't sure she had. There seemed to be so many parallels between those two men.

"So you're not going to Patagonia?"

"No, I'm probably not going anywhere. It's just"—and she made a wide, spreading gesture—"Bud's deception, the public shame—"

"It's not your shame," Ralph said quickly.

"But even Timmy feels it, all the same. I know he does. And he looks so bad, so frail." Now her worries poured out of her. "The funeral was very hard for him, the emotion, the church so stifling, and the heat these last two days. This morning I sent him to spend the day with a friend of his who has a broken leg. That way I can be sure he'll be quiet. But I never know what's coming next."

"I understand. I lived through it all with the Crawfields until Peter died," Ralph said gently, looking straight at Laura.

She said very low, yet not allowing herself to flinch, "I think of Peter so often. You knew him. What was he really like? Tell me the truth. Margaret said—"

"Margaret told you the truth. He was a very quiet, thoughtful boy and young man. He was much the way you've described your Timmy."

"They look alike."

"They do. I took particular notice of Timmy when I was at the funeral." Ralph smiled suddenly. "Perhaps it will interest you to know that Peter was a religious Jew."

"Tell me."

"He was more observant than anyone else in his household. They still talk about it. Perhaps it was his age, or maybe it was his illness, or maybe he simply was a spiritual person. I was there when he became bar mitzvah, when he was confirmed, and when he was buried."

In the cemetery under the Star of David, Laura thought. A strange journey from his conception and his birth to that resting place.

"It's easier for me than for Margaret and Arthur. Peter is gone, and there is nothing I can do about that, but if he were living and didn't want me—" She stopped for a moment. "It would be unbearable. Yes. Unbearable."

"And so it is for them. They want so much to see Tom, Laura."

"Poor people. Well, tell them from me that they're welcome to come to this house. There's no reason anymore why they can't."

"Shouldn't you ask Tom first?"

"I don't know. I don't know what to do with him. What's to become of him! He hardly speaks. We eat in silence. I know he has, or had, a girlfriend, but he doesn't even see her, he doesn't see anybody. Of course, I know it's very soon after and we're all still in shock, his life has been overturned, but still I am just so worried. If you had heard him talk to the minister the night Bud was killed, you would know what I mean. It was dreadful."

"I've heard him enough," Ralph said.

"Here's the mail."

Tom had entered so suddenly that it was certain he had heard the last remarks. He gave Ralph a nod and confronted Laura.

"You're not wearing black."

"It's too hot for it, Tom."

"Not for me."

He was still dressed in a dark suit and black tie. Equally black was the look that he gave to Laura and Ralph.

Resentment and alarm rose together within Laura. "Where are you going?" she asked as he strode toward the front door.

"Out."

"You've just come back from being out."

"I'm going for a walk. I can't stand staying in this house looking at Dad's things. Maybe I'll go to the cemetery, I don't know."

"I don't think you should do that." Now pity wiped out the

resentment. "Don't be so hard on yourself. Your father wouldn't want it."

"I think he would. Especially since I seem to be the only one around here who really feels his death, except maybe Timmy, and he's a kid, so that's different."

"That's not fair, Tom. You shouldn't talk this way to me."

"I'm only speaking the truth. Even Jim Johnson seems to have more feeling."

Ralph interrupted. "Yes, for the Klan."

"Not at all!" Tom said indignantly. "I was referring to the letter he sent me, sympathy over the loss of my father. He has no connection with the Klan anyway, and you know it."

"No, I don't. His ideas are only a clever disguise for the Klan's ideas."

Tom snapped back. "That's your opinion, Mr. Mackenzie."

His voice and his very stance, with chin up and hands in pockets, was enough to infuriate an older adult. And Laura felt a mother's shame because he was a reflection upon her.

Ralph flushed. Clearly his anger was rising, but he answered evenly.

"I'd like to talk to you about Johnson. Have you ever wondered where all the money's coming from to support his high style of living?"

"No, I haven't. You drive a pretty expensive car yourself, and I imagine you live well. Does anybody ever ask you where your money comes from?"

"Tom!" cried Laura, aghast at such impudence.

Ralph raised his hand. "Please. He's asked a valid question. Tom, I can easily and will gladly account for every dollar. I practice law, and the IRS knows where to look if it wants to. I doubt whether Johnson can say the same. I know he hasn't turned down any Arab money. They love his anti-Semitism."

"I'm not on the campaign trail, although I intend to be as soon as I can, but today's not the day and I don't want to talk about Jim Johnson."

"Okay, Tom. Why don't you sit down and let's talk about something else?"

"Frankly, Mr. Mackenzie, I don't want to talk to you about anything," replied Tom, still standing.

"You might be interested in this. As of an hour ago we found the man who drove the car through the Klan meeting."

Laura started, and Tom's eyes glowed as he cried out.

"Who? Who is he?"

"Some fanatic, unbalanced as the Klan, only at the opposite end of the spectrum. Otherwise, little difference."

Tom ignored that. "What's his name?"

Mackenzie demurred. "You'll see it in the papers. I just thought you'd be relieved to know that he'll be brought to justice."

"I'd be relieved to know that he'd been strung up by his heels."

"That's not what is done in America. He'll have a trial and if he's found guilty, he'll pay a penalty."

"Hogwash," Tom said. "I wish I could get at him. He'd pay a penalty all right. You want to hear what I'd do to him?"

"Not particularly."

Where was this going to end? Laura's beseeching glance went back and forth between the two.

"I wish you would let me talk to you," Ralph said. "I believe I could help you if you'd give me a chance."

"I don't need help, not your politics, and especially not the kind you've been giving me. All you want is to turn me over to those—those people. It beats me why you're such a great friend of a pack of Jews, anyway. I suppose you've got black friends, too?"

"As it happens, I have."

There was a silence. And Laura saw that each of the two, sensing an impasse, would like to bring the discussion to an end and was on the verge of doing so. Tom was the first to make a move.

"Well, I guess that's enough of this. I'm going out."

"I'm truly sorry that you lost your father," Ralph persisted. "Mine died, though not so horribly, when I was not much older than you. Maybe sometime when you're feeling more inclined, we can talk about that."

"No, let's not kid ourselves. I'd rather be impolite than hypocritical, Mr. Mackenzie. I don't ever want to talk to you about anything, and you can tell that to the Crawfields, too," said Tom.

He remembers to close the door without a sound, Laura thought irrelevantly, just as Bud always reminded him to do. Bud hated slammed doors.

"I'm sorry," Ralph told her. "I came to bring you what cheer I could, and instead I've created a disturbance."

"No, this is the way he's been, that's all. He was like this before Bud died, but Bud defused him. They were always together. The trouble is, the trouble will be, the Crawfields and nothing else."

"They're not going to disappear, Laura."

"I know." The blood tie. It was a curse or it was a blessing, but always it was a tie unless both ends were willing to let it go. And the Crawfields were not willing. Nor would I be, thought Laura, if I were in their place.

"I wonder how he'd feel if they weren't Jewish," Ralph mused.

"I'm pretty sure he wouldn't want to leave this house. But he'd probably be more willing to know them, probably even curious, even wanting to know them after the first shock was over."

Ralph was troubled. He frowned, concentrating and hesitating; putting his fingertips together and pursing his lips, he nodded to himself. Presently he said, "They're determined to see Tom to work things out. I can predict, I can promise, that they'll be calling and writing. They may simply ring the doorbell one day as I did now. And if they do that, you can be sure it won't be pleasant for anyone."

"He'll be going back to college soon."

"They'll go there, too, and more easily. It's nearer to them."

"Perhaps we really should leave for Patagonia after all," Laura said bitterly.

"No," Ralph answered. He was thoughtful. "I think what you might try is another visit, this time here. You said before that they were welcome in this house—"

"I wasn't thinking. You can't believe Tom would welcome them, can you?"

"No, but he's practical, and if you put it to him that an arranged visit would be much more satisfactory than a lot of unexpected interruptions, I think he'd see the sense in that. He'd be coldly polite, very coldly, but I don't foresee disaster. The presence of Holly and Timmy would help. It would divert attention."

Doubtfully, Laura conceded that it might be worth a try.

"And if it should be a disaster, perhaps they will give up trying, at least for a while. But Margaret," Ralph said, shaking his head, "Margaret is pitiful."

Frustrated, Laura clenched little fists and shook them in the air.

"If I could get my hands on whoever it was who mixed up those babies, I'd—" Then she thought of something. "All right, I'll invite them to Sunday lunch. Will you come, too?"

Ralph stood up to leave. "No, Laura. I'm bowing out. Tom and I are like oil and water, as you've seen. It's best for us all that I bow out of this. Good luck," he said.

She opened the front door. Smiling, he turned to go down the steps.

She watched his car back down the driveway and turn into the road. "Bowing out." Permanently? Thoroughly? The feeling of loss was bleak. But to think of "loss" was absurd, after all. You couldn't lose what you had not possessed. It had been like window-shopping and nothing more; admiring, vaguely wishing, and knowing you were being foolish, you moved on.

But she felt loss, nevertheless.

Shortly afterward, Tom came home, sweating in his proper suit and tie.

"So he's finally left. I thought he was planning to move in."

"Tom, don't. Don't badger me. What do you gain by it? Unless you get some enjoyment out of adding to our misery."

"He's on the make, that guy. I saw how he looked at you."

"That's a nasty cheap shot. Your father's hardly a week in his grave, and you actually believe a decent man would be coming here with—with *thoughts*, even if I could possibly be interested," Laura said hotly, "which I'm not."

"Well, I hope you aren't," Tom grumbled.

"I only want to see you happy again. You and Timmy."

"Then keep the pests away, Mom. Mackenzie and those Crawfields. Keep them away."

She pleaded now, "How can I do it? You know I can't. When they want to get in touch with you, they will. That's why I thought maybe it would be a good idea to have them here next Sunday for a talk, to work out some sort of arrangement that you can tolerate."

"No, Mom!" The cry was almost hysterical. "I don't want them here! No, Mom!"

"God help me," Laura said, and added very softly, "They are your father and mother, darling, whether you like it or not."

Once more came the hysterical cry. "No! I don't want to hear it! Never say it! No!"

He ran out of the room. She heard his footsteps tearing up the stairs, and then the slam of his bedroom door.

"God help me," she said again.

CHAPTER
15

Margaret left the telephone and returned to the table, where Arthur and she were having a cup of after-dinner coffee.

"It's all set for Sunday. She wants us to be there for one o'clock lunch. She insisted on lunch, although I told her not to bother. Poor woman, no matter what kind of man he was, he was still her husband. Such an awful death, all those gruesome photos in the paper, and the cruel publicity."

"She's worried about the business besides, Ralph tells me. He advised her to sell it. I remember the property. It's a fine one, but the market's bad. Still, you never know."

Over the raised cup, Arthur looked out into the gathering dark. Often lately he found himself apt to fall silent, gazing at nothing.

"But Tom's in a worse state, Ralph told me."

"I know." Arthur brought his eyes back to meet Margaret's; the two pairs met in familiar understanding. "He has been clobbered from every side. No matter how much he denies it, he must have been shocked out of his wits to learn that Rice was a Ku Kluxer."

"Do you believe it's possible that Laura didn't know it, either?"

"Ralph says she didn't."

"He certainly seems to know a lot about her, considering the short time he's known her. Do you think there could be anything—anything there? She's a charming woman. I'd call her beautiful, wouldn't you?"

Arthur smiled. "Yes, but you can bet your last dollar there hasn't been 'anything.' Ralph is hardly the man to complicate his success by having a messy affair with a married woman."

"She's not married anymore."

"Good Lord, haven't we got enough to think about without fantasizing over Ralph's love life? Stick to next Sunday. Are your parents included?" Arthur said, changing the subject quickly as Holly came in.

"Not this time. Let's not overwhelm Tom again. I've been thinking, perhaps that was our mistake. It must have been formidable to face such a lineup, with Papa so emotional, too. The three of us will be enough."

"Enough for what?" asked Holly. When Margaret explained, her jaw dropped. "You surely don't expect *me* to go, do you?"

"Why, of course," Arthur said mildly. "Why not?"

"Because I don't want to. Because Tom's loathsome, Dad. If you ask me, whoever switched those babies did us all a favor. When I think of Peter and then of that miserable—miserable *thing*, I could barf."

"You're not helping us with such talk," Arthur said.

"I tried to be decent to him, even though I knew all those things about him. I showed him the dog, I tried to make conversation, but he didn't want it. I'm too Jewish for his royal highness, I suppose."

Margaret chided softly, "Don't, Holly. It will take time and patience, that's all."

"You're deluding yourself, Mom. He's full of hatred. When he was at this table at lunch that day, I saw him looking at the Sabbath-candle holders. You'd have thought he was seeing a bomb or a rattlesnake or something."

"You know you're exaggerating," Margaret countered. "Try

to put yourself in his place. And now with the awful death of Mr. Rice—"

Holly sat down, propped her elbows on the table, put her chin in her hands, and regarded her mother. "I have tried. But let's leave me out. Think about Peter instead. If he were still alive, now that this has been found out, how do you think you would behave?"

Margaret shook her head. "I can't answer that. Each of us is an enigma. I can't even tell you what I myself would do in any new, given circumstance."

She has grown older, Holly thought. She hasn't done her hair properly for days. She's beaten down, and that damn Tom is the cause. Until this happened, she looked like a girl; people said we looked like sisters, and I used to hate that, but now I wish people could say it again.

Arthur, gazing out of the window, spoke without turning his head.

"This is a time of crisis, Holly. You were so strong all through the last crisis when Peter was in the hospital. And when we lost him, you were our comfort. I don't think you can realize how, in our hearts, you were our hope. And you still are."

A wave of sorrow passed over Holly. In these last months she had been drowned in sorrow, as if some fate were trying to make up for all the easy years of her childhood. As if it were trying to teach her something, maybe?

Her father had still not turned from the window. What was he seeing out there? Most probably the face of the sullen, hostile rebel who was his son. Dad must know, she thought, because he is both shrewd and wise, that there is nothing to be expected from that son but rejection and pain.

Suddenly he turned back to the room. His eyes that could so often moisten with either tears or laughter were now dry and weary. "We'll try one more time, Margaret," he said. "If it doesn't work, well, that'll be just one more death in the family. And besides, we can't make more trouble for Laura. She's had too much." He leaned down and kissed his wife's cheek. "And

Holly, about Sunday. You do whatever you want. We shan't force you."

Quietly, she replied, "I'm going with you, Dad and Mom."

Laura waited until Friday to announce the impending visit. The truth, she admitted to herself, was simply that she had delayed because she did not want to face another explosion.

During the few days since Ralph Mackenzie's and Tom's confrontation, little change had occurred, except that Tom had finally given up the dark suit, and Timmy had again developed an alarming cough. The heat wave, having reached a new height, made it dangerous for him to be outdoors at all, so he had become irritable under confinement to books and television. Moreover, he had retreated into silence, not a hostile silence like Tom's, but a melancholy one, forlorn and vague, in which he refused to be drawn into conversation. Laura had, therefore, no idea what he was really thinking about Bud, other than that he grieved over Bud's death.

They had just finished their dinner when she told them. Tom shoved his chair back so hard that he shook the table.

"Not those people again!" he cried.

Laura drew a long breath to gather strength and proceeded. "Tom, I understand how you feel. Believe me, I really do. But listen to me. The fact is, and I've told you this, if I don't set a date, they're bound to get to you anyway. Would you rather have them surprise you one day at your dorm with all your friends around, or satisfy them now with a quiet visit here at home?"

He was flushed, and not only with anger, although there was plenty of that; she saw again how fearful he was.

"Tell me. If you had to make a choice, and you do have to, which it would be."

"Oh God Almighty, is this the pattern for the rest of my life?"

"Let's take one step at a time, Tom. That's what I'm doing." And she could not refrain from adding, "Seeing these people isn't exactly painless for me, either, you know."

Then a shadow of resignation seemed to pass over Tom's face, softening its rigid lines. "Okay. I'll sit there if that's what it'll make it easier for you, Mom. But I will not, I cannot, talk to them. I'm warning you now. I'll sit there despising them, and I won't care whether they know it or not."

"They already know it," Laura said.

Lunch at the Crawfield house had been elaborate, she remembered. While it was certainly not necessary to match it, for this was no competition, it was only right to take more pains than she usually would take for a couple of old friends who were dropping by to lunch. It was just as well, too, that she would have something to occupy her other than the conflicts that had been raging within her day and night.

Betty Lee offered to come to work on Sunday. "You're having special company, I can see that. You never ask me for anything, and I can surely give you a few hours of Sunday, what with all the trouble you've had."

With careful, tactful appreciation, Laura declined help. It was strange to think that Betty Lee, who had held Tom in her arms when he was three days old, still knew nothing of his dread secret. But even Timmy desperately wanted it to be kept from anyone.

So she prepared in stages. On Friday a strawberry soufflé went into the freezer, on Saturday she put together the ingredients for Cajun baked chicken and Tom's favorite corn pudding. All that remained for Sunday morning were the salad and hot biscuits. Of these preparations no notice was taken. No relieving breeze disturbed the thick funereal air that had filled the house since the night of Bud's death—and indeed before Bud's death. She moved with her tasks through hours that were almost soundless. Only the rain, which had been falling for two days, disturbed the silence.

Tom clung to his room, reading and listening to his stereo. He was well enough acquainted with popular psychology to diagnosis his ailment; depression was anger turned inward. After grievous explosions, his nerves were worn thin, and anger now had no place to go but inward. Like a prisoner in a cell, looking out a barred window onto a dreary wall, he was trapped. Mom had caught him in a moment of weakness, just as a sudden surge of pity for her had risen. Now another terrible Sunday loomed.

And then on Saturday Robbie telephoned.

"Miracle of miracles!" he shouted. "How did you know I've had you and nothing but you in my mind all day? From the minute I opened my eyes, Robbie, I swear."

"How did I know? Guess what? You've been in my mind all day every day. I've been so sad for you. It's a physical ache. I can feel it in my heart. It must be awful for you."

"It's pretty bad."

"But I'm sure your dad would want you to get back to living as soon as possible."

"That's true." And he thought, I want to lie in your arms and tell you everything.

Her voice picked up a cheerful tone. "Guess what? I finished a day early and here I am, back at old state U. I've got my new room, and it's gorgeous. When are you coming? Today, maybe? Tomorrow?"

Back at college? He had actually lost track of the date. Oh my God, Sunday—

"Robbie, I want to, but let me see what develops here in the next couple of days. My mother—"

"Yes, yes, of course. Your poor mother. Well, honey, I'm here. Just give me a call when you know."

They talked. And the more they talked, the more powerful became the returning surge of Tom's anger. He was to give up Robbie in exchange for a day of mental torture with those— those interlopers, unwanted, aggressive, persistent—there were no words.

When he hung up, he lay back in the bed and pounded the pillows.

The house was too quiet. Laura tried, as she was dressing on Sunday, not to look toward Bud's closet where his clothes were still hanging. They would have to be sorted and given away. Eventually she would have to do it.

Bud Rice, the man "not interested in politics"! And in a subtle way he had, all these years, been preparing Tom to fit into his mold. All of that going on, she thought, as termites gnaw away until the beam collapses. Oh, she was bitter.

And yet, so complex are we all that she could not look at the clothing he had worn so proudly and so well, he who now lay, silenced forever, under the earth.

By nine o'clock, the kitchen work was finished and the table had been set. When she went out to the cutting garden to get flowers for the centerpiece, the sun was merciless. The temperature was already at oven heat, and by noon they predicted it would reach one hundred.

Timmy came out to the garden offering to help. Such a good kid, he was, a peacemaker in spite of his worries, torn between Tom and herself.

"No," she said kindly, "thanks, but it's much too hot. You're still coughing, and I don't want you to start sweating. Go back in and have a cool drink. Is Tom up yet?"

"I don't know. His door's closed."

By half-past ten, Tom had still not come downstairs. Laura's heart began to pound. This undertaking was another terrible mistake. She should never have weakened and given in. Yet Ralph was right when he said that the Crawfields weren't going to go away. If only Tom doesn't make a nasty botch of it again as he did at their house! She had wanted to dig a hole in the floor and crawl into it.

"Tom," she called, knocking at his door.

There was no answer, so she tried again, and when there was still none, she opened the door. Even before she read the large white sheet of paper that lay on the neatly made bed, she knew what would be on it.

3 a.m., she read. *Mom, I'm sneaking out. It's easier for both of us. I'm going away for a couple of days. Don't worry. I just can't face those people. You know how I feel, or maybe you really don't know. I love you, anyway.*

"I do know how you feel," she said loudly. "But do you know by any chance how I feel? And what am I to say to 'those people,' as you call them? Coming from the other end of the state to see you and it's left to me to explain? Explain what? How? This isn't fair of you, Tom."

The photograph that had stood on the desk had been moved to the night table, where it would be the last thing he'd see at night and the first thing in the morning. That's where he's gone, she thought, to the girl.

And as if it could tell her something about the person behind itself, she examined the face again. It was not beautiful, but it was piquant, and very small, enclosed as it was by swoops of dark hair. There was intelligence in the eyes, pert humor in the mouth, and a determined set to the chin. On the whole, nothing remarkable. Yet to him at nineteen, she was unique. She was the Only One. That's how it is at nineteen. You remember, Laura, don't you?

A sudden thought shook her into action. Find an excuse, somebody's not feeling well, call them off. And she ran to the telephone. But it rang and rang without answer, so they had already left. What on earth was she to tell them?

"The truth," she said aloud, surprised at her own hesitation. There was never anything else to say but the truth. Then perhaps they would see how hopeless their attempts were.

Timmy was in the kitchen taking his medicine. And she asked him whether he had known that Tom was leaving.

"No, Mom, I didn't." He paused and added, "I think of Tom all the time. I'm so sorry for him, and I'm so lucky not to be like him because I'm the son who really belongs here."

She did not correct Timmy's choice of words, didn't say that of course Tom belonged here, too, for his meaning was clear. She said only, "This is a dreadful mess today. I hope you will help me by being friendly. You must be the host."

"No problem, Mom. Those people don't mean anything to me one way or the other. They can't touch my life. I can be the friendliest guy you ever saw. I might even like them."

* * *

When Timmy, who had been watching out, called, "Here they are," Laura went to the door. With greater consideration than many people showed, rather than block the driveway, they had parked on the street. Very slowly, they walked up the path. They're as nervous as I am, she thought, still undecided whether to give them the news the moment they entered the house, or whether to wait until they had been sitting for a while.

The decision did not take long to make itself. Coming indoors out of the brilliant light, the three stood for a moment in the hall blinking, then, smiling, shook hands with Laura.

"And this is Timmy," she said.

They shook Timmy's hand. Their eyes looked beyond him into the depth of the house toward the stairs and came back to Laura.

"We were all so sorry to hear of your trouble," Margaret said.

"Thank you."

Mechanical courtesies passed between them.

"I hope you had no trouble finding the house."

"No, not at all. Your directions were perfect."

"I'd hoped we might eat on the back veranda. There's a lovely view of the garden, but not today in this weather."

"Yes, the heat is fierce, isn't it?"

In the front parlor, the banjo clock on the wall struck one.

"You couldn't have timed it better," said Laura.

"The credit is Arthur's. If it were up to me, we'd always be late," Margaret replied.

From Mrs. Edgewood's roses, which were still fresh, a subtle fragrance floated between the two groups, Laura and Timmy on one side of the fireplace, the other three facing them. American Gothic, Laura thought, stiff as the figures in the famous painting. It is pathetic.

"I love these old-time roses," observed Margaret. "The hybrid teas may be more flashy, but they have no fragrance."

"These aren't ours. Someone gave them to me," Laura said

desperately. It was at this moment that the decision made itself.

"Tom isn't here. He left in the middle of the night. I didn't know until this morning. I tried right away to phone you, but you had already started."

"Left!" cried Margaret.

"I'm sure he's all right. There was a note. I think he probably went to see his girlfriend."

"Girlfriend," repeated Margaret.

"Yes, he seems to have a girl at the university. I don't know exactly. He never talks about things like that."

There was no comment. And Laura, still desperate, went on talking. "Of course, I know that boys—young men—never do tell their parents much, do they? I mean—" She stopped. What was the use? They looked stricken.

Then Arthur spoke. "He must have said something."

"Nothing new. Just the usual about not wanting to see you. Until finally he said all right, he would. I never thought he would do anything like this. No, I never thought," she finished.

Margaret was biting her lip. Holly was turning her head from her father to her mother and back, questioning, asking without words what was to come next.

A good question, thought Laura. These people were obviously too well-bred to get up and leave, although you could be sure that was what they would like to do. And she would hardly be so outspoken as to say, "I know you want to go, so please don't be afraid of offending me. I'll understand."

It was Timmy who broke through the frozen silence with a loud announcement: "I hope you're all hungry for lunch, because I am."

Darling Timmy! She could have hugged him for his sensitivity and his funny, clumsy attempt at tact.

"Are you? Can you survive for another three minutes while I run to the kitchen?"

So now there was no choice but to sit down together and behave normally, that is, to resume mechanical courtesies and a stiff American Gothic pose, around a table this time, each with an organdy place mat and two Irish crystal goblets in front of him.

"I do love an old house," said Margaret, "the high ceilings, the woodwork, and so many fireplaces."

"Well, this is home, and I can't imagine leaving it," replied Laura, pouring wine out of Aunt Cecile's Irish crystal decanter, "but still, on a day like this I wouldn't object to a fully air-conditioned house."

And Holly remarked, "Oh, there is a wonderful breeze in this room. I don't feel hot at all."

The girl was well-bred, helping the conversational ball to roll. That cerise linen was perfect on her. She had Tom's paper-white skin. She must be careful not to look at her so much, because of course they would all know what comparison was being made. But then, they were making their own comparisons with their surreptitious glances toward Timmy.

Peter, thought Laura. The name was always a stab, an electrical shock.

"This corn pudding is delicious," Margaret said. "I've never had one like it before."

"It's from a handwritten recipe book, my grandmother's recipe, or maybe even her mother's, I'm not sure."

As if it mattered who had first made the pudding.

On a branch at the window, a catbird sat and squawked. Forks touched porcelain, lightly. Someone broke open a biscuit; you could almost hear it crumble. Margaret opened her lips as if to speak and closed them, as if she had forgotten what she wanted to say. Arthur said nothing. Men never helped to keep the conversational ball rolling. If it was up to them, the ball would drop on the floor and lie there. The catbird squawked again. And suddenly Laura put her fork down.

Without prior plan, she cried out, "Why don't we all talk about what's really in our minds?"

Startled, as if she had said something surprising, all except Arthur turned toward her.

"Yes," he said, "I have been thinking that, too, and dreading it because our thoughts, our questions, have no answers and no future."

His wife chided him gently. "It's not like you to be so pessimistic. You're always the hopeful one who props me up."

"Good enough in its place. But there comes a time when you have to be a realist. The injustice that was done to us all remains a mystery. I personally think it must have been that nurse who disappeared in Hawaii. We can't find her, but if we should, what good would it do us? What good now?"

Timmy's mouth hung open, as it was apt to do whenever his attention was completely caught. "Why would she want to do that?" he asked.

"She wouldn't want to," Arthur explained. "It was a stupid, careless accident in a poorly run little private hospital that closed down not long afterward."

"I wasn't born there," said Timmy, reassuring himself.

Laura smiled at him. "A thing like this is almost as rare as putting a man on the moon."

"Yes," said Margaret, "I remember reading about a case that happened in France. It was ten years ago, I think. I remember being so shocked. It was in all the newspapers."

"It's a miracle it hasn't been in the papers here," Arthur remarked. "I don't understand it."

Laura said, "Our lawyer has influence. Since everything happened here in this city, you see . . . He knows everybody, the hospital board, the two papers." After faltering a moment, she resumed, "And Bud knew everyone. He was determined to plug every possible leak. He thought it was all a lie, anyway."

Timmy insisted, "But it isn't a lie, Mom, is it?"

"No, dear, it isn't."

"Well, so far, so good," said Arthur. "But I wouldn't count on keeping it quiet forever."

"Oh," cried Holly, clapping her hands together so hard that her bangle bracelets clinked, "if it's ever in the news, I'll die. I swear I will."

"No, you won't," said her father. "You'll put up with it like the woman you are."

Margaret soothed. "Anyhow, you'd probably be away at college when it happened. If it ever does."

"What the world thinks is of no importance," Arthur said, almost angrily. "There's only one person who's important now, and that's Tom. What's to become of him."

"He'll always be my brother!"

The exclamation resounded; it was a cry of defiance, of pain and fear. The two mothers' glances met in immediate comprehension.

"Of course he will," Margaret said heartily. And then, addressing Laura, she added, hesitating a little, "It's bothered me that perhaps you might have some worry about our trying to influence Tom someday, to take him away from you. If you've ever had such a thought, dismiss it. It's the last thing we would ever do, even if it were possible, which hardly seems likely. Tom is yours, not ours, and we wouldn't have it otherwise."

"Thank you for being frank," Laura said. "Yes, I've had some worried moments. But I won't anymore—not about that, anyway." She stood up. "Who would like iced coffee with dessert? Or hot coffee, or tea? I have them all."

"Let me help you," Margaret offered.

"No, no thanks, you sit still."

Once more, the tension passed, and conversation was moved to neutral ground, stiffer, and yet unquestionably safer. The dessert was praised. When Margaret expressed a wish to see the garden, they all went out into the broiling sun, beneath which petals curled and leaves drooped.

Now, surely, they will want to go home, Laura said to herself. With this mission unaccomplished, why do they want to stay?

"Why do you have this wire fence around your fishpond?" inquired Holly.

She was being attentive to Timmy, which was rather sweet of her because she could hardly find an eleven-year-old boy that interesting. She is sorry for him, and for herself, Laura thought, because he reminds her of Peter.

"It's to keep the dog from drinking the water," Timmy told her.

"Oh yes, Tom — I mean, someone said you had a dog."

"Not anymore. He was killed with Dad."

"I'm sorry," Holly said softly.

A nice girl. A nice girl.

The telephone was ringing in the kitchen. "Do answer, Timmy," Laura said. "Whoever it is, say I'll call back later."

The message was not for her. It was Mr. Mackenzie calling to talk to Mr. Crawfield.

Everyone followed Arthur into the house. When he turned from the telephone, he reported with his hand over the speaker, "Ralph only wanted to know how everything was going. I wondered — he's in the city today — whether I might ask him to join us here for a few minutes."

"But of course," said Laura.

I bow out, he had told her, and she had taken that to mean that their relationship — no, you could hardly call it that — their friendship, then, was to dwindle easily away, as water trickles off into sand. And that was surely what he had meant. This visit today was for the Crawfields' benefit.

"How like Ralph." Margaret sighed. "He's made such an effort to bring us all together, and now he's feeling our pain."

"He's a prince," said Arthur. "We're agreed on that. But enough of pain. Are you perhaps planning to get another dog, Timmy? Holly volunteers at an animal shelter, you know. That's where we got the dog we have now. Our first one, who came to us when Holly was two years old, died of old age. We went right out and got another one."

Timmy said, "I don't know whether I'm ready. Earl was a special dog. I don't think I could ever love another that much. I don't know. Would you like to see pictures of him, Holly? I have a whole album in Dad's den."

"I'd love to," Holly said enthusiastically as she went with Timmy, followed by Laura's grateful glance.

"There is something especially touching about boys that age," Margaret observed. "A girl that age is almost a woman. There's very little of childhood left in her. But in a boy, even when he's very bright and can surprise you with adult opinions, the little child still shows through."

"Timmy is very much like a child in some ways. I have to watch him so carefully. For instance, he knows that if he spits blood when he coughs, he'll have to go back to the hospital, so I'm sure he'll try to hide it from me if it happens. This heat's the worst thing for him, too. He hasn't been feeling well, but he won't admit it. So I have to watch. It's difficult . . ."

Margaret nodded. "Yes, they hide things. Sometimes they wait till the lungs fill up and it's almost too late, or it is too late."

"Last year he wanted to try out for the track team. He pestered and pestered, so finally we said he could. Of course he didn't make it, he almost suffocated from the effort."

Arthur, who had been staring at nothing while they talked, came awake. "It must be hard for him to compare himself with someone as vigorous as Tom."

"Yes," Laura said simply. "Yes, it is. But Tom has always tried to make it easier. He's taught Timmy to lift weights, which is good enough for the muscles, but better still for the spirits. It's an adult male activity, and they can do it together."

No one commented. Darn catbird, Laura thought. He, or one of his relatives, had followed them from the other side of the house to squawk into their sudden silences.

Then Margaret said, "I have a sense of unreality. Do you feel how unreal it is for us to be sitting here like this talking about Tom?"

And Laura answered, "I do. And I also feel how remarkable it is that we don't hate each other."

Arthur spoke. "There wouldn't be much use in that, would there?"

At that moment, Ralph Mackenzie came in. When he had sat down, he looked around at the three solemn, quiet faces, and making no false attempt at useless cheer, said bluntly that he had not expected this meeting with Tom to work, but had thought it worth a try.

"I think," he said, "you have met with an immovable object."

"Yes," said Arthur, "a stone wall. And one doesn't batter one's head against stone walls. If Tom doesn't want to talk to us, we'll have to accept it. It will be easier all around."

Margaret was biting her lips again. When she saw Laura glancing at her, she stopped and asked with an assumed brightness, "How is the campaign going, Ralph?"

"Pretty well. Two more of the men at the KKK meeting have been identified as Johnson men. The link is getting tighter and tighter, which is all to the good for our side."

Arthur, addressing Laura, asked, "Your manager Pitt didn't do your company any good, did he?"

Margaret remonstrated, "Arthur! Please!"

"Laura's not a weakling," Arthur replied. "The facts are there, the whole affair is horrendous, she's had to face it, and she seems to have faced it rather well."

"Thank you," Laura said. "I try."

"So what is happening with your company? Ralph says you have problems, that they—"

"It's all right," Ralph said. "Laura can know that I told you. I thought maybe you might have some ideas for her. You've got business contacts that I haven't got."

"I may have both, some ideas and some contacts."

"I would be very grateful," Laura said. "We can't last too long like this. The wages and the expenses continue, but business has dropped way off."

"Will Tom want to take it over someday?" Arthur inquired now. "I understand he's been working there."

It was as if, in spite of his remark about Tom and the stone wall, he was unable to stay away from the subject.

"No," replied Laura. "That was only a summer project to please Bud. Tom still wants to be an astronomer."

Arthur persisted. "No politics?"

Laura felt the heat tingle up her neck and onto her cheeks. "I can't tell. It is all up in the air. Everything is."

"Didn't Holly come with you?" Ralph asked quickly.

"She's with Timmy, looking at pictures of Timmy's dog," Margaret said.

Laura went to call the two. Her body was rigid from the strain of the day. But they would soon be going home, and the house would be empty of all their questions; she would go to the piano, she would play Monopoly with Timmy, she would lie down . . .

"You people had a long talk about dogs," said Margaret. "I didn't know there was so much to say about dogs."

Margaret struggled too hard. She was on the verge of tears, anyone could see that, yet she was so determinedly upbeat. It was irritating. And yet I suppose I do the same, Laura said to herself.

Holly answered, "We didn't talk that much about dogs, we talked about Peter."

"Oh," said Laura.

"I asked whether he knew he was going to die," Timmy said, "whether when he was eleven he knew he would be dead in a few years."

They were all stunned. There was no "proper" answer to give because, of course, Timmy was really asking whether he, too, would be dead at eighteen. What could one answer?

It was Arthur who replied. First he removed his glasses and wiped his forehead. Then he sighed. Finally, having moved his chair nearer to Timmy's, he smiled and began to speak to the boy as though there was no one else in the room, only they two, man to man.

"Listen," he said. "Listen to me. I don't truly know what Peter actually thought. He certainly must have worried about it, and probably he put it out of his mind as best he could. We're all going to die, but we don't know when. Your father didn't know it the night he left here in his car, intending to come back in a couple of hours."

Oh no, thought Laura. He's too blunt, too rash. He's tearing the bandage off the fresh wound. But she did not know how to stop him.

"All of us are prey to accident or sickness. The only difference in your case is that you already know what it is that you have to fight. Most of us don't know, so we're caught by surprise."

Timmy looked doubtful, yet kept his eyes focused on Arthur.

"The good news for you is that people with your disease are living much, much longer than ever before. The better news is that—well, have you ever heard anything about gene therapy? Do you know anything at all about it?"

"No, but Tom does. Tom reads about science things all the time."

"Well," said Arthur, pausing. "Well, you can ask Tom to look it up for you. There are things going on in the universities and the National Institutes of Health, experiments with packaging the cystic fibrosis gene in a cold virus. It's complicated stuff, more than I understand myself, because I'm not a scientist. The only thing I do understand is how hopeful it all is."

"Why didn't they use it for Peter?"

"It's brand, brand new. It wasn't ready yet."

And it isn't ready yet now, thought Laura, with tears prepared to flow in another minute, prickling the backs of her eyes.

"But it will be, soon?" asked Timmy.

Arthur made a skillful evasion. "They expect so. Soon enough for you, at any rate."

"In the meantime," Laura prompted, "he has to take care of himself."

"By all means," agreed Arthur.

"He has to obey all the rules. He knows them, but sometimes he forgets. He has to watch his diet, not overexercise, and not get overheated."

"Absolutely," Arthur said.

"I wish I could get him out of this awful heat," Laura complained. "But I can't possibly go anywhere now. There are things to do. Lawyers and papers. Things."

Timmy was uncomfortable, and she became aware that she had been discussing him as if he weren't present, just as one speaks about a little child who cannot understand what is being said.

"I wonder," Margaret began, and looked toward her husband.

He nodded and smiled again. The smile used up his whole face, forehead and cheeks. "Go ahead."

Margaret began, "I don't suppose Laura would, or even that Timmy would—"

"Would what?" asked Timmy.

"We have a cottage near the lake," Margaret said. "We were planning to go up for a week, but we postponed our departure till tomorrow because we were coming here. If you would consider it and your mother would let you," Margaret said, turning to Laura, "it would be fun. It's cool, at least ten degrees cooler than here."

Now Holly interjected. "We go sailing and fishing in the river nearby, and there are two boys in the next cottage who are about your age."

Timmy looked interested. He needed a change, he needed to have something good happen, Laura told herself. And yet she hardly knew these people. Unconsciously she looked toward Ralph, who promptly answered her silent appeal.

"Lake Mohawk's a great place. Beautiful white sand beaches, hills all around, beautiful. Timmy would love it."

Oh, she remembered the hills and the white sand beach, the sun and the wind, the bee-buzz in the flowers along the stairs rising to the cottage . . .

"I guess I'd like to go," said Timmy, surprising her. Apparently these strangers attracted him. "Mom, yes, I'd like to go."

"All right," she said, giving in. And to the Crawfields, "You are just so incredibly kind, that I don't know what to say."

"Say nothing. It will be our pleasure. What we'll do is, go

back to our house from here, pack a few things, and make an early start in the morning."

"Then, Timmy," Laura said, "you'd better get your things now. Take two swim trunks, and don't forget a sweater."

As soon as he was out of the room, Margaret assured Laura, "You mustn't worry for a minute. We know how to take care of him."

"I know you do."

When they had driven away, Laura remarked how strange it was that they had come here to be with their son, only to leave with hers instead.

"What really happened to Tom?" asked Ralph. "Although perhaps you don't want to talk about it."

"The same as always. He said it was just too much for him. It was the worst moment when they arrived and I had to tell them he wasn't here. I didn't know what to expect, whether Margaret would cry or they'd be furious, but they took the disappointment very well."

"They do their crying in private."

"I feel so sorry for them. It's amazing that they wanted to take Timmy."

"He's Peter all over again, and they can feel for him."

Ralph was still standing at the door. And when he turned to her, she, expecting a polite leave-taking, was about to respond when he remarked instead, "I look around at these huge old trees and all this space, and suddenly I miss what I grew up with. I think of a garden, a hammock, and a book. My apartment begins to feel like a box."

"Would you like to see our garden for a minute?" A second after giving the invitation she was embarrassed. She had presumed on the man's good manners. Had he not made clear his decision to "bow out"?

"I'd like to," he said.

They went through the house onto the rear veranda. The afternoon had waned, and here in the shade the air had cooled enough to be bearable. A fine spray from the lawn sprinklers glistened on a broad perennial border, a well-tended melange of larkspur and phlox, of lilies, asters, and cosmos.

"Who takes care of all this?" asked Ralph.

"Bud and the boys, mostly Tom when he's home."

But they would not be home, Bud never again and Tom only rarely, more rarely than ever now, things being what they were. This awareness swept over Laura with the sudden force of wind, chilling the long lawn in front of her and the lonely house at her back. She closed her eyes.

When she opened them, Ralph was looking at her. "I said if you needed help you should ask me," he said gently. "You still haven't asked."

"But you also said you were 'bowing out,' and I understand why."

"I was talking about Tom. Did you think I meant you?"

"It seemed that way."

"I didn't mean you," he said quietly.

If she had been frail and weepy, she would not have touched him so, he believed. He had felt the strength of her, the iron under the velvet, from that very first day when he had brought his shocking message to this house. It seemed like years ago, but it had only been weeks. And he remembered that he had gone away wondering what could have brought such a woman and such a man together. What a waste! he had thought, and thought now. That man had corrupted the boy, or at least, having seen the creeping corruption, had done nothing to stop it. Indeed, he had encouraged it, and must have rejoiced in it. And now she stands in mourning, for he recognized the black blouse and white skirt as a kind of discreet mourning—not because the death had crushed her, but because she knows what this particular community expects. And while she's here, she will properly meet expectations. He understood her.

He wished he could foresee what was to happen between them, whether anything could. Tall as she was, he was still much taller, and she had to look up to meet his eyes. Two round, heavy tears gathered in hers. *I didn't mean you.* He was moved to the heart.

"Tell me," he said, "let me help you. You never complain."

Laura shook her head. Totally unable to say that he was too much in her thoughts, that he had reawakened in her all the longing, the fierce sickness of desire that she had once had— only once—and then lost, she shook her head.

"You keep everything locked up inside."

"No. Well, yes, I guess I do."

And now as her tears rolled freely, she spoke.

"How can I sort it out? Everything is tangled into everything else. I think of Bud and how he died. They say he was killed instantly, and maybe he was, I don't really know, and I hope he didn't suffer. But I didn't love him. He was good to me, and he loved the boys, but he wasn't honest with me, and I know my life with him wasn't honest either. I covered up with my joy in music and my sons. Now I wonder what will become of my sons—" She stopped and drew back. "Are you shocked that a widow in these circumstances should say such things?"

"As you say, 'in these circumstances.' So no, I am not shocked," he said gravely. And putting his arm around her shoulder, drew her to him.

The contact was tentative, the intent was only to strengthen and console; she knew that. Yet she knew, too, that with a slight, responding turn of her body or his, there would be consequences. Already her heart was beating rapidly . . .

She pulled away. It wasn't possible, not here and now, with a pile of black-bordered stationery on the desk waiting to be addressed, no, nor with the boys still wounded and grieving for their father; nor with Tom and Ralph at loggerheads . . .

He read her mind. Releasing her, he murmured, "There is a time, Laura. A right time for everything."

The evening had darkened into a hazy blue when she accompanied him to the door. Neither of them spoke. He kissed her cheek and went quickly down the path.

She went to the back of the house to lock up for the night.

A chorus of those insects who grow louder as summer moves toward fall now burst the quiet, making her aware before long that she had been there for minutes gazing, thinking and gazing at the night. The hedgerow at the garden's end was deep as a forest, where, wandering in circles, one might be lost forever.

CHAPTER

—————— 16 ——————

On Saturday night Tom had sprung up out of bed, switched on the light and seen that it was almost three o'clock. Actually it was already Sunday.

At one o'clock in the afternoon those people would be coming up to the front door, the whole kit and caboodle of them, as Aunt Lillian used to say; remembering the old aunts and their sayings that had used to seem so boring and outdated, he longed for them now, those neat, proper American ladies. They would take his part, he was sure. Damn. He had to get out of here.

Enough was enough. No doubt it was mean to run out on Mom at the last minute, but he had never been mean to her before and must be forgiven a first time. Anyway, he felt bitter toward her. Deny it as she might and as she had done, there was something between her and Mackenzie, the bastard who was pushing him over to the Crawfields. He sensed it. Hadn't Mom herself always said he had "an uncanny nose for people's secrets"?

He folded his best slacks and a good sport shirt. Tonight they'd go out to dinner, he and Robbie, to a great lobster dinner. He folded some bills and zippered the pocket. At the last minute before turning the light off, he remembered the polar bear, tucked it under his arm, and crept downstairs.

The house was too still, Mom was alone in the big room without Bud, and Timmy was alone without his dog.

He took Bud's car. Mom's sleek Mercedes stood between it and the van, so he didn't have to see the van. He had purposely not let himself look at it since that night. Poor Bud.

At seven o'clock, having the key to the house door, he climbed the stairs to the topmost tower room that Robbie had described and knocked.

He heard the flurry of her feet and her startled, still sleepy cry, "Who is it?"

"Polar bear," he growled, and when she opened the door, thrust the animal into her face.

Laughing, she half crying, they fell together onto the bed. Her hands caressed his cheeks and his hair. The blood drummed in his ears. Her arms twisted around his neck.

"My God, I've missed you! My God, I love you. Tom, Tommy, it's been a hundred years."

Her fingers twisted, unfastening, unbuttoning, stripping, until he was as naked as she. He had for an instant a queer sense of being an observer, of seeing two bodies entangled in each other, arms, legs, and lips, a sense of seeing himself, as in the last moment before the plunging darkness, he caught the morning light on her moist, glistening eyes and her glistening teeth; then he sensed no more, neither Robbie nor himself, only that vast, sweet, thoughtless dark.

All day they lay together, sleeping, making love and once more sleeping. When late in the day the sky dimmed and the room went blue with dusk, they woke up rested, enlivened and starving. Unwilling to leave the room, they settled for doughnuts and coffee.

"Why are you smiling?" Robbie asked.

"Because you're so delightful, so beautiful and so smart, and I'm so happy."

"When are you coming down here for good?"

"I'll stay tonight, go home to pack up and be back for registration on Friday."

"We'll have a great year. Very busy," she warned, suddenly earnest. "The campaign people expect us to produce on this campus. After all, practically everybody here is over eighteen. I'd like to see a good turnout. It'll take work, though."

"I'm ready."

"We're going to go places with Johnson, you and I. We've already caught his eye, you know that. And he wants young people to build beyond this campaign, to build for the future."

"I'm ready," he repeated.

She said softly, "I didn't want to do anything to spoil our day, but I just have to tell you again how sorry I am about this whole rotten time you've had, Timmy almost dying, and then losing your dad that way. They ought to boil that guy alive. No trial, no lawyers, nothing. Just boil him alive."

Tom nodded.

"I know you must have times when you're right down at the bottom of a pit. I really love my dad, and when my parents split up, not that there's any comparison with what's happening to you, I was so hurt to think he could leave me and go so far away. And then when my brother got on drugs, I was right down at the bottom of that pit. It took a long time for me to climb out. Times I thought I never would, but I did. It gets better after a while, believe me. You don't think so, but it does."

He started to open his mouth, to say, "Robbie, I need to tell you something," but stopped. Maybe later the words would come more easily.

"Isn't this a lovely room?" asked Robbie for the third or fourth time.

He understood how much this little haven meant to her. She must have lived in miserable conditions, he thought tenderly, and thinking so, said, "Robbie, you haven't said what you pay for this room, but since I'm going to enjoy so much of it, too, it's only right that I help pay."

"Well, I won't say no, and yet are you sure you can afford it? I mean, are things going to be different for you now?"

"I can afford it," he said firmly.

"You're so good to me, Tom. The little things you think of, like this bear." She picked it up and hugged it. "I'm going to call him 'Tom, Jr.' Look at his big brown sexy eyes." And she caressed the bear, holding its plump white head between her pink satin breasts.

"Oh, Robbie!" he cried, "I wish I could stay here in this room with you forever and forever."

Then he knew he must have frightened her with his cry because she dropped the bear and stared at him.

"What is it? What's the matter? You look so desperate all of a sudden."

"I am desperate," he said. "I have a lot of trouble."

"Oh, tell me. Let me help you. What is it?"

His hands had begun to sweat, yet his mouth was dry. He got up for a glass of water, drank it all down, and then began.

"You're not going to believe this, but, well, have you ever heard of a case where an infant was switched with another at birth and was given to the wrong family?"

"Yes, I think I even read about it once in the papers or some magazine. Why?"

A large lump had formed somehow in his throat, making it hard to talk. Trying to swallow it, he took more water.

"Well," he began again, made a gesture of despair and stopped. "I don't even know how to tell you properly."

"What do you mean?" Robbie's eyebrows rose, and her eyes were stretched wide in alarm. "You don't mean yourself, that you—"

For a moment, unable to answer her, he propped his elbow on the chair's arm and rested his forehead in his hand. Robbie sprang up and knelt on the floor at his chair.

"Tom, Tom, is it you? Is it?"

"Yes," he mumbled, not looking at her.

There was a long silence. When at last he looked up at her, she was crying.

"My poor guy. My poor guy. You don't have to talk anymore now if you don't want to. It can wait till you feel better."

When she put her cheek against his, he felt her wet lashes,

felt her compassion, and suddenly it became possible to let the whole incredible tale spill forth.

"Ironic, isn't it, that the messenger should have been Ralph Mackenzie, of all people?" he said when he had finished, after long minutes during which she had sat spellbound.

"Yeah. A bearer of good tidings, as usual. God Almighty, of all the weird things to happen to a person. You live nineteen years, and then one day just like that"—and she snapped her fingers—"you find out you've been in the wrong place the whole time. I can't imagine it. Can't imagine myself."

"The awful thing is that it feels like the right place."

"Tell me, how do your parents—I mean, how did your father take it? I can't imagine them, either. It could almost drive a person crazy, I think."

"Mom's broken up, but you wouldn't think so if you didn't know her. She's a very controlled person, always keeps the lid on, tries to hide her red eyes for my sake, tries to reason things out. You know the type. And you have to admire all that. At the same time, it can also make you mad as hell."

"And your dad? Was he—"

"Oh," Tom said, "it was pathetic. Poor Dad, he refused to believe it. Almost the last words he ever spoke to me were, 'It's all a tricky pack of lies, Tom. Don't let them fool you.' Almost the last words before they—"

Robbie's forehead crinkled into an anxious frown. "But is it possible that he was right, though?"

Tom drew a long sigh. "How I wish! No, it's not. Actually, I'm almost sure Dad knew the truth, too. He simply didn't want to accept it, so he talked himself into denial. Look, we went through two weeks' worth of medical tests, blood work, DNA and mitochondria, the way they identified the Czar's bones. The works. Then there's the business about the other guy, the one my age, having the same disease Timmy has. Dad was too intelligent to discount all that. It came down to the question of accepting it, that's all. And he couldn't."

"Do you think he ever would have?"

"Who knows? But yes, I think he would have had to in the end."

"And have you accepted, Tom? I mean as much as anybody ever could? I mean, are you over the worst, mind-boggling shock of it?"

He bent down and stroked the heavy hair back from the tiny, anxious face. "I've had a lot of mornings when I was sorry I had woken up, and I mean that, Robbie. The thing that kept me going was knowing that I would be able to talk to you."

"My Tom, my Tom, what you've been through!"

"It isn't over yet." He spoke quietly now as he began to recognize in himself the return of his usual optimism. "Those people, those other people, they want me to—I don't know exactly what they do want—to recognize them, I suppose. Just recognize, whatever that involves."

"Don't you want to at all?"

"No. And I don't know how to handle it. They pressure me. Even Mom does. I'm supposed to be home today to meet them. That's why I sneaked out. Maybe you have some advice for me. I hope so, because I need it. God, how I need it."

"Who are they?"

"Well, it's a small world, as they say. You know that department store downtown not two miles from where we're sitting right now?"

"Sure, Crawfield's, where I bought my new curtains and black lace nightgown. Is that where they work, or where the man works?"

"They don't work there, they own it."

"Own it? Crawfield's? Still the original owners?"

"The grandfather founded it, I think, and they still have it."

Robbie was puzzled. "But they're Jews. Everybody knows they are. They can't be your—"

"Oh yes, they can be. My luck. My luck, Robbie."

"I don't believe it," she said, staring at him. "I don't believe it."

"But it's true."

She sprang up and stood leaning against the window frame, still staring at him. "It can't be. You can't be."

"You and my poor dad," Tom said sorrowfully.

"A Jew," she said.

He saw that she was trembling. Just so had he trembled, with his arms and his legs gone weak while his very heart had seemed to gasp in his breast, that day when Mom had called him to her and told him. And now, comprehending Robbie's anguish, he was very, very gentle.

"I'll get through it," he said consoling her. "Don't be afraid. I'm not going to let anything like this ruin my life—our lives together."

"A Jew," she repeated. "You. How does it feel?"

"Feel?" A puzzling question. "Why, no way, really, that I can describe except stunned. People came and told me, that's all, the way I'm telling you."

"You must feel different." Her voice was flattened with a tone he had never heard from her before.

"Different? Not *inside* myself. No, *I* haven't changed. I'm myself. What I've always been, no matter what anybody tells me."

"But something tells me you've known it all along, and you've hidden it." Tears started in her eyes.

He was astounded. "My God, Robbie, what are you saying?"

"That you knew it and you were afraid to tell me."

"My God, Robbie, I swear I've told you the whole truth. If I had wanted to hide it, why would I have revealed it today?"

She did not answer. When he moved toward her, she recoiled, flattening herself against the wall. Her tears spilled over, shining on her cheeks.

"Listen to me. Help me," he pleaded. "I counted on you."

Still she did not answer. An alteration had occurred. This that he was seeing in her eyes was not only shock and grief; it was also anger. She frightened him.

He pleaded again. "I'm Tom, the same Tom I was five minutes before you heard my story." And he tried to laugh, a wan,

weak apologetic laugh, as though this were all some sort of
foolish joke.

"You tricked me, Tom," she said, "and I hate myself."

He didn't want to believe he had heard her. And he
stretched out his hand.

"Come here. Take my hand. It's clean, it's kind, it has
touched you softly and loved every part of your body."

"Stop it. Do you have to remind me? Do you think I shall
ever forgive myself?" She began to sob. "What am I going to
tell people? What am I going to do now?"

"You'll tell people that I haven't committed any crime, and
we're going to go on as we were before."

"This has nothing to do with a crime. It's not what you ever
did or didn't do, it's what you are. Do I have to explain? You
don't need an explanation, you know what I'm talking about."

Yes, yes, he knew, but this was different . . . And putting
his arms around her, he pulled her to himself, murmuring her
name.

"Robbie, Robbie darling, don't talk like this. Robbie darling—"

Her sudden shove was so fierce that he went stumbling.
Appalled, he grasped the back of a chair, crying, "This can't
be you! What's happened to you? The way you look at me—"

"It's me, all right," she said grimly. "Do you really think it's
possible for me to look at you the way I did before I knew
this? Do you?"

He was desperate, and desperately he tried an appeal to
reason.

"Listen to me. Listen. I'm the same Tom. Look at my face,
my hands . . . I'm the identical person. They've given me a
new label, that's all . . . How can that change me? You
loved me, Robbie."

"What was, was. This is now."

"I was part of you. We were part of each other. And we
worked together. You respected me. You've said so a hundred
times."

"I didn't know, did I? That was all under false pretenses."

"Why don't you call Jim Johnson? Or we can both talk to him together. He's an intelligent man. He'll straighten this out. He'll understand the situation I'm in."

"Are you kidding? He'll advise me to get rid of you in the next five minutes."

He was frantic. And glancing around the room as if he was seeking for something, an iota of common sense, he saw a copy of Hitler's book lying on a chair. When he picked it up, her eyes followed him.

"So would you," he asked slowly, "so would you have had me killed if we had been living at that time, in that place?"

"Don't ask useless questions. I'm not killing you now, am I?"

"You are. You're doing it slowly."

"We're not getting anywhere with this talk. It's melodrama, and it disgusts me," she said with a shudder.

"It isn't melodrama, it's real life."

And they stood there facing each other as two people who, meeting in an unfamiliar place, might be not quite sure of each other's identity.

Then suddenly Robbie fell apart, and her voice screamed out in shrill, contemptuous laughter.

"Crawfield! Wouldn't my mom be happy to hear that! She'd kill you for laying a hand on me, and me for letting you do it."

He looked at her blazing eyes and her contorted mouth. It seemed to him that the world was crazy, and he said so.

"The world is crazy, and you've gone crazy, too."

"You think so? No. I'm very, very sane, and you'd better believe it. And what's more, you'd better get out. Fast, too. Hear me?"

She was screaming loud enough to be heard in the basement. In a minute somebody would be knocking at the door. He reached for his clothes; all this time he had been in his underwear and must look absurd. She hadn't even the decency to turn away while he put his pants on. She just stood there watching him.

He hated her. Hated, and understood how a law-abiding human being can be driven in one mad moment to murder. Let him get the hell out of here. . . . He picked up his duffel and went to the door.

"Wait," she said, "take this, too." And she handed him the polar bear, Tom, Jr., with the beautiful brown sexy eyes.

And he left without a word.

What was it that he felt back on the highway speeding home? Hatred was too simple. There had to be much more to it: rage, shame, and grief. Which of them was uppermost, he did not know. He only knew that he had been crushed and trampled on, that he was in despair. His Robbie, whom he thought he knew! He began to sob, and hoped no one would see him lest he be arrested as a drunken driver. He drove and drove, with hours ahead of him, going home to he knew not what. Recriminations, probably, because of the damned Crawfields again. But he had no other place to go.

Suddenly he was hungry. At a diner he stopped and ordered a hamburger with french fries. Yet when the plate was put in front of him, he did not want it.

The waitress, a tired young woman, inquired whether anything was wrong with the food.

"No," he said, "I made a mistake, that's all." He paid the bill, left a tip, and suddenly asked, "Do you have a child?"

"Why, yes—" she began, and then, suspiciously, demanded, "Why? What's it to you, anyway?"

"Don't worry," he said, "I'm not being personal. It's just— Wait a minute."

He ran out to the car and came back with the bear. "Here," he said, "this is for your kid."

Astonished at the obviously expensive toy, she apologized. "I didn't mean to give you a nasty answer. This is so nice of you. I really didn't mean—"

"That's all right. You were being careful, and you have every right to be, the world being what it is and people what they are."

And he ran out, leaving her staring after him.

It was almost midnight when he turned into the driveway and put the car into the garage. The house was dark except for the ceiling light above the piano where his mother was playing. And recognizing the fragmented, wandering strains of Debussy, he knew that she was still deeply sad.

Not ready to go inside, he sat down on the steps of the veranda. It was a dark night, and the stars were brilliant, there the Big Dipper, there Ursa Major, there, beyond and beyond, another universe and yet more, unnamed, unseen, unknown. His eyes roved in a circle through the unfathomed glitter and returned to the backyard where suddenly a bird, no more ignorant than a man about the Ultimate, gave a startled cry.

The world is crazy, he thought again as he had thought in the moment of Robbie's transformation. She despised him! His Robbie! And Dad's bloodied face was smashed. And a Rice was turned into a Crawfield, a damned Crawfield. Everything had gone wrong from that poisonous day when Mackenzie brought the message.

After a while, he got up, quietly unlocked the back door, and as quietly crept up to his room. There again he sat some more and tried to think. But no thoughts came other than that he most certainly would not, could not go back to college. He could not see himself passing her in a corridor or existing within sight or sound or cognizance of her, ever again.

On the table next to the bed where he was half sitting, half lying, stood the photograph. There she was, smiling at him, showing her perfect teeth and her lavish windblown hair. Happy, she had been. Happy! And hard, hard, without mercy.

He seized the picture, to shatter the glass on the floor. Then he ripped it in half, into quarters, eighths, and scraps.

So much for you, Robbie. May someone someday do to you what you did to me.

The vague, dreamy music that had been filtering up the stairs now stopped. He turned off the light and closed his door. The morning would be time enough to let Mom find out that he had come home.

She knocked and called, "Tom, I heard you. You can't be asleep yet. May I come in?"

"I'm falling asleep," he lied.

She opened the door and switched on the light. Now she would see the debris on the floor, and he would have to explain. In her nice way, she would force him to.

But she made no mention of it, although it was right in front of her. Instead she expressed a mild surprise. "I thought from your note that you'd be gone for a few days at least."

"I'm sorry, Mom. It wasn't the most decent thing to do, running out like that. I only hoped you'd understand why I had to do it."

"I understood."

Her patience made him more sorry for her, more guilty for causing her so much pain.

"You didn't have to creep in like this. Didn't you want to talk to me? Did you think I'd be too angry?"

"That wasn't it. I didn't want to wake Timmy."

She smiled. "You never fool me, Tom. Any more than I can fool you. Just because I don't say anything, it doesn't mean I don't see things."

He gave her a weak smile in return. "The mess on the floor? Well, I'm through with my girlfriend. We had a big blowup and it's all over."

"I'm sorry. Was she a wonderful person?"

"No, as I found out. It hurts all the same. To be rejected," he said, hearing his own bitterness, "to have somebody just turn about and walk away from you. It hurts like hell."

"Yes, it feels as if the world has come to an end."

"How can you know? You never—"

"People your age forget that everybody was your age once."

"You're a good mother," he cried out suddenly, astonishing himself with the outburst. "And to think that you're not really, not really—" He could say no more.

"But I am your mother. I am and I always will be," she said.

Her eyes filled. She gave a rueful laugh and wiped the tears away with the back of her hand. "Too many tears around here lately, don't you think?" She looked down at the floor. "Do you want to tell me what happened?"

"It's too long a story. She found out, or I told her, about myself, the Crawfields and all that business."

"I see. Found out that you were born a Jew."

"Don't say that, please, Mom."

"I guess she doesn't think that you belong on the staff of *The Independent Voice* anymore. Well, I don't think you do, either. It's a vicious, dirty rag, fit for the KKK and nobody else."

He gave a long, tired sigh. "I guess it is. But Dad—"

"When someone in my family is or has been wrong I have to say so."

"I wish Dad had been—been different. I wish he hadn't been in the KKK. I loved him so."

"It would have been better for you if he hadn't, to say nothing of being better for himself. He threw away so much that was good in him."

He wanted to silence her, to silence the buzzing in his confused, exhausted brain.

"The door's open. You'll wake Timmy," he said.

"He's not here. He'll be away till next Sunday."

"Away? Where's he gone?"

"The Crawfields took him along with them to the lake."

He was astounded. It seemed to him that nothing was too absurd to be possible.

"Yes, we had a very nice lunch. Holly was really sweet to Timmy. She's a lovely girl. Ralph—Mr. Mackenzie—joined us later, and since he knows them so well and he seemed to approve, I let Timmy go."

"Did he want to go?"

"Of course. I wouldn't have sent him otherwise, would I? He obviously liked the family. It'll do him good."

Liked the family. They're moving in on us. Taking my

brother. It's like lying in the arms of an octopus. There's no escape.

"So it seems that you're all on their side now, you and Timmy both."

"Don't be silly, there are no 'sides' here."

"I hate them," he said, through clenched teeth. "If you knew how I hate them. And I'm never going to see them. Never."

"Well, we can talk about that another time if you want to. It's late, and the subject's too deep for the hour. Good night, dear Tom."

He would become a recluse. He'd stay here for a while, he told himself, do Bud's work around the house and Mom's garden, take Bud's place, a father's place with Timmy, read, study astronomy, and maybe when he felt ready for it, find some kind of job, probably a simple one, in an observatory; he'd find the most remote location that there was, away from people.

Yes, he knew very well that worse things could befall a human being than had just now befallen him. Take cystic fibrosis, for one. An innocent like Timmy, to be so threatened! Still, if your leg was broken, you felt the pain, and it didn't ease the pain to be told that somebody else had two broken legs.

And suddenly *her* face, Margaret Crawfield's face, appeared before him again, bright and clear in the darkness of his room. Why did her face persist in such exact detail, as if he had actually wanted to memorize it, which, God knew, he hadn't? Her gold earrings were shaped like little shells, one of them partly hidden because of the way her hair fell over it. Her cheeks were round, her eyes bewildered, her lipstick faintly russet . . .

Damn to hell the morons in that hospital who put me where I am today! And yet don't damn them, because I'd a thousand times rather be where I am than where I would have been if they had not done what they did. . . .

On the next day the doorbell rang while Tom and Laura were having a silent breakfast. Tom answered it. Two men stood before him.

"Thomas Rice?" inquired one.

"Yes, what is it?" he answered, wondering; then, seeing the camera slung around the other man's neck, he suddenly knew and was struck by panic. Nevertheless, he asked, "What do you want?"

At that moment, the camera caught him, openmouthed and fearful. The first man handed him a newspaper.

"Your paper. I guess you haven't seen it yet."

Tom glanced. It was folded in half, but what the left-hand column disjointedly revealed was enough to justify his terrified, racing heart.

Local family . . . hospital mix-up . . . two infants . . .

"We'd like an interview," the man said, pleasantly enough.

"No!" he cried, so despairingly that Laura came running.

She saw at once what the matter was. "Tom, go inside," she commanded.

She must have expected this, he thought, retreating into the shadows of the hall.

She was quite calm. "No interviews," she said as the camera caught her, too.

"It's news, ma'am. Unusual news."

"That may be, but it's human suffering besides."

He took out his notebook and began to write.

"You were here a while ago when my husband was killed. I remember you. Don't you think this family has had enough for a while?" she asked quietly.

"It's my job. For me, it's just a job, and I do it."

"I understand. And it's my job to protect my son, you see."

"He's not really your son though, anymore, is he? How does it feel to find that out after nineteen years?"

"A whole lot better than your face will feel, because if you don't get it out of the way, I'm going to slam this door on it. And you may print that."

She slammed the door. Tom ran to the window and watched the men drive away.

"I was afraid they might stay and peer in at the windows," he said, trembling.

"They'll be back, Tom, and there'll be more of them, here and at the Crawfields' house. Be sure of it."

"If it's in the papers already, what more do they want from us?"

" 'Human interest story,' " she said shortly. "That's what it's called. I wonder how—I'm going to call Mr. Fordyce."

In the library, Tom sat with his head in his hands, listening to his subsiding heartbeat. When he raised his head, he found himself looking into the eyes of the "black Irishman," supposedly his ancestor.

Human interest, he thought. Yes, very. It probably is very interesting unless you happen to be the object of the interest.

From the kitchen across the hall, Laura's telephone conversation was audible.

"I thought you had it all fixed, Mr. Fordyce . . . Yes, yes, I understand there can be no guarantees . . . I know, but it's so awful for Tom. And such a short time after the other horror . . . Yes, I'm thankful, too, that Lillian and Cecile aren't here in the thick of it. The Paiges have always been so private . . . Die down? In time, of course. Nothing is forever, is it?"

Tom heard the telephone click and waited for Laura's report. It was several minutes before she came back, and when she spoke, he sensed reluctance.

"The story came from the wire service. That means it goes all over the country, and no paper will hold it back. The editor here feels bad about it, Mr. Fordyce said. He had concealed it so nicely up till yesterday. Fordyce knew yesterday that this was coming, investigated, and did his best to stave it off. But there's no help for it now."

"Do they know who reported it?" he asked.

"A woman. They don't know her name. She sounded young. She was apparently informed of every detail, the time and place of the births, the names, the DNA tests, everything. And the hospital confirmed what she said."

Tom winced. "She betrayed me, didn't she?" he cried.

Laura laid her hand on his shoulder and began softly, "She betrayed more than you alone, Tom. She was untrue to basic human decency. What made her think"—and now Laura's voice rose almost passionately—"that she was so much better than other people, that she dared judge and condemn? Betty Lee, for instance, or the Crawfield family, or—or you, Tom? What?"

He said miserably, "She was so intelligent, a scholar, worked her own way, so energetic, so unusual—"

"Yes, some of Hitler's most powerful Nazis had their Ph.D.'s. But they had no morals, no human heart."

The phone rang, and Laura went to it, saying, "Don't you answer it. I'm going to take charge of it today."

He heard her speak. "Yes, this is Mrs. Rice. No, I'll take the message for him."

When she put the phone down, it rang immediately again. "Who was it?" he asked.

Laura was grim. "Pigs. Filth. Boys'—men's—voices. From college."

Yes, he could imagine the guys on *The Independent Voice.* They'd be mocking him, laughing, whooping it up. *Jeez, Tom Rice! Jeez, can you beat it?*

Again the phone rang. Was the whole world, with all that was happening both here and abroad, going to focus on Tom Rice?

"This horrible girl, this Nazi," Laura was saying. "And he doesn't want to go back to college—"

He got up and started to walk out of the house. Then it occurred to him that more newspaper people might be lurking there, so he went up to his room instead and sat staring out the window at the heap of stones on Earl's grave.

And he thought about Bud. He thought about the Klan, their vile talk of bullets and blood. He remembered how, watching them that night, he had been afraid and curious, but how most of all, he had had an urge to laugh at their stupidity. It was only that Bud had been so proud—

He thought of the promise he had made to take Bud's place, to avenge him. Now finally he knew it was a promise he would not keep. Whatever had happened to turn Bud in that direction it was too late to learn, and he regretted that with all his heart.

Whatever had turned Robbie, he thought perhaps he understood: anger at her life, a slatternly mother, the loved father who had put as much distance between himself and his quarreling family as he could—rage at them had turned into rage at the world.

The telephone and the doorbell rang intermittently all that day. More papers, dailies and weeklies, national magazines, and a talk show, all wanted the story.

"But you have the facts already, all there are," Laura told them. "What you want is our reaction, an X ray of our hearts, and you're not going to have it. And as to making a display of ourselves on television, you can forget it."

At noon she called Tom to the kitchen to have lunch. He wasn't hungry, he protested.

"Take half a sandwich, at least. You can't let this situation break you down."

They were sitting at the kitchen table when Betty Lee's face appeared at the upper half of the door. From her expression they knew at once that she had read the paper. As it turned out, she had heard the local news on the radio.

The two women put their arms around each other and Betty Lee cried.

"I felt in my bones that there was trouble in this house even before Mr. Bud was killed. Then my head said no, I was imagining it. But you see, the bones were right. Oh Tom, I don't care what any old science men or lawyers or anybody says, you are my Tom-baby. Your mother came home from the hospital and put you in my arms. You had on a blue sweater that your aunt Cecile crocheted, and you were the prettiest little boy baby, your daddy's and your mother's pet. And I'm coming back here again to stay. Yes, I am."

Dear Betty Lee. She meant so well with her kind, tearful recollections. And he was thankful that the aunts were not here also, with more tears and recollections.

Tired as Laura was, her head stayed high all through that long day. He wished he was able to hold his own head as high, but he was not able and was back at his window looking out into the yellow afternoon when Laura came to him again.

"That was Ralph on the phone." He noticed that she now omitted "Mr. Mackenzie." "He just heard from Arthur Crawfield. Some reporters managed to find out that the family was at the lake and they've been there taking pictures, asking a thousand questions. They may come back earlier. At home it will be easier to avoid reporters."

Tom was silent, and Laura continued, "But Ralph thinks we all might just as well give the reporters what they want, and they'll go away. We've nothing to hide, he said. We've nothing to be ashamed of, and he's right." She paused a moment reflectively. "Ralph is usually right, I've found. I told him you don't want to go to college, but of course, you know you must go somewhere. He has connections with Stevenson, a small college in New England, and he's pretty sure they'll take you in the circumstances and late as it is."

In the circumstances. Because I'm some sort of freak, that's why, with a father who isn't my father, in the Ku Klux Klan.

"Will you go there if he can arrange it, Tom?" Laura asked. "It's supposed to be a very fine place."

Her eyes were anxious. He couldn't let himself hurt her anymore.

"Yes," he said, "I suppose I'll have to."

Timmy was brought home on Saturday. Tom was in his room—he had spent most of the week in his room reading or sleeping—when he heard the car and the voices. From the sounds he ascertained that there were two women and a man.

Then he heard Timmy's shout, "Where's Tom?" and a few seconds later, Timmy burst through his door.

"Look! Look!" he shouted.

A small, bedraggled dog came after him. Part terrier and part unknown quantity, it made the late Earl seem handsome.

"Isn't he beautiful? I named him Earl the Third."

Tom had to smile. "Why the Third? He's only the Second."

"I don't know. It just sounded better. Isn't he beautiful? He's housebroken and comes when he's called."

The dog sat up and, with his whiskered head cocked to one side, regarded Tom as if he were a curiosity to be studied.

"We got him this morning at the shelter where Holly volunteers. Somebody had found him on the roadside, hungry and scared. The lady said probably he had been dumped there. People do that, can you believe it? Anyway, he's had a week at the shelter to be washed and fed, and he's in good shape. Right, Earl?"

Wise brown eyes turned toward Timmy. The scrap of a tail wagged.

"There was a purebred Airedale there that Uncle Arthur thought I should take, but I really wanted this one. Uncle Arthur gave them a nice contribution, too."

"So it's 'Uncle Arthur.' Who told you to call him that?"

"He said I might call them both 'Mr.' and 'Mrs.' or 'Uncle' and 'Aunt,' and I liked Uncle and Aunt, since we don't have any of our own except Mom's, and they're our greats. And they're really nice, Tom. I had an awesome time. We sailed around the lake and anchored on an island, we had a picnic there, then we even went back to their house yesterday and went to the shelter this morning. They've got a neat house, it has a barbecue in the kitchen —"

"I've seen their house."

"I forgot. Anyway, I had a great time. They're nice, Tom, they really are. Let me tell you what we —"

"Look, kid, I know you mean well, but I don't want to talk about them." He knew he was being brusque, but this net was drawing too tight. "Uncle and Aunt!" Tighter and tighter, as if he didn't know they were trying to pull him in.

To Tom's surprise, Timmy just shrugged. "Okay, you don't have to. You think they're after you," he said, with rather a shrewd expression, Tom thought, "but we were all talking one night, and Uncle Arthur said you're a man, you can do what you want with your life, and if you don't want to have anything to do with them, you don't have to."

"He said that?"

"On my honor, Tom. He's a very smart man. He knows a lot of new things about cystic fibrosis, too. He studies about it, and—"

"Well, Mom and Dad did too. What do you think, that they didn't?"

"I know that," Timmy said impatiently, "but this is brand, brand new, only a few months old. Uncle Arthur explained what they're doing with genes; they're going to try putting better genes into our airway tissue, they expect to try it on some people next year, it'll take a few years, maybe five, Uncle Arthur says, but—"

Tom wanted to interrupt again with the remark that "Uncle Arthur was no scientist," but the boy's eyes were so alive with hope, so gay with excitement, that he refrained.

"Well, that's good news," he said.

"And I'm young enough so that even if it does take that long, it won't be too late for me."

No, pray God it won't, little brother.

"It's called 'genetic manipulation,' and it'll really be a cure, not just a medicine. If they'd only had it, then Peter wouldn't have died."

Oh yes. Peter, the Other One.

"They talk about Peter a lot. He looked like me. Holly says he was a wonderful brother. They hardly ever fought. He was very good-tempered."

Like you, Tom thought. Like your mother.

"I like her. We played chess. I wasn't much good at it to start, but she taught me a lot."

How innocent, Tom thought. A game of chess wins him over.

"Come on downstairs, Tom. You can't stay up here."

"Why can't I?"

"Dad taught us manners, didn't he? Even Aunt Margaret said I have good manners, and I told her Dad was strict about manners."

"Yes? And what did she say to that?"

"She said that was good of Dad."

Tom prodded now. "Did they have anything else to say about Dad?"

Timmy appeared to be reaching into his memory. Then he said, "Well, I don't know what started it, maybe I said something first, but Uncle Arthur said that Dad's being in the Klan was terribly wrong, yet we should thank him for the good things he did for us."

That sounded like Dr. Foster at the funeral.

"Come on down, Tom."

"It's so hard for me, Timmy. You don't know how hard."

"Yeah, I know. You're all upset about that girl. I see her picture's not here."

"For Pete's sake, who told you about that?" Tom cried indignantly.

"Mr. Mackenzie told Uncle Arthur and we talked about it. Aunt Margaret said how hard it must be for you to accept, or something like that."

His private affairs laid open to be chewed over . . . Had they all nothing better to do?

"She stinks, Tom. She lied, too. I read all the stuff in that paper you had on your desk. That stuff about blacks. And I thought about Betty Lee. The stuff about foreigners, and I thought about Mr. Foutiades at the pancake shop and Mr. Bruno the barber. The stuff about Jews. Why, you're one yourself, Tom! You see how she lied? She stinks."

The innocent, decent kid, holding his dog in his arms, kid with an earnest plea . . .

"Come downstairs, Tom. Please come."

"Okay. Okay, I will," he said.

They were gathered on the long back veranda, the three women at one end seated, while Arthur Crawfield stood alone at the far end, looking out toward the garden. Timmy promptly went to him, while Tom, after minimal greetings, sat down on a bench by himself, halfway between the two groups. And he realized that there must be some agreement, tacit or otherwise, among them all, including Mom, to let him alone.

He wanted that, yet every nerve in him was alert; his ears and the corners of his eyes paid attention in both directions.

The women were talking about jewelry. Mom was saying something about her aunts on their round-the-world trip.

"They love to shop, and Lillian, especially, has a connoisseur's eye. This necklace arrived last month from Bangkok."

"A lovely present to arrive in the mail," said Margaret.

"Yes, but the funny thing is I'm really not all that wild about jewelry, and they've still not caught on. Everything I own came from them."

In a high, pretty voice Holly exclaimed, "But it's gorgeous. Look how it's made. Do the petals move?"

Laura's answering voice had a smile in it. "Come, feel it."

They made a picture, the girl's glossy head bent toward Laura's neck, the gold flashing through her fingers.

Only Jews like jewelry, Robbie had sniffed. Lillian and Cecile would be surprised to hear that.

Holly said, "It happens to be perfect on you. You have the right neck to show it off, a beautiful long neck. I wish I had a longer neck. It's so graceful."

Mom obviously liked this girl. And she had been so nice to Timmy . . .

Arthur strolled past Tom down the length of the veranda, ignoring him.

"I think I may have a buyer for your property," he said to Laura. "We buy from a furniture manufacturer who wants to expand in this area. From what I remember, your plant could be adapted easily."

Tom's thoughts were on other things. He was feeling all

queer and sad. How could this have happened to him, this double blow: new parents, Jewish parents, a Jewish sister?

Yet it wasn't their fault any more than it was Mom's. He ought really to be asking why they, this pair of parents, should have been the victims of some stupid nurse. Surely they were just as badly hurt as he was, to be fair about it.

"Yes," he heard Laura say briskly. "First it was Paige alone, then Paige and Rice, then Rice and Son. Now we move on."

"It's the only way," replied Arthur.

When he stood before Tom, he seemed to be waiting for him to say something first. When Tom did not, he began.

"I'm sorry about—" and Tom knew he was hesitating between "your father" and "Bud," which would be too familiar, so that he ended by saying, "what happened. It was a terrible death, wicked and cruel."

"But he was a Klan man. I should think you would say he deserved it," Tom said bitterly.

"Violence is never the answer, even toward Klansmen, who teach violence."

"They want your destruction," Tom said.

"I know that."

"Then I don't really understand you."

"No, but someday you will."

This was an odd individual. My father! he thought with the same pounding shock he had felt at the first encounter. This time he tried *absorbing* the man, his laconic speech, his habit of blinking behind his glasses, and the slight frown that could mean disapproval or else that he was trying to solve a puzzle.

"You're not thinking, are you, that I see myself as some kind of Holy Roller? Not at all. I only know that once people are allowed to drive a car through a crowd of living bodies, we'll all be living in a jungle. But enough of that. I want to talk about you, Tom. About us."

Tom said awkwardly, "I should thank you for giving Timmy the dog. He's so happy with him."

"That's fine. But I said I want to talk about you. Listen, Tom. You don't have to be close to us if you don't want to. I've already made that clear. But I worry about your prejudices, not for my sake, but for yours. They're acid, they'll eat you up, and in the end, destroy you somehow as they did the man who was your father."

"He wasn't a bad man," Tom protested.

"No, he was just dreadfully misled. Foolish enough to allow himself to be, as so many in Germany were misled. You heard Albert, my father-in-law, you heard what he endured. And do you know that, like Anne Frank, he still believes in human goodness? It's a question of education, he says. One must be taught right."

Strange people, Tom thought, and then, recalling Dr. Foster, felt a slight smile on his lips.

"Why are you smiling?" asked Arthur.

"Because that's what they taught when I went to Sunday school."

"Of course. Because it is right."

The women had stopped talking and were listening, so that Tom became the object of attention, and it made him uncomfortable. His hands began to sweat again.

And a shock went through him, much like the one he'd had on the first morning when, on waking, he'd remembered that Bud was dead. This girl, this Holly on whose arm Mom's hand now rested as they listened, would, if she had gone to state U, been one of those who received the anonymous dirty messages that Robbie's group sent out. He winced, thinking suddenly that he had never done anything like that. In his mind's ear now he heard again Robbie's jeering laugh; in his mind's eye he saw the contempt on her face; contempt for him whom she had so "loved," whose scholarship she had so admired, a scholarship far superior to her own. And again a terrible anger flared in him. But this time it was not merely on his own behalf.

"As to your faith, if you have any and I hope you have," Arthur said, "I also hope you will keep it. In your heart, I mean, not just give lip service to it. Peter kept his—ours—till the last." A cloud came briefly over his face and passed. "Are you still interested in astronomy?" And when Tom nodded, "A person who studies the universe will enlarge his mind and hatred will become picayune, stupid, impossible. Did you enjoy the book we sent to you?"

"I tore it up," Tom said, and not trying to hide his shame, looked straight at Arthur.

Arthur looked straight back. "That's understandable. Well, we'll get you another one, if you want. Shall we? You tell me, and don't be polite. Tell the truth."

"I'd like another one," Tom said.

And he thought once more that this was an unusual man. You could be sure that Bud's attitude toward Arthur would not have been like Arthur's toward Bud, if the situation had been reversed. Yet he wondered whether, if he had been brought up by Arthur, there could have been the closeness he had had with Bud, the hunting, fishing, playing ball, the jokes . . . Perhaps, but he rather thought not. They were so different.

At any rate, it didn't really matter, did it? Now was now.

"Life has treated us very strangely," Arthur said, as if he was musing to himself. "Think of it. A nurse's carelessness gave Peter to a family that made a good Jew out of him, and gave you to your good mother Laura and to Timmy. Incidentally, he and I are friends, do you know that?"

"He told me," answered Tom.

"Give me your hand, Tom."

Arthur took it and held it for a moment in both of his. "God bless you," he said.

Tom needed to cry, but he wouldn't let himself. It wasn't manly to cry. Bud had taught him that as far back as when he'd skinned his knee falling off his three-wheeler. Yet in spite of this resolve, his eyes filled with tears.

"I don't know what to feel," he blurted.

And suddenly Margaret rushed to him. She was so small, half a head shorter than he, so that he had to look down at her as she held him, down at the face that had been appearing in his dreams, the round, flushed cheeks, the big wet eyes, the hair curved over one cheek, and the earring, the little golden shell.

And he was struck, struck by a shaft of light that dazzled his brain, while at the same time he was aware of what was happening to him. An epiphany, he thought, like the conversions one reads about, the ancient miracles and revelations.

"I'm sorry," he murmured. "I'm sorry about what I've done."

She put her fingers over his lips. "No, no. It's all right. It's all right now."

Over Margaret's head he saw Mom watching and crying, too. And with the instant comprehension that was so much a part of her, she read his fear that this scene would grieve her, after all.

"Oh, Tom," she cried, "there's room for more than one in your heart! We'll all do well together. I'm not afraid."

It was Holly who relieved the overwhelming emotion of the moment. "Goodness, there's enough water in this place to turn all the dead brown grass out there to green." She flapped her own damp handkerchief in the air.

Then, just as the mood broke into laughter, Earl the Third raised his leg against the veranda's railing.

"More water!" shrieked Holly.

Timmy quickly picked him up and set him out on the lawn. "I'll have him trained by next week, Mom," he called back. "Don't worry, I will."

By now everyone was laughing, and Tom was thinking that Timmy was right and Holly really was okay.

"What about telephoning Ralph?" suggested Arthur, and asked Laura, "Do you mind?"

"Why, not at all," she said, hoping her face would not betray her.

"He tried so hard to bring all this about," said Margaret.

And Laura directed Tom, "Run down to the cellar closet, will you, dear? If ever a day deserved it, this one deserves champagne."

CHAPTER

—— 17 ——

Five after five, Laura read on the glowing dial of the bedside clock in Aunt Cecile's old room. It would have been unthinkable to bring Ralph into the room she had shared with Bud; indeed, that room was now being dismantled, awaiting a complete renewal. In the high bird's-eye maple bed, Ralph was still asleep. He did not stir while she got up, found her robe in the dark, and went downstairs.

Her slippered feet had not evaded the sharp ears of Earl the Third, who now came swiftly to join her in the kitchen. Most likely, he had been restless, sleeping alone in Timmy's room this night. And as she bent down to pat him, she felt the smile that began to creep over her face. She couldn't say she had actually planned to have Ralph stay here, when she had suggested to Timmy that it might be fun to spend election night at his best friend's house. She hadn't planned it, but she had definitely hoped.

The smile broadened. "Well, Earl, you never know, do you?" she said, and went to put a pot of coffee on the stove. "Not that I need waking up," she added.

It had been a long time since she had felt this peculiar joy, actually not since girlhood, she thought, so long a time that she had forgotten how it felt, remembering only the marvel of it. Slowly, slowly, the memory, too, had lost its color and gone gray, how gray she had not even realized until now.

And, as the sky began to lighten toward another mild November morning, and bare treetops grew distinct behind the hedge and behind the roof of the old Alcott house, she sat there sipping the good warmth and musing. Forward, back, and forward again, the film runs . . .

Yesterday at headquarters, watching the screen as the returns came sweeping in, and the telephones jangled without stay. Anxious faces floating, anxious feet hurrying, and rumors spreading, only to be denied.

And the evening at last, waiting and hoping until, near midnight, the hope became reality and uproarious celebration broke loose into a pandemonium of music and balloons and noise.

Then Ralph coming to her after an hour of all that. "I've been looking all over for you in this crowd. Enough! I've thanked everyone I can think of, so let's get out of here. There's nobody I want to be with except you."

And the weeks before this, the last glimpse of Tom at the airport, willing to go, revivified, with his head up. His assurances over the telephone; new friends, astronomy, his first sight of a near blizzard, and more.

"Don't worry about me, Mom. Honestly, I mean it."

And Timmy, hopeful now, without the vague, anxious look that had always lurked even at his most cheerful moments. Please God, let the hope be warranted.

And the aunts, who took three full days and nights of talk on their way back to Florida to absorb the story of Peter and Tom—not that they had absorbed it fully yet, or that anyone ever really could.

Figuratively, they had wrung their hands over Bud. "The Ku Klux Klan! And he such a gentleman," mourned Cecile, who, so clever at business, could also be so naive. "Such a gentleman! I would never have believed it if anyone had told me."

Lillian, who had been enthusiastic about Jim Johnson, assured Ralph that "If we still lived in this state, we'd all vote for you." Ralph had given Laura a surreptitious wink. But he liked the aunts.

"I suppose you'll be getting married someday," Lillian said privately. "You'll wait a year at the very least, naturally."

"Do have it in the house," advised Cecile. "Elegant, but small in the circumstances. He's a very fine catch, dear."

So women really do still talk that way, Laura thought, amused.

"You're leaping way ahead," she had replied. "No one said anything about a wedding."

"Oh, but I see it coming," had said Cecile, the romantic.

"What are you doing?" asked Ralph, coming now into the kitchen. "It's almost the middle of the night."

"Just thinking. I'm so grateful that you won."

"I won the battle. But the war against the Johnsons is never won, neither here nor in Bosnia."

"It's as bad as that."

"Of course it is. You know they've got all sorts of groups under other names, selling neo-Nazi literature, corrupting the young. They spread themselves like a disease, a virus."

"Thank God, Tom conquered the virus."

"Yes," Ralph said soberly. "What do you hear from him?"

"Nice things. Holly's college is a three-hour-ride's distance, so he borrowed a car last weekend and went to take her to lunch. It was funny, the way he tells it. It seems some fellow he knew saw him with her and asked him later who 'the cute girl' was. So he simply told them the whole story, and it didn't seem to bother him in the least to tell it. Naturally, they were amazed, and that's all there is to it."

"He's a good guy. I always suspected he was. But was he ever angry at me! At one point, I didn't see how I'd ever get to you, with all that anger directed at me." Ralph waited a moment, searching through the past. "I'll never forget the day I brought that terrible news to this house. My heart was racing so that I didn't think I'd manage to get the words out."

"You were very calm, though."

"That was my legal training."

"You were very kind. That isn't legal training, it's you."

He squeezed her hand. "We've come a long way in a short time, Laura."

He looked at her so intently, so earnestly, and yet so eagerly, that she was struck with a kind of pain.

"I told you once, or maybe I only think I did, that I believe there is something like an alter ego, the *other self*, and that's what I was looking for. And I felt it that first day when I saw you here."

"Had you never felt anything like it before?"

"I told you, I've had my full share of women, but that way —no. You have, though."

"Once."

"I won't ask you about it."

"It's ancient history. Finished and over. Everything is. Myself as Mrs. Homer Rice—that's all over, too. And probably was long before I realized it."

Before I knew the extent of his deceit, she thought, knowing what I have just found out.

Later, sometime today, she would tell Ralph the rest of the story. But the whole day lay ahead, and later would do as well as now.

"You're not going to work today, are you?" she asked him.

"No. A man's entitled to recuperate from all his politicking on the day after he has won an election."

"What would you like to do with the day?"

"Do you want to know? I'd like to go back upstairs."

It was so *right* to go "back upstairs." This night, their first night, had been completely *right,* the last step in an orderly progression from the hour when they had sat in the coffee shop at the Hotel Phoenix and she had thought, or could she possibly actually have told him, that he looked like Lincoln. A funny thought for a person born south of the Mason-Dixon Line . . .

"You're laughing. At what?"

"Not really. Just smiling."

At the bedroom door he opened his arms wide to summon her into them. His eyes were bright with his happiness. And she thought, as he held her breast to breast, I never want to lose him.

Late in the afternoon they went to sit on the veranda. Ralph was examining an old guitar that Aunt Cecile had left on the closet shelf years before. A thin twang trembled as his fingers moved on the strings.

And suddenly Laura interrupted him. "I have something here, a letter. It came three days ago, but I didn't want to trouble you with it until the election was past."

"Trouble me? Is it bad news?"

"I'll let you decide. Will you read it? Or shall I read it to you?"

"You read it to me, please."

She took it out of the envelope and in a strange, tense voice, unfamiliar even to herself, began to read.

"The stationery is headed: Francis Alcott, with an address in New York. Here it is.

" 'Dear Laura,

" 'When you read this, I shall be dead. Tomorrow I am to undergo surgery on my heart, and I do not believe I will survive it, but will go as my father did, at his same age. The Alcotts don't make old bones.

" 'My attorney will destroy this letter if I should survive because I want now, at long last, to come to you myself and tell you, along with everyone else concerned, what you will be reading here.

" 'Since I left home I have gone back every two or three years with the intention of seeing you. Perhaps you will not believe me, and I cannot blame you if you do not, but it is true that I have walked around and driven past your house time and time again, trying to find courage enough to ring the doorbell. I used to visit my parents' graves and my most distant relatives, but when the last day came, I would still not have found the courage to ring the bell.

" 'In the past few years my heart has been having "episodes," and after each one, I have resolved again, before it should be too late, to see you, but as with the embezzler who is determined surely to return the money "someday," the day never came.

" 'Dear Laura, I have loved you, or shall I say "the memory of you," all my life. I know now that I must have loved you when you were still a child, perhaps only ten years old, but since it was not "right" to do so, my conscious mind did not permit me to. But when I came home that weekend after four years away, then you were twenty, and it would have been, it was "right"; and *recognition* when you came through the hedge and crossed the lawn toward me was like an explosion, like fireworks soaring into that summer night. When you played *A Little Night Music*, when you threw crumbs to the birds on the beach the next day, and when we— But you know the rest.

" 'So now I must get to the core of the matter. I have kept up with the news at home; I know that you are a recent widow, and I know the circumstances. Also, I have the newspaper stories about the Crawfields' and the Rices' babies. Dear Laura, it is at this point that my pen wants to stop, but I will not allow it to.

" 'The exchange of the babies, the frightful, cruel, unspeakable deed, was done by me.

" 'I can see you now as you read these words, your trembling hands, your horror, your outrage and your grief. Why? you will demand. How is it possible for a human being to plot such a wanton, brutal thing?

" 'I will tell you. It was not plotted or planned. It was a spontaneous act that, ten minutes afterward, I would gladly have undone if I safely could have. It was an inexcusable act, born out of desperation.

" 'On the evening when I went to visit you and your newborn boy at the hospital, I was carrying a burden of information that you did not have and that I could not possibly have given to you. I had returned, as you must remember, because of my father's death. In going over his papers to see what records had to be transferred and what discarded, I came upon one, going back for years, of your husband's family. You probably know that he had a sister who died in early childhood and an uncle who died at twenty-one, as well as a cousin in the prior generation who died young. What you may not know is that they all had cystic fibrosis. And I found a note in my father's handwriting about a discussion he had had with Homer Rice before he married you, in which he, my father, had advised him strongly never to have children. Laura, if your husband were still alive, I would never tell you that part of the story, lest it affect what I hope was a good marriage.'"

She put the letter down, appealing to Ralph, "Why am I not in a rage? I only feel numb, too dull to understand how Bud could have tricked his unborn children. Why am I not in a rage?"

"Because it would be futile. If he were living and you knew this, you'd be in a rage, and he'd know it, all right. Not that it would do any good. Read on," Ralph said.

" 'Anyway, you in your natural pride asked me to look at your baby. So when I left you, I went to the nursery. The staff of that little place was shorthanded, for whatever reason I do not know, and there was only one nurse in attendance. I introduced myself. Your baby was crying; it was a distressful cry, I thought. The nurse told me he cried a good deal, that the doctor had said it was probably colic and that they were going to change his formula. They had taken X rays, which showed nothing wrong.

" 'It was then that she asked me whether I could do her a favor, there being a problem in her family, by staying in the nursery for ten minutes so that she might make an important phone call. She knew my father and had no reason not to trust me. When she left, I saw the X-ray plates with your name lying on the desk, and I examined them. There it was, as I had feared: the dilation of the small intestine, the narrowed colon, and all the rest. Soon the ilium would fill; this baby's future was writ clear. His doctor hadn't known what he was looking at. I was acquainted with him, an agreeable, decent old-timer who had learned almost nothing new since leaving medical school some forty years before. It was a wonder he had even known enough to order the X rays.

"'I guess I lost my reason. I only know I wanted to save you from tragedy. I looked around, and seeing another bassinet that held a boy, I made an exchange. The bead bracelets were so carelessly loose—it is no wonder that this inefficient little clinic eventually had to close its doors—that with the aid of some lubricating jelly, I was able to slip them off. After that, I moved the bassinets. By the time the nurse came back, all was as it had been except that each of a pair of red-faced, bald male infants now had a new identity.

"'And no one ever questioned anything. Why should they have? What I had done was unthinkable, so why would anyone have thought of it?

"'Two or three times in passing your house, I've seen the boy, the vigorous son who was not yours, and I imagined your pleasure and pride in him. Later, from neighborhood friends of my father's, I learned about your second child. Now my feelings were mixed. I began to think more and more about those other people whom, for your sake, I had robbed of their rightful child, and I was afflicted with such pain and guilt as no one can comprehend who has not been in my place.

"'And then one day, incredibly, the Crawfield family came to me, of all people, traveling to New York because they had learned of my work with this disease. I should have told them then and there, but I did not have the courage. Coward that I was, I wanted somebody else to do it, somebody who could not possibly implicate me, so I recommended a medical center nearer to their home, and the rest you know.

"'So here it is. Think what you must of me, Laura. If it means anything at all—not much, I'm afraid—know that I have spent my life trying, through charity to my patients and to the poor in general, to repay the world in some way for the evil thing I did. Forgive me a little if you can, and I pray that those other people may forgive me a little, too.'"

Laura stopped. A crow cawed once, and Earl barked at it

once. Otherwise, the proverbial dropped pin would have disturbed the silence of the pair on the veranda.

Then she said, "That's all. There's just his name."

"Francis Alcott. So he was the one."

"He lived there in the house beyond the hedge."

"Do you think of him very often?"

"Not often. It's a long-healed wound. Lately, though, since I've known you—will you mind if I tell you that you remind me of him?"

"You forget. You have already told me. But you never told me what happened, why you didn't—"

"He didn't take me. It's that simple. He had promised someone else."

"Fool! I would have thrown the whole election away for you if I'd had to. I'd give up anything and go away anywhere with you. You know that, don't you?"

She looked at him. Although the light was dimming, she saw plainly the anxiety in his eyes.

"I know it, Ralph."

"What a tragedy to have such lifelong guilt because of a moment's aberration!"

"With all the fame, the knowledge, and the respect."

"I wonder what Arthur and Margaret will say when you tell them."

"I already have told them. And Tom, too. They all said that in an odd way, it is a relief to know, even though it can't change things. And Margaret said, 'Let us all rest now and try to put it behind us.' She is the soul of kindness."

"How different things would be if she were not."

"And they are so crazy about Timmy. They want to take him to Washington to see the Smithsonian, the Holocaust Museum, the Capitol, and everything. Isn't that nice?"

"She still worries that you might be thinking they'll try to win Tom away from your home and your ways. She wants you to be sure that will never be done, not by gesture or word."

"They've said so, but I'm glad to hear it again. Because I'm not angelic, Ralph, and that would tear me in two. But I'm not worried now. I've asked the Crawfields to come here for Christmas weekend."

"Are they coming?"

"Of course. And we are all to go there in the spring for the Passover Seder. It would be interesting. I've never been at one."

"It is. It's a freedom festival, very happy. They always invite me. It's a day for family and good friends."

A few drops fell, and Laura sprang up. "It's going to pour tonight. I should cut these roses before the rain beats them down."

They were the lingerers, last of the season, no more than a dozen, dark red and fragrant with a tartness faintly like pine. She cut and lifted two handfuls to her face. Ralph was gazing at her.

"I want to be with you forever," he said. "When can we start?"

"Appearances, you know. The aunts would say, 'after a decent interval.'"

"Like what? Tomorrow?"

They both laughed, and Laura said, "Next month, when Tom's home for vacation."

"I wonder how he'll take it."

"Well enough, I'm sure. He's been suspecting us, anyway."

"He's a good guy. I know I've said it a couple of times today, but I'll say it again."

And they sat there close together, she with the flowers in her lap, as the evening drew in and a small wind came to rustle what was left of the leaves. After a while, he picked up the old guitar and began to play.